The New England
Town Meeting

The New England Town Meeting

Democracy in Action

JOSEPH F. ZIMMERMAN

PRAEGER

Westport, Connecticut
London

Library of Congress Cataloging-in-Publication Data

Zimmerman, Joseph Francis, 1928–
   The New England town meeting : democracy in action / Joseph F.
Zimmerman.
     p. cm.
   Includes bibliographical references and index.
   ISBN 0–275–96523–6 (alk. paper)
   1. Local government—New England. 2. Democracy—New England.
3. New England—Politics and government. 4. Political
participation—New England. 5. Politics, Practical—New England.
I. Title.
JS431.Z56   1999
320.4744—dc21   98–31074

British Library Cataloguing in Publication Data is available.

Library of Congress Catalog Card Number: 98–31074
ISBN: 0–275–96523–6

First published in 1999

Praeger Publishers, 88 Post Road West, Westport, CT 06881
An imprint of Greenwood Publishing Group, Inc.

Printed in the United States of America

The paper used in this book complies with the
Permanent Paper Standard issued by the National
Information Standards Organization (Z39.48–1984).

10 9 8 7 6 5 4 3 2 1

For Ronald M. Stout
Colleague and friend

Contents

Contents

Tables and Figures

FIGURE

Preface

The New England town meeting and school district meeting are the only direct democracy institutions in the United States involving law-making by assembled voters. Although the town meeting has influenced political thought and been praised by eminent observers, including Thomas Jefferson and Alexis de Tocqueville, political scientists, with a few exceptions, have not studied this form of law-making.

There are two profoundly different views of the primary assembly. Proponents emphasize that town meeting government is the purest form of democracy that ensures that all policy decisions are in the public interest since no intermediaries are placed between the voters and the public decisions. Furthermore, advocates argue that the meeting maximizes citizen participation, allows ordinary voters to hold administrative officers directly accountable, provides psychological benefits for attendees, preserves local customs, including the town meeting supper and citizen service as town officers, and performs citizen education and community-building functions.

Critics of this law-making institution are convinced that, in practice, it is not the purest form of democracy. A number of critics, in essence, agree with Greek philosophers who feared that an assembly of voters would become an ocholocracy, and James Madison specifically described the ancient Athenian assembly as a mob.[1]

Supporters of representative law-making maintain it is superior to citizen law-making and point to town meeting voter participation, which is exceptionally low in other than very small towns and, in general, has been declining during the past four decades. Rational-thinking critics assume that the small town meeting attendance facilitates control of the decision-making process by interest groups that promote their special goals and therefore conclude that the assembly is an unrepresentative body. These critics, however, have not studied the quality of town meeting decisions.

This book examines the open town meeting in each of the six New England states and analyzes the reasons for the decline in participation and the role played by town meeting committees as counterpoises to special interest groups and draws conclusions relative to the quality of town meeting debate and decisions. In addition, recommendations are advanced to make the meeting more participant-friendly in order to increase attendance.

Alternatives to the open town meeting also are examined. A chapter is devoted to the representative or limited town meeting, and conclusions are drawn with respect to this form of town meeting, the official ballot referendum type of town meeting, and a town council as the law-making body.

NOTE

1. James Madison, *The Federalist Papers* (New York: New American Library, 1961), p. 342.

Acknowledgments

Collecting data and information on the operation of town meeting governments in the New England states would have been impossible without the cooperation of numerous town clerks, town moderators, other town officers, municipal associations, and townspeople in each of the six states. Town officers, in particular, willingly completed questionnaires and answered telephone questions.

While it is not possible to acknowledge every individual and organization that provided assistance, a special debt of gratitude must be expressed to colleague Ronald M. Stout for his suggestions to improve the manuscript, Chief Legal Counsel H. Bernard Waught, Jr., of the New Hampshire Municipal Association for critically reviewing Chapter 4, Professor Frank M. Bryan of the University of Vermont for his constructive review of Chapter 5 and authorizing use of his data on town meeting attendance, Molly K. Duggan of the Vermont League of Cities and Towns for her extraordinary helpfulness, Michael Starn of the Maine Municipal Association for reviewing Chapter 5, and Terence Elton of the Connecticut Conference of Municipalities and Finance Director Donald Goodrich of Portland for assistance in collecting and providing information for Chapter 7. The research was supported, in part, by a faculty research grant awarded by the State University of New York at Albany.

I would be negligent if I failed to acknowledge the research assistance of Stephen D. Koczak, Troy E. Smith, and J. Cherie Strachan and Addie Napolitano's excellence in preparing the manuscript.

Chapter 1

Law-Making by Assembled Citizens

Law-making by assembled adult males dates to the age of Pericles in Greece in the fifth century B.C., but there is no evidence that the New England open town meeting, as an egalitarian institution, has a direct lineage to classical Greek democracy (see Chapter 2). The only other currently assembled voters' law-making body is the Swiss *Landsgemeinde* in the half-cantons of Appenzell Inner-Rhoden and Outer-Rhoden, Nidwalden, Obwalden, and the canton of Glarus, where the traditional annual open-air meeting of voters is held to decide issues.[1] These half-cantons and the canton of Glarus have populations ranging from 14,500 in Appenzell Inner-Rhoden to 53,400 in Appenzell Outer-Rhoden.[2]

In common with the classical Athenian *ecclesia* and the Swiss *Landsgemeinde*, the New England open town meeting is a *de facto* representative body because the majority of the eligible voters do not participate in the meeting except in small towns. New England open town meeting voters who do not attend, in effect, have elected the self-selected participants to represent the interests of all town residents. The absentee problem is not a new one in New England towns. The Boston records early in the nineteenth century referred to "thinly attended" town meetings and noted:

it is very seldom, that men of the best intelligence and most capable of conducting publick business will leave their important private concerns to attend affairs in which they have only a general interest; it therefore unavoidably happens that the affairs of a large town are conducted by a very small number of persons, who represent and act for the whole, but who are not chosen by them, who do not possess their confidence and act under no or a very slight responsibility.[3]

Law-making by voters in the United States is not restricted to the New England town meeting. Unassembled voters can employ the referendum to approve or disapprove proposed state constitutions and state and local laws. Furthermore, voters in seventeen states may utilize the initiative to place proposed constitutional amendments on the referendum ballot and in twenty-one states may place proposed laws on the ballot.[4] Similarly, the electorate in twenty-four states also may employ the protest referendum by petition, which suspends a statute until a referendum is held to determine whether the statute should be repealed.[5]

A New England town meeting, except in Rhode Island, is called by the Board of Selectmen—the town's plural executive—which issues a warrant or warning of the place, date, and time of the meeting. The warrant also contains business articles, a fixed agenda to be acted upon by assembled voters. Should the selectpersons fail to include in the warrant an article requested by a group of voters, the latter may employ the initiative to place the article in the warrant. The financial town meeting in Rhode Island is called by the town clerk.

VIEWS OF ADVOCATES AND CRITICS

Town meeting government developed without official authorization in the Massachusetts Bay Colony in 1629 (see Chapter 2), and few citizens criticized this form of citizen law-making until late in the eighteenth century, when the population of the town of Boston was growing rapidly. The Massachusetts town meeting played an important part in the events leading to the Revolutionary War. General Thomas Gage, who was appointed governor of the Massachusetts Bay Colony in 1774, forbade the holding of town meetings without his specific consent.[6] Salem selectmen nevertheless posted a warning for a town meeting that was held in the presence of the governor and two regiments.[7] Although seven town leaders were arrested, they were not punished. Shortly thereafter, the town of Danvers held a town meeting, and Governor Gage responded: "Damn 'em! I won't do any thing about it unless his Majesty sends me more troops."[8]

Similarly, Lord Germain, who was scheduled to become secretary of state for the colonies, decried town meetings in the following terms upon being informed of the Boston Tea Party:

This is what comes of their wretched town meetings—these are the proceedings of a tumultuous and riotous rabble, who ought, if they had the least produce, to follow their mercantile employment and not trouble themselves with politics and government, which they do not understand.[9]

Political thought in the United States has been influenced greatly by the New England town meeting, which has been praised and/or advocated by a number of prominent observers, including Thomas Jefferson and Alexis de Tocqueville, and ordinary citizens. Commencing with Madison's derision of direct democracy, however, town meeting government has been criticized primarily for low attendance by registered voters and the alleged domination of the meetings by special interest groups.

Advocates

Thomas Jefferson, a leading anti-federalist, was an opponent of a strong national government and praised the New England town meeting on a number of occasions. In 1782, for example, he wrote that "every government degenerates when trusted to the rulers of the people alone. The people themselves therefore are its only safe depositories."[10]

In a letter to Joseph C. Cabell dated February 2, 1816, Jefferson elaborated on his concept of the ward-republic as follows:

Where every man is a sharer in the direction of his ward-republic, or of some of the higher ones, and feels that he is a participator in the government of affairs, not merely at an election one day in the year, but every day; when there shall not be a man in the State who will not be a member of some one of its councils, great or small, he will let the heart be torn out of his body sooner than his power be wrested from him by a Caesar or a Bonaparte.[11]

In a letter to Samuel Kercheval on July 12, 1816, Jefferson expanded his comments on the New England town meeting by declaring that such governments "have proved themselves the wisest invention ever devised by the wit of man for the perfect exercise of self-government, and for its preservation."[12] Jefferson particularly was impressed by the ability of citizens to manage directly public affairs, which cements them together as a community.

Referring to his town of Concord, Massachusetts, Ralph Waldo Emerson in 1835 explained that "the great secret of political science was uncovered" in the town meeting; "how to give every individual his fair weight in the government, without any disorder from numbers. . . . Here the rich gave counsel, but the poor also, and moreover, the just and the unjust."[13] Emerson reported that the town meeting produced general contentment, "and the people truly see that they are the lords of the soil."[14]

Alexis de Tocqueville, a keen French observer of governmental systems in the United States, noted the similarities between the New England town meeting and the Athenian assemblage of voters that made laws in the fifth century B.C. and was impressed by the New Englanders' understanding of governmental problems. He acknowledged that "the government may have defects, and indeed they are easy to point out, but they do not catch the eye because the government really does emanate from the governed."[15]

Tocqueville elaborated on the advantages of governance by assembled voters and their self-imposed obligations to members of society and concluded that although they were religious sectarians, they held no political prejudices against others.[16] He reported:

The New Englander is attached to his township because it is strong and independent; he has an interest in it because he shares in its management; he loves it because he has no reason to complain of his lot; he invests his ambition and his future in it; in the restricted sphere within his scope, he learns to rule society; he gets to know those formalities without which freedom can advance only through revolutions, and becoming imbued with their spirit, develops a taste for order, understands the harmony of powers, and in the end accumulates clear, practical ideas about the nature of his duties and the extent of his rights.[17]

Tocqueville also was convinced that direct democracy in New England towns avoided "the commotion of municipal discord."[18]

The themes of citizen education and community building appear frequently in the writings of observers impressed with law-making by assembled voters. Lord James Bryce, a British observer, in 1888 accentuated the first theme by concluding that "the primary assembly is admittedly the best. It is the cheapest and the most efficient; it is the most educative of the citizens who bear a part in it. The Town Meeting has been not only the source but the school of democracy."[19]

Similarly, the education theme was highlighted in a 1909 lecture at Johns Hopkins University by President A. Lawrence Lowell of Harvard University, a political scientist, who cited the distinct advantage of decision-making following popular debate in a town meeting in contrast to a referendum not preceded by such debate.[20] Noting that issues in a town meeting are subjected to considerable debate, he argued that the citizen voter cannot reach conclusions on how to vote on warrant articles "merely after hearing one side stated by his friends, or reading one side in his newspaper, or being simply told by his party, or by some other organization, how to vote."[21] Furthermore, Lowell emphasized that town meeting voters are able to question town officers and their proposals prior to voting on warrant articles and can hold the officers accountable.

These observers, in effect, were agreeing with Aristotle, who explained:

For the many, of whom each individual is but an ordinary person, when they meet together may very likely be better than the few good, if regarded not individually but collectively, just as a feast to which many contribute is better than a dinner provided out of a single purse.[22]

Many non-academic and academic observers have agreed with the conclusions of numerous participants in New England town meetings relative to the positive values of law-making by voters. In a book on small town governments, Granville Hicks in 1947 contrasted the organization of civilian defense during World War II in his New York town with the organization of civilian defense in a neighboring Massachusetts town where one of his friends was a selectman.[23] Hicks reported that the people of the two towns were similar, but the Massachusetts town residents were accustomed to assembling to make collective decisions and "knew how to conduct themselves when a special town meeting was called for the purpose of electing defense officials and appropriating money."[24] In contrast, the New York town "was still blundering through a tangle of conflicting authorities and contradictory directives" at a time when the Massachusetts town had a well-organized civilian defense system.[25]

Neil G. Kotler completed a Ph.D. dissertation at the University of Chicago in 1974 on politics and citizenship in Springfield, Vermont, an industrial town that attracted many immigrants who did not speak English in the period 1865 to 1930.[26] He explained that voters desiring to participate readily did so, and deliberative bodies provided a range of information and opinions on issues.[27] He concluded:

The institutions of town government enabled citizens to exercise their political liberty. As long as the rules remained in force, proponents of the resolution could not be denied their right to a hearing. The rules and traditions of town meeting were a common ground for all parties. Attachment to the institution proved stronger than divisions over the issue at hand.[28]

The preceding individuals, with the exception of Emerson, were observers of town meetings and not participants. Their views, however, have been echoed by many town meeting participants who are convinced that this law-making system is the ideal. John Gould of Brunswick, Maine, summarized town meeting government in his town in 1940 in the following terms:

Absolute independence characterizes Town Meeting. No one tells a Yankee how to vote, no one dictates; and only another Yankee can persuade. In a world where Democracy perishes, and in a country where self-government occupies every thinking mind, it is startling and refreshing to find New England Town Meeting alive and able and in the hands of a right-fisted people who keep their heritage well.[29]

Raymond P. Clark of Sudbury, Massachusetts, in 1985 agreed with critics that the town meeting often is dominated by special interest groups but noted that "in open town meeting . . . you are eligible to join a special-interest group merely by showing up and, at the appropriate time, raising your hand. Those who have no interest in a particular issue prove it by not bothering to come out."[30] Clark also lashed out at critics who "can figure out the flaws, but can't think of anything better."[31] He stated that he would remain a supporter of the open town meeting, which he described as "sprawling, sloppy, amateurish, hilarious, mawkish, and the best form of local government ever devised."[32]

A different perspective on town meeting government was provided by selectman Joseph Ford of Lee, New Hampshire, who in 1986 stressed democratic scrutiny of administrators at town meeting:

If you give up town meetings, you give up a lot. Selectmen and mayors often take positions that clearly don't represent the views of the town. A town meeting makes town officials more accountable. It lets people see their officials in action.[33]

In 1995, executive director Barbara Anderson of Citizens for Limited Taxation expressed the view that Massachusetts town voters who do not attend town meetings have no basis for the complaint that attendees make the decisions and added: "It's the best type of government for making decisions. And town meetings are fun. There's still that thrill when that gavel comes down. You are part of your own government."[34]

A New Hampshire town clerk in a town of nearly 5,000 population with a 10 percent turnout of voters at the annual meeting wrote to the author in 1996 that she makes it a point to observe participants and concluded that "a good representation of citizens participate, listen carefully to the debate, and make the best informed decision. It is still the best democratic process and those not attending are giving up a valuable liberty."

The members of the Plymouth, New Hampshire, Board of Selectmen and school board in 1996 attributed the desirability of the town as a place of residence to the vitality of school district meeting and the town meeting and noted:

Much of this vitality is the result of the dialogues and discussions (sometimes heated) that we have during school district and town meeting time. It is at these meetings that we come together to determine how to maintain and improve the town. . . . Ideas are exchanged, adjusted, and affirmed in an open democratic manner. In fact, the town meeting and school district format are the purist form of democracy.[35]

Critics

James Madison in *The Federalist Number 10*, in arguing that New York state should ratify the proposed U.S. Constitution, commented on the inability of a direct democracy to cure "the mischiefs of faction."[36] He maintained:

there is nothing to check the inducements to sacrifice the weaker party or obnoxious individual. Hence it is that such democracies have ever been spectacles of turbulence and contention; have ever been as short in their lives as they have been violent in their deaths. Theoretic politicians, who have patronized this species of government have erroneously supposed that by reducing mankind to a perfect equality in their political rights, they would at the same time be perfectly equalized and assimilated in their possessions, their opinions, and their passions.[37]

Madison continued his disparaging remarks regarding law-making by assembled voters in *The Federalist Number 55*, where he wrote: "In all very numerous assemblies, of whatever characters composed, passion never fails to wrest the scepter from reason. Had every Athenian citizen been a Socrates, every Athenian assembly would still have been a mob."[38] In *The Federalist Number 58*, he asserted that "the ascendancy of passion over reason" is greater in a large than in a small legislative assembly because of the higher proportion of "members of limited information and of weak capacities."[39] He concluded that in ancient assemblies "a single orator, or an artful statesman, was generally seen to rule with as complete a sway as if a scepter had been placed in his single hand."[40]

Madison's negative views were the first and last major published criticism of the open town meeting until 1897, when an unsigned article appeared in *The Nation* with the title "The Decay of Town Government."[41] The article noted that New England town government had been "extolled as very nearly perfect" and that until twenty-five years ago "to question the excellence of New England town government would have seemed like questioning democracy itself."[42] Reference was made to towns "filling up with millionaires and magnates from the city, who add to the taxable wealth of fine houses, stock farms, and other improvements, and who expect to be plundered a little."[43] This description, which apparently referred to southwestern Connecticut, was not accurate for the vast majority of New England towns. Nevertheless, the article continued as follows:

The "ring" in the village rests upon the same basis as it does in the city—a little rural machine of a few dozen voters who are supported by labor furnished by the town, and in return go to the town-meeting and keep in office the selectmen who furnish them support. They are a mere handful, generally outnumbered by the property-owners who, however, stay at home and let them do it. These property-owners have the matter in their hands, and the misrule which exists is the measure of their indifference.[44]

In 1912, Delos F. Wilcox opined that the town meeting could function successfully only in small rural towns and "is a sort of national memory, a regret of days gone by and conditions that have passed. . . . The town meeting belongs essentially to the past."[45] Wilcox placed his faith in the initiative, protest referendum, and recall as popular devices to protect the public against abuse by legislative bodies.

Writing in 1932, Professor Orren C. Hormell of Bowdoin College in Maine noted that during the previous two to three decades most New England towns with a population exceeding 5,000 had debated whether the town meeting could be reformed.[46] Acknowledging that small rural towns might find merit in direct democracy, he concluded that the larger towns were finding town meeting government to be unworkable, and he "wondered whether the people in the free-for-all of a town meeting were at all times in a position to formulate and give expression to the *will of the people*."[47]

Journalist Kendall Banning in 1935 reported town meeting voter attendance had declined sharply and in the average town approximated 8 to 10 percent of the taxpayers.[48] He agreed with Hormell that the small number of voters attending town meetings did not reflect accurately the will of the people.[49] Banning concluded that the will of the people could be determined best by mailing a referendum ballot containing warrant articles to each registered voter, thereby allowing all voters to participate in the decision-making process by means of a postal ballot.[50]

John W. Alexander and Morroe Berger in 1949 bluntly maintained in the

American Mercury that the town meeting is "a sacred cow that deserves to be laid to rest."[51] They based their assessment upon observation of town meetings in three Connecticut towns and attributed the decline of the town meeting to the expansion of the powers of the state and federal governments, which were making major decisions affecting the daily lives of citizens. Nevertheless, they noted that town meeting government in many towns is "an expression of the townspeople's community spirit, a reaffirmation of their solidarity. This kind of vitality, however, appears to characterize mainly the meetings in small towns."[52]

Political scientist Robert C. Wood of the Massachusetts Institute of Technology published a highly acclaimed book in 1958, based, in part, upon observations of the town meeting in his suburban town of Lincoln, Massachusetts, that were severely critical of direct citizen law-making in town meetings.[53] He asserted that meaningful consideration of warrant articles did not occur because opposing views were not discussed, and there was no "effective opposition."[54] Wood became convinced that "an excessive reliance on direct popular action can lead . . . to no popular action at all with the citizens baffled and perplexed and the expert and small clique in charge."[55]

Wood concluded that the town meeting does not measure up well in terms of democratic theory and, agreeing with Madison, maintained that the outnumbered minority cannot be faulted for failing to make a vigorous case for its stand on issues. He pessimistically feared suburban residents might become apolitical because the theory of town meeting government places too many time demands on them, and they have decided to leave the solution of town problems to the experts.[56]

Criticism of town meeting government continued in the 1960s. A 1965 editorial in the *National Civic Review* opined that the open town meeting "still lingers on as an instrument of control by small groups of self-seekers and without participation by 90 percent of the voters."[57] The Committee for Economic Development, composed of prominent businessmen and educators, in 1966 concluded that the town meeting "met the needs of simpler earlier times, but was not designed to handle the complex modern problems confronting rapidly growing areas."[58]

Jane J. Mansbridge studied town meeting government in a Vermont town with a population of 350 in the 1970s and concluded that the small number of voters who attended town meetings on a regular basis were not representative of the citizenry; "informal channels of influence will come to dominate decision making; and a large number of those excluded from the informal processes will feel manipulated, angry, or apathetic, cursed with self-blame."[59]

The Granite State Taxpayers Association, with representation in forty-three New Hampshire towns, was distressed by low voter attendance (5% to 10%) at school district meetings, conducted in the same manner as town meetings, which vote to appropriate funds that consume 65 to 75 percent of all town property tax revenue. District meetings approve contracts with teachers' unions and all school spending. The association estimated that at least 60 percent of district meeting participants were teachers and other school district employees and their families and friends.

The association arranged for the introduction in the General Court (state legislature) of an official ballot (OB) bill (Senate Bill 2, or SB2) that applied only to school district meetings. Pressure grew for the inclusion of town meetings, and the bill was amended and enacted by the General Court in 1995 to include both types of meetings.[60] A three-fifths vote of town meeting participants is required to adopt or repeal the OB acceptance statute, which authorizes a referendum form of school district meeting and town meeting, with the first session devoted to discussion of the warrant and possible amendment of the articles. A public hearing is held on the amended warrant, and in April of each year the voters go to the polls to vote, via a referendum, on the warrant articles (see Chapter 4).

Professor Frank M. Bryan of the University of Vermont in 1995 agreed with Mansbridge's conclusion that town meeting attendees were not representative of the citizenry, by writing that a Vermont "town meeting is dominated by middle class and professional people. In most towns the number of blue collar and working class people equals that of upscale professionals. The most affluent and the least affluent are less likely to attend and participate."[61]

Selectman Larry Blacker of Sudbury, Massachusetts, was disappointed that the 1996 annual town meeting rejected two zoning articles that he favored and commented that "(w)hen a town meeting gets packed, it gets packed more by NIMBYs [proponents of not-in-my-backyard philosophy] than anyone else. It's an oligarchy, and that is not what was intended."[62]

Ian Menzies, a Massachusetts critic of town meeting government, stated in 1996:

It's no more the purest form of democracy than the Red Sox are pennant contenders. Often the disabled can't come, the elderly can't come, single mothers can't come. If you can't get out on the night of town meeting, you're cut off.[63]

Melanie B. Gross, a member of the Woodbridge, Connecticut, board of finance, wrote a 1996 op-ed article for the *New York Times* in which she explained that "not many years ago" the town hall was packed by 300 to 400 residents attending a hearing on the proposed town budget, but in 1996 "barely 50 came . . . and most were employees and officials who were there to answer questions. Some people who came in the spirit of civic pride were chased away within minutes by the hostile atmosphere."[64]

DEMOCRATIC LAW-MAKING

What is the most democratic system for local government law-making? Answering the question is a difficult task, although it is easy to give a superficial answer based on the two Greek words that form the roots of the word "democracy'' and translate as "power of the people." The derivation of the term suggests that law-making by assembled citizens is the most democratic form of enacting statutes.

The New England open town meeting comports with the classical definition of democracy. However, the relatively small percentage of registered voters who attend town meetings, with the exceptions of towns with very small populations, raises the question whether the participants are representative of the electorate at large and make *pro bono publico* decisions that promote and protect the public weal.

Town meeting critics, in effect, suggest that an important interest group, such as town employees or schoolteachers, conspires to undermine the public interest by packing town meetings and approving warrant articles promoting their special interests. The pressure groups' victims, according to the conspiracy theory, are the non-participating, taxpaying voters, who are forced to finance the policies approved by the interest group-dominated town meetings. The key questions are whether there is an inherent bias in town meeting decision-making today and whether an effective counterweight to special interest groups exists.

All venerable political institutions should be re-examined periodically to determine their viability and whether they deserve to survive. Are the eulogies of the open town meeting deserved or folklore? Is the New England town meeting a viable example of "pure" democracy in action or a degenerate descendant of a formerly great institution of local government? Do poor attendance by voters, relative lack of debate, and influential interest groups constitute its syndrome? Is law-making by assembled voters devoid of merit, and have population growth and development of a megalopolis undermined the *raison d'être* of the town meeting?

As noted, a plethora of seemingly plausible evidence has been marshaled by vociferous critics to document the deficiencies of the open town meeting, label it an anachronism, and conclude that superintendence of town affairs by voter assembly is impossible today except in towns with a very small population. The stereotypes of the open town meeting advanced by its ardent supporters and its severe critics cannot both be accurate. To evaluate the town meeting, it is essential to examine its organizational development from its very informal beginnings in 1629 and the emergence of committees that act as counterforces to interest groups.

Major economic and social changes have occurred in New England since the development of town meeting government in 1629. Towns in metropolitan areas, such as Hartford and Worcester, have become highly urbanized and experience many of the problems found in large cities. Voters have more demands placed upon their free time, particularly if both parents with children work full-time. Television and the Internet occupy the free time of many town residents, and other residents devote their free time to athletic, social, and other activities, thereby limiting the time they can devote to participating in voter assemblies. Furthermore, federal and state government mandates and restraints limit the scope of town meeting discretionary decision-making and may lead to the attitude among a significant number of town voters that the town meeting no longer addresses major issues that affect their lives.

Population growth in Boston persuaded voters in 1822 that the open town meeting no longer was functional, and they decided to adopt the only existing alternative—a charter establishing the city of Boston with an elected council as the law-making body. By 1915, however, an alternative to converting a large town into a city became available when a special charter was enacted by the Massachusetts General Court (state legislature) providing for a representative town meeting (RTM) in Brookline. Adoption of such a charter, however, meant that law-making by an assembly open to all voters was abandoned. Currently, forty-two Massachusetts towns, seven Connecticut towns, one Maine town, and one Vermont town have an RTM or limited town meeting, an institution examined in Chapter 9.

The major thesis examined in this study is that the traditional New England open town meeting is a *de facto* representative legislative body, with changing membership, that considers all viewpoints on warrant articles and makes decisions that generally are in the best interests of the town. In particular, we seek to determine whether New England towns have an adequate and credible policy-making institution capable of effecting the goals of the thesis as they enter the twenty-first century with institutions fashioned in the early decades of the seventeenth century. Our study examines countervailing forces at town meetings that may neutralize or reduce the power of special interest groups and ensure that town meeting decisions are sound ones that promote the common good.

In particular, we explore the operation of the open town meeting in each of the six New England states and the adoption of modifications designed to improve the performance of the primary assembly of voters. We also assess the representative town meeting and the Australian or official ballot (OB referendum) variation of the town meeting, adopted by thirty-five New Hampshire towns and eight Vermont towns, which modifies the traditional open meeting by providing for a deliberative session allowing voters to consider warrant articles and ask questions, but decisions are not made until another day, when voters go to the poll to act on the articles by referenda.

Chapter 2 examines the origin of town meeting government and its early development as elected and administrative town officers begin to appear.

NOTES

1. Georg Thürer, "The 'Landsgemeinde' of Switzerland," *Pro Helvetia*, July 1972, pp. 1–7.
2. *Switzerland* (Berne: Kümmerly & Frey, 1994), p. 23.
3. *A Volume of Records Relating to the Early History of Boston Containing Boston Town Records, 1814–1822* (Boston: Municipal Printing Office, 1906), p. 43.
4. For details, see Joseph F. Zimmerman, *Participatory Democracy: Populism Revived* (New York: Praeger Publishers, 1986), pp. 68–104.

5. Ibid., pp. 45–67.

6. Ralph V. Harlow, *Samuel Adams: Promoter of the American Revolution* (New York: Henry Holt and Company, 1923), pp. 246–47.

7. Ibid., p. 247.

8. Quoted in Ibid.

9. Quoted in Cass Canfield, *Samuel Adams's Revolution: 1765–1776* (New York: Harper & Row, Publishers, 1976), p. 58.

10. Paul L. Ford, ed., *The Writings of Thomas Jefferson* (New York: G. P. Putnam's Sons, 1894), vol. 4, p. 64.

11. *The Writings of Thomas Jefferson (Monticello Edition)* (Washington, D.C.: Thomas Jefferson Memorial Association of the United States, 1904), vol. 14, p. 422.

12. Ibid., vol. 15, p. 38.

13. Ralph Waldo Emerson, *Miscellanies* (Boston: Houghton, Mifflin and Company, 1904), vol. 11, pp. 46–47.

14. Ibid., p. 49.

15. Alexis de Tocqueville, *Democracy in America* (New York: Harper Perennial, 1988), p. 70.

16. Ibid., pp. 44, 47.

17. Ibid., p. 70.

18. Ibid., pp. 62–63.

19. James Bryce, *The American Commonwealth*, 2nd ed., rev. (London: Macmillan and Company, 1891), p. 591.

20. A. Lawrence Lowell, *Public Opinion and Popular Government* (New York: Longmans, Green and Company, 1926), p. 153.

21. Ibid.

22. Benjamin Jowett, trans., *Aristotle's Politics* (New York: Carlton House, n.d.), pp. 145–46.

23. Granville Hicks, *Small Town* (New York: Macmillan Company, 1947).

24. Ibid., pp. 49–50.

25. Ibid.

26. Neil G. Kotler, "Politics and Citizenship in New England Towns: A Study of Political Participation and Political Education" (Unpublished Ph.D. dissertation, University of Chicago, 1974).

27. Ibid., p. 300.

28. Ibid., p. 303.

29. John Gould, *New England Town Meeting: Safeguard of Democracy* (Brattleboro, Vt.: Stephen Daye Press, 1940), p. 10.

30. Raymond P. Clark, "Maybe It's Sloppy, but It's Good Government," *Boston Globe*, February 22, 1985, p. 14.

31. Ibid.

32. Ibid.

33. David Shribman, "The Town Meeting, New England Staple, Faces Tide of Change," *Wall Street Journal*, March 7, 1986, p. 24.

34. Robert Preer, "Meeting Needs of a Democracy?" *Boston Globe*, May 13, 1995, p. 13.

35. Allen MacNeil et al., "Official Ballot Bill Tears Away at the Wrong Things," *The Citizen* (Laconia, N.H.), March 2, 1996, p. 7.

36. *The Federalist Papers* (New York: New American Library, 1961), p. 81.

37. Ibid.

38. Ibid., p. 342.

39. Ibid., p. 360.

40. Ibid.

41. "The Decay of Town Government," *The Nation*, September 2, 1897, pp. 180–81.

42. Ibid., p. 180.

43. Ibid.

44. Ibid., p. 181.

45. Delos F. Wilcox, *Government by All the People or the Initiative, the Referendum, and the Recall as Instruments of Democracy* (New York: Macmillan Company, 1912), pp. 5–6.

46. Orren C. Hormell, *Maine Towns* (Brunswick, Maine: Bowdoin College Bulletin, 1932), p. 17.

47. Ibid., pp. 16–17.

48. Kendall Banning, "Is the Town Meeting Democratic?" *National Municipal Review*, March 1935, p. 153.

49. Ibid., p. 154.

50. Ibid., p. 155.

51. John W. Alexander and Morroe Berger, "Is the Town Meeting Finished?" *The American Mercury*, August 1949, p. 151.

52. Ibid., p. 148.

53. Robert C. Wood, *Suburbia: Its People and Their Politics* (Boston: Houghton Mifflin Company, 1958).

54. Ibid., p. 283.

55. Ibid., p. 284.

56. Ibid., p. 197.

57. "The Fading Town Meeting," *National Civic Review* 54, October 1965, p. 522.

58. *Modernizing Local Government* (New York: Committee for Economic Development, 1966), p. 30.

59. Jane J. Mansbridge, "Town Meeting Democracy," in Peter Collier, ed., *Dilemmas of Democracy* (New York: Harcourt Brace Jovanovich, 1976), p. 167.

60. *New Hampshire Laws of 1995*, chap. 164 and *New Hampshire Revised Statutes Annotated*, § 40:13.

61. Frank M. Bryan, "Direct Democracy and Civic Competence," *The Good Society*, Fall 1995, p. 41.

62. Tom Moroney, "Modern Life Challenges Town Meeting Tradition," *Boston Sunday Globe*, April 21, 1996, p. 9.

63. Ibid.

64. Melanie B. Gross, "Political Poison at the Grass Roots," *New York Times*, May 4, 1996, p. 19.

Chapter 2

Genesis of
the Town Meeting

The first English colony in New England was the Popham colony, established on August 29, 1607, at the mouth of the Kennebec River and abandoned the following spring.[1] Prior to the landing of the Pilgrims at Plymouth, Massachusetts, in 1620, fishing settlements existed along the coast but were not of the nature of permanent settlements and possessed no organized local government.[2] Relatively little is known about these settlements other than the fact that they were temporary abodes of fishermen who maintained their permanent homes elsewhere.

The first permanent settlement of Massachusetts may be attributed, in large measure, to the bitter animosity that developed between the Church of England and two dissident groups: the Pilgrims and the Puritans, who sought a more complete reformation of the Church of England.[3]

The Pilgrims originally were a small group of farmers and artisans of the lower and middle classes living in Scrooby, England, who were called "Separatists" because they had separated from the Church of England and in the autumn of 1606 formed their own church.[4] The Pilgrims believed that the Church of England retained too many features of the Church of Rome.

Roland G. Usher maintained that the Pilgrims were not persecuted actively by the Church of England or the government, but by their neighbors.[5] The Pilgrims concluded that England was contaminated and a hazard to their spiritual welfare. In consequence, they decided in 1607 to emigrate to the Netherlands, where they had heard freedom of religion existed for all. How many made the trip is not known, but their community was established in Leyden in 1608.

Life in Leyden was hard for the Pilgrims, whose lack of skills restricted them to the lowest-paying positions. The fun-loving Dutch by their lighthearted behavior on Sundays shocked the Pilgrims, and the danger was ever-present that the Pilgrims would be absorbed by the Dutch. By 1620, many Pilgrim children were speaking Dutch, and several members of the church had become Dutch citizens; the Pilgrims feared that their children might lack the dedication to resist the influence of Dutch society and that the great reform movement might die. Consequently, a decision was made to emigrate to America and settle with the permission of the Virginia Company of London in Virginia, where they could practice their religious beliefs freely without being molested by neighbors, and life would be easier and more conducive to the establishment of a utopian society. The Pilgrims journeyed to England and set sail from Plymouth for Virginia on September 6, 1620.

The Pilgrims landed in Massachusetts, which was outside the jurisdiction of the Virginia Company of London. The reasons for the Massachusetts landing are not clear; adverse weather conditions may have been a factor. Of course, the possibility exists that the landing may have been pre-determined by the Pilgrims because there was no established church in New England or for other reasons. The lack of a charter was remedied by the signing on November 11, 1620, of the Mayflower Compact, which established the basis of government in the colony.

The compact reads, in part, as follows:

In the name of God Amen! We whose names are under written . . . do by these presents, solemnly and mutually, in the presence of God and one another covenant and combine ourselves together into a civil body politic for our better ordering and preservation, and furtherance of the ends aforesaid; and by virtue hereof to enact, constitute and frame just and equal laws, ordinances, acts, constitutions, and offices from time to time, as shall be thought most mete and convenient for the general good of the colony; unto which we promise all due submission and obedience.

The Mayflower Compact governed the Plymouth Colony, which was never granted a royal charter until it was merged with the Massachusetts Bay Colony in 1692. Fragmentary evidence available indicates that the leaders of the Plymouth Colony possessed complete power over the colonists and could refuse permission to newcomers to locate in the colony unless they were considered to be prospective members of the church. The Pilgrims exhibited relatively little interest in political philosophy or institutions. Their apparent disinterest in government resulted from the great importance they attached to the doctrines of their church designed to promote their spiritual welfare.[6]

Relatively little is known of the early government of Plymouth Colony, but it is certain its contribution to the development of the Massachusetts town was minor, because Plymouth was directly ruled by the governor and council of the colony and not allowed to develop as a direct democracy. With the exception of Scituate, which in 1636 was authorized ''to make such orders . . . for the convenient and comfortable living as they shall find necessary,'' Plymouth performed all governmental functions until 1651, when Sandwich was permitted to be governed by an elected Board of Selectmen authorized to call town meetings.[7]

In addition to this theocratic government established on the south shore, several fishing villages were established on the north shore but were of a temporary nature. An attempt was made by the Dorchester Company to establish at Cape Ann a permanent fishing base, but it was abandoned in 1626; no civil government had been established at Cape Ann.[8]

While the Pilgrims were meeting in Scrooby, there was in England a group of men who were not Separatists but wished to reform the Church of England and "purify" its liturgy. The Puritans were men of wealth and station in England who were feeling the distress of the times, including the political uncertainties resulting from the continuing struggles between the Crown and Parliament. The Puritans did not suffer persecution in England yet concluded they had little chance of achieving victory in their campaign to reform the Church of England and decided to emigrate to Massachusetts Bay. Although a number of writers have held that theology was responsible for the settlement of the Massachusetts Bay Colony, it would appear that the motivation was religious, economic, and commercial.

Charles I granted the royal charter of the Massachusetts Bay Company, a joint stock company, which created "one body politique and corporate in fact and name, by the name of the Governor and Company of the Massachusetts Bay in New England."[9] The charter, which passed the seals on March 4, 1628–1629,[10] provided for a governor, deputy governor, and eighteen assistants who were authorized to hold a General Court—composed of these officers and freemen of the company—to admit freemen, elect officers, and make laws governing the inhabitants of the colony.[11]

The charter was similar to ones possessed by other commercial and trading companies of its day and led some to conclude that the motivation for the foundation of the company was principally commercial. Yet the charter authorizes the General Court to make orders, laws, and statutes "whereby our said people inhabitants there, maie be soe religiously, peaceablie, and civilly governed, as their good life and orderlie conversacon maie wynn and incite the natives of the country to the knowledg and obedience of the onlie true God and Savior of mankinde, and the Christian fayth, which, in our royall intercon and the adventureers free profession, is the principall ende of this plantacon."[12]

The Puritans brought to Massachusetts Bay a carefully conceived concept of an ideal society and a plan for its future development. This concept included political and economic institutions borrowed from England and adapted to the exigencies of life in Massachusetts Bay.[13]

The records of the Massachusetts Bay Company unfortunately are not as complete as desired by scholars. The first few entries deal primarily with securing supplies for the plantation and authorizing Governor John Endicott and council to make necessary laws and orders for the governing of the plantation. It appears the Puritans believed their new commonwealth could be successful only if the government was controlled by the colonists. If the stockholders resided in England, they might be pressured by the Crown to adopt policies injurious to the new colony, and the danger existed that control of a majority of the stock of the company might fall into the hands of persons unsympathetic to the noble purposes of the Puritans. John Winthrop and others planning to migrate to Massachusetts Bay purchased the shares of those who desired to remain in England. On May 22, 1629, the question of transferring the government to New England was raised for the first time, and on August 29, 1629, the transfer was voted.[14] The form of government for the new colony was established at the third meeting of the General Court in the New World when it voted on October 19, 1630, to authorize freemen to choose assistants empowered to elect from among themselves a governor and deputy governor, who with the assistants would have the power to enact laws and select officers to execute the laws.[15]

Sites for towns were selected on the basis of available springs and defensibility against Indian attack. The territorial area of the town was small and was determined primarily by the convenience of getting to the Sunday meeting, as attendance was compulsory, and absence was subject to a fine or other penalty.[16] The General Court on September 2, 1635, ordered that no dwelling house could be built more than one-half mile beyond the meetinghouse in any new plantation without the permission of the court.[17] As the houses were clustered close together around the common and the meetinghouse, the individual lots were necessarily small, and each lot contained enough space for a house, small outbuildings, and a small garden. Land suitable for cultivation near the center of the town was divided among the settlers in an equitable manner. Each man was responsible for keeping his fields "sufficiently fenced," and town meetings appointed individuals to see that fields were fenced adequately. The penalty in Dorchester for failing to fence properly a field was three shillings.[18] The common land situated near the extremities of the town was used at first for pasture and a source of wood but later was distributed to new settlers.[19]

The completeness of the early records in the towns varied considerably. In general, the early records are sketchy and provide only an approximate picture of town government. Yet they indicate considerable diversity in governmental practices in the various towns. Consequently, it is difficult to arrive at valid generalizations for all early towns.

THE *FOLKMOOT*

The charter of the Plymouth Company, the Mayflower Compact, and the charter of the Massachusetts Bay Company did not contemplate town government and, consequently, made no reference to towns or their government.

The first towns in the Massachusetts Bay Colony were governed by a *folkmoot*, an extra-legal and informal assemblage of the freemen. All matters affecting the welfare of the town, such as the division of land, building of a church, hiring of a minister, and admission of new inhabitants, were discussed, and decisions made. Attendance at town meetings was compulsory; absentees were punished by a fine, and early records contain the names of citizens who failed to attend the meetings. No town officials were elected during the earliest stage of the development of the New England town form of government, which at this stage had not become institutionalized and was completely informal. No town charters existed, no permanent organization was established, the number and frequency of meetings were indeterminate, and no specific duties had been established for the town meeting or town officials as they began to make their appearance.

The distinguishing characteristic of the first New England towns was the primary assembly of adult males as the ruling body. The assembly in the beginning in several towns was held weekly but soon gave way to a monthly meeting. Cambridge at a meeting held on December 24, 1632, established the policy of monthly meetings.[20] Meetings were held in Boston during 1635 on January 23, February 13, September 30, October 4, October 14, November 4, November 23, and December 19. Six meetings were held in Boston during the year 1698.[21] In 1663, Watertown decided to hold an annual town meeting on the first Monday of September.[22]

The practice at the early town meetings was not documented adequately and undoubtedly varied from town to town. It appears that all adult male residents of the town generally were permitted to attend town meetings and speak. However, only freemen usually were allowed to vote. They originally were the shareholders of the Massachusetts Bay Company and later included men who were granted political freedom. An entry in the company records dated October 19, 1630, contains the names of 110 men who desired to be made freemen but fails to mention if any action was taken.[23] The General Court on May 18, 1631, voted that men could not be admitted as freemen ''of this body polliticke'' unless they were ''members of some of the churches within the lymitts of the same.''[24] On March 3, 1636, the General Court ordered that no person shall be admitted as a freeman if he is a member of a church that was organized without the approbation of the magistrates and a majority of the existing churches.[25] On May 18, 1631, 116 men took the oath of freemen, and between March 6, 1632, and March 4, 1636, 340 men took the same oath.[26] Available evidence indicates that freemen constituted a very small percentage of the adult male population in the Massachusetts Bay Colony.[27]

On April 1, 1634, the General Court required every male over twenty years of age who had lived in the colony and was not a freeman to take an oath acknowledging that he and his family were subject to the government of Massachusetts and would be obedient to the magistrates and all laws enacted. Furthermore, he was required to pledge to notify the authorities if he heard of any sedition, violence, or treachery being plotted against the government.[28] If any man twice refused to take the oath, he was banished from the colony unless the court granted him a respite.

The General Court on May 14, 1634, voted to require freemen to take the following oath, which grew out of experimentation with earlier oaths:

I, A.B., being, by Gods providence, an inhabitant & ffreeman within the jurisdiction of this comonweale, doe freely acknowledge my selfe to be subject to the gover^t thereof & therefore doe heere sweare, by the greate & dreadfull name of the euerlyveing God, that I will be true & faithful to the same, & will accordingly yielde assistance & support therevnto, . . . submitting my selfe to the wholesome lawes & orders made & established by the same; and furth^r, that I will not plott nor practice any euill against it, nor consent to any that soe doe, but will timely discover & reveale the same to lawful aucthority nowe here established, for the speedy preventing thereof . . . I will giue my vote & suffrage, as I shall judge im myne owne conscience may best conduce & tend to the publique weale of the body, without respect of psons, or fav^r of any man. Soe helpe mee God, in the Lord Jesus Christ.[29]

The early towns were ethnocentric in character, and their records contain numerous reference to the admission of individuals to towns and the treatment of ''strangers'' by the citizens of a town. In some towns the town meeting empowered the selectmen to admit men as ''townsmen.'' The town frequently would require a newcomer to find a sponsor among the town's residents or post a bond guaranteeing that he would not become a poor relief burden to the town. The *Dorchester Records* contains an interesting reference to the receiving of strangers in the town in 1658:

Not to p'vent such inconuenience as may come if euery one be at liberty to receiue into this towne whom they please. It is ordered therefore by the select men of this towne that if any maner of p'son ore p'sons in this towne shall intertaine anyh soiorour ore inmate into his or ther house ore habitation aboue one weeke without lisence from the selectmen ore the maior parte of them first had and obtained, shall forfeit fiue shillings, and for every weekes Continuance three shillings foure pence.[30]

The *Dorchester Records* also reports that in 1662 ''Daniel Eliers came to the select men and intreated to be an inhabitant in Dorchester; the selectmen would not accept of him to be an inhabitant unless he did bring a sufficient man or men to be bound to secure the towne of him, or to be in couenant for one yeare with some honest man.''[31]

Foreigners coming into Watertown had no rights ''either of commonage, or land vndivided'' but were authorized to buy an inhabitant's rights.[32] During the late 1600s fewer references to strangers or land disposition appear in the official records of the towns.

It appears that many early town meetings were lively affairs and in some instances disorderly. The following entry in the *Dorchester Records* dated ''The 18 of the 10 month 1642'' is of considerable interest:

Whereas it hath beene obserued diuerse tymes, in our general Towne meetings, that some Confusion and disorder hath happened in the agitation of our publicke matters and plantation affaires, by reason that men haue used thire libertye to p'pound theer matters to the Plantation without any fore knoledge of the seauen men, and theere matters have been so followed that diuerse things haue beene spoken of and few matters haue beene issued by reason that new matters haue beene vpsterted and lytle worke don, and moreouer the spirits of som men trobled and offended by reason that thire matters could not be hearde, it is thearefore ordered by the 7 men that al matters and questions which any man hath agitated and petions to be answered by the Plantation shall first be brought to the 7 men or to some tow or more of them, and by them Consydered and orderly p^r sented to the plantation who shal follow the busines, together with the Plantation, without any interruption, by any matters incerted, to the Conclusion and determynation theareof, except it be vnreasonably refused by the 7 men otherwyse euery person ofending against this order shal forfeyt for the same syx pence for euery such offenc to be leuyed by distresse for the use of the towne.[33]

EMERGENCE OF TOWN OFFICIALS

The town meeting soon proved inadequate for the governing of town affairs, and officials began to appear. With their appearance town meetings were held with less frequency and often only once a year to elect officers and conduct town business; special meetings were held if needed.

The first town official to appear in the records of the Massachusetts Bay Company was the constable. The court of assistants on September 28, 1630, appointed the constables of Salem and Dorchester.[34] On October 19, 1630, the General Court appointed the constable in Charlton, Rocksbury, and Watertown.[35] The constable undoubtedly was considered the most important town official in the early days of the town, as he was selected by the General Court and was the only town official referred to in the records of the company until April 1, 1634, when the General Court ordered the constable and four or more "of the cheife inhabitants" of every town to survey the houses, cornfields, and other lands and enter their findings in a book, a copy of which was to be transmitted to the General Court.[36] He warned the inhabitants of all town meetings and also acted as the tax collector in smaller towns.

The first locally elected town officials to make their appearance in the early town records were the selectmen. The *Dorchester Records* first refers to them on October 8, 1633.[37] Terms of office usually were either annual or semi-annual.

The Massachusetts town started with a plural executive: the selectmen. During the early years of town government selectmen were not called by their present title but were called "townsmen" in Cambridge, "selected townsmen," "the seven," the "nine" men, or "chosen men for managing the prudential affairs," and in Dorchester "The names of such as were chosen for the ordering of the affares of the plantation."[38] An entry dated "This 24th of the 1st mo., 1642" in the *Boston Records* contains the first reference to the term "selectmen."[39] An entry in the *Cambridge Records* dated November 20, 1665, is entitled "At a meeting of the selectmen" but refers to "The townsmen" issuing orders.[40]

The number of selectmen varied from town to town and from time to time within a town, ranging from three in Charlestown to twelve in Dorchester. The October 8, 1633, Dorchester town meeting agreed that there should be twelve selectmen, but the following year on October 28 the town meeting decided that there should be ten.[41] The selectmen frequently met in the home of one of their members, and the clerk recorded their proceedings in the same book in which he recorded the proceedings of the town meeting.

The duties assigned the selectmen by the town meeting differed to some extent from town to town. Their duties in Watertown included the division of town lands, repairing and enlarging the meetinghouse, surveying the inhabitants relative to their knowledge of God, and ensuring that children received an education.[42] In Dorchester, their duties included regulating the presence of strangers in the town, laying out ways, appointing a captain and lieutenant to be in charge of the ammunition, regulating the sale of cider and the cutting of trees, and selecting a schoolmaster.[43] Selectmen in the early days also performed certain judicial functions.[44] Decisions could be made by a majority of the selectmen present, provided there was a quorum. In Dorchester in 1634, there were ten selectmen, and a quorum of seven was established.[45] The town meeting, however, kept ultimate power in its own hands, and the selectmen acted principally as an executive committee of the town meeting.

The *Dorchester Records* contains a curious document referred to as "The Directory," which gives charges to the selectmen:

Fourthly we require that our 7 men shalbe careffull to meet 8 tymes in the yeare viz the 2 monday of euery month in the yeare except the 2:5:6:8 at some place which shal be certainly knowne vnto all the Tow and there be Resident from 9 oclocke in the aff ore noone vnto 3 oclocke in the afternoone: that so all such haue any Complaints or Requests to make or any information to giue or anything what soeuer to doe with them moie Certainely Find all or 5 of them at the Least.[46]

One of the seven selectmen in Dorchester was appointed the moderator because of "intemperate clashings in our towne meetings."[47]

The most complete early record describing the government of a Massachusetts town is contained in the report of the town meeting held in Dorchester on October 8, 1633:

Inprimus it is ordered that for the generall good and well ordering of the affayres of the Plantation their shall be every Mooneday before the Court by eight of the Clocke in the morning, and p^r sently upon the beating of the drum, a generall meeting of the inhabitants of the Plantation att the meeteing house, there to settle (and sett downe) such orders as may tend to the generall good as aforesays: and every man to be bound thereby without gaynesaying or resistance. It is also agreed that there shall be twelve men selected out of the Company that may or the greatest p't of them meete as aforesayd to determine as aforesayd, yet so as it is desired that the most of the Plantation will keepe the meeteing constantly and all that are there although none of the Twelve shall have a free voyce as any of the 12 and that the great(r) vote both of the 12 and the other shall be of force and efficasy and aforesayd. And it is likewise ordered that all things concluded as aforesay shall stand in force and be obeyed until the next monethly meeteing and aferwardes if it not contradicted and otherwise ordered upon the sayd monethly meete (ing) by the greatest p'te of those that are p^r sent as aforesayd.[48]

Although the selectmen were the first elected officials documented in early town records, the existence of the records is conclusive evidence that someone was charged with the duty of keeping them. In 1656, the *Dorchester Records* refers to the choice of a "recorder" for the town, and the *Boston Records* under an entry dated "12 March 9/23" refers to the "towne clarke."[49] The functions of the town clerk in many respects were similar to those of the church vestry clerk in England.

Not only was attendance at town meetings compulsory, but officeholding was compulsory for those elected. The records of the October 28, 1634, Dorchester town meeting contain the following entry: "It is agreed that whosoever is chosen in to any office for the good of the Plantation, he shall abide by it, or submit to a fine as the company shall thinke meete to impose."[50] In Boston in 1653, "Joseph Rock was fined twenty shillings for refusing to accept the office of a Constable, being legally chosen thereunto."[51]

THEORIES OF ORIGIN

A considerable dispute raged among historians during the latter quarter of the nineteenth century over the question of whether the Massachusetts town was (1) indigenous in origin, (2) a lineal descendant of the ancient Anglo-Saxon *tun*, or (3) an adaptation to a new environment of English institutions with which the colonists were familiar.

The first theory is a parthenogenetic one, holding the town developed spontaneously as a new political institution on the rocky shores of Massachusetts as the colonists faced an environment completely foreign to them. Evidence to support this theory is completely lacking.

Herbert B. Adams held that the Massachusetts towns were descendants of English local institutions that, in turn, had descended from Germanic prototypes. Writing in 1882, he reported that the villages in southern Germany were physically similar to New England rural towns.[52] Adams came to the conclusion that the New England town meeting grew out of the primordial field meetings of German farmers held for the purpose of distributing land and regulating crops; the village elders were the forerunners of the constable and selectmen of the Massachusetts town.[53] Adams wrote:

The original idea of New England Towns, like that of their Old English and Germanic prototypes, was that of a village community of allied families, settled in close proximity for good neighborhood and defense, with homes and home lots fenced in and owned in severalty, but with a common Town Street and a Village Green or Home Pasture, and with common fields, allotted outside the Town for individual mowing and tillage but fenced in common, together with a vast surrounding tract of absolutely common and undivided land, used for pasture and woodland under communal regulations.[54]

Whether a lineage can be established descending from the ancient Germanic *tuns* through Anglo-Saxon institutions to the New England towns is debatable. Certainly, the similarities between the New England town and the Germanic *tun* may be partially or completely coincidental rather than evolutionary. The records of the early Massachusetts towns are fragmentary regarding the origin of the town form of government but contain nothing suggesting a conscious copying of Germanic institutions.

The third theory posits that the colonists upon their arrival in Massachusetts adapted the English manor and vestry with which they were familiar to a totally new situation. Many similarities exist between the New England town and older English institutions that suggest a continuity between them. In England, prior to the settlement of colonies in Massachusetts, parishioners met in the vestry to make decisions concerning the support of the church and elected churchwardens who were placed in charge of the property of the church.[55] Following the break with the Church of Rome, laws were passed imposing many civil duties upon the churchwardens, including the hiring of schoolmasters and the administering of laws. The vestry meeting and the churchwardens correspond, in certain respects, to the town meeting and the selectmen, respectively.

Support for the third theory is found in the records of the court of assistants held at Charlestown on August 23, 1630; the court stipulated that justices of the peace shall have "like power that justices of the peace hath in England."[56] Further evidence is the fact that churchwardens in England were referred to in the records as "the four," "the twelve," or "the sixteen," and selectmen in the early Massachusetts towns were referred to as "the ten" and the "seven men."[57]

Sumner C. Powell's study of the settlement of Sudbury, Massachusetts, shattered a number of generalizations about the early Massachusetts towns.[58] Powell pointed out that the settlers of Sudbury did not emigrate from the same English village but rather from a large number of boroughs, parishes, and towns.[59] The early Sudbury leaders evidently borrowed from each of these systems of local government in constructing the Sudbury governmental system. Powell reached the conclusion that "there were multiple origins and many distinct early towns, and that all of these towns and their relationships need careful examination."[60]

Available evidence supports the theory that the settlers in each town adapted a number of familiar English institutions to the exigencies of life in Massachusetts Bay. It is not unreasonable to conclude that town institutions were forged by experimentation over a period of years.

Chapter 3 examines in detail the operation of the open town meeting in Massachusetts.

NOTES

1. *Tercentenary of the Landing of the Popham Colony at the Mouth of the Kennebec River, August 19, 1907* (Portland: Maine Historical Society, 1907), pp. 2–28.

2. Samuel G. Drake, *The History and Antiquities of Boston, From Its Settlement in 1630 to the Year 1770* (Boston: Luther Stevens, 1856), p. 29.

3. Francis S. Drake, *The Town of Roxbury* (Boston: Municipal Printing Office, 1905), p. 2.

4. See Roland G. Usher, *The Pilgrims and Their History* (New York: Macmillan Company, 1918).

5. Ibid., p. 17.

6. Francis Baylies, *Historical Memoir of the Colony of New Plymouth* (Boston: Wiggin & Lunt, 1866), vol. 1, pp. 256–57.

7. Nathaniel B. Shurtleff, ed., *Records of the Colony of New Plymouth in New England* (Boston: From the Press of William White, 1855), vol. 1, p. 44; Henry C. Kittredge, *Barnstable: 1639–1939* (Barnstable, Mass.: Tercentenary Committee, 1939), p. 12.

8. Clifford K. Shipton, *Roger Conant* (Cambridge: Harvard University Press, 1944), pp. 50–59.

9. Nathaniel B. Shurtleff, ed., *Records of the Governor and Company of the Massachusetts Bay in New England* (Boston: From the Press of William White, 1853), vol. 1, p. 10.

10. The Julian calendar was in use at the time, and the year legally commenced on March 25. The first date in a double date refers to the legal year, and the second date to the historical year.

11. Shurtleff, *Records of the Governor and Company*, vol. 1, pp. 10–17.

12. Ibid., p. 17.

13. William Haller, Jr., *The Puritan Town-Planting in New England Colonial Development 1630–1660* (New York: Columbia University Press, 1951), p. 13.

14. Shurtleff, *Records of the Governor and Company*, vol. 1, pp. 49, 51.

15. Ibid., p. 79.

16. James K. Hosmer, *Samuel Adams, the Man of the Town Meeting* (Baltimore: Johns Hopkins University Studies in Historical and Political Science, 1884), vol. 2, no. 4, pp. 8–9.

17. Shurtleff, *Records of the Governor and Company*, vol. 1, p. 157.

18. *Dorchester Town Records*. Fourth Report of the Record Commissions of the City of Boston, 2nd ed. (Boston: Rockwell and Churchill, 1883), p. 3.

19. George L. Haskins, *Law and Authority in Early Massachusetts* (New York: Macmillan Company, 1960), pp. 69–70.

20. *The Records of the Town of Cambridge (Formerly Newtowne) Massachusetts 1630–1703* (Cambridge: Printed by order of the City Council under direction of the City Clerk, 1901), p. 4.

21. *Second Report of the Record Commissioners of the City of Boston* (Boston: Rockwell and Churchill, 1877), pp. 2–9, 222–40.

22. *Watertown Records* (Watertown, Mass.: Press of Fred G. Barker, 1894), p. 78.

23. Shurtleff, *Records of the Governor and Company*, vol. 1, pp. 78–80.

24. Ibid., p. 87.

25. Ibid., p. 168.

26. Ibid., pp. 367–70.

27. Haller, *Puritan Town-Planting*, p. 22.
28. Shurtleff, *Records of the Governor and Company*, vol. 1, pp. 115–16.
29. Ibid., p. 117.
30. *Dorchester Records*, p. 95.
31. Ibid., pp. 113–14.
32. *Watertown Records*, p. 2.
33. *Dorchester Records*, pp. 50–51. The term "plantation" was utilized to designate a colony or a town. The term is employed only in Maine today.
34. Shurtleff, *Records of the Governor and Company*, vol. 1, p. 76.
35. Ibid., p. 79.
36. Ibid., p. 116.
37. *Dorchester Records*, p. 3.
38. *Cambridge Records*, p. 50; *Dorchester Records*, p. 19.
39. *Boston Records*, p. 68.
40. *Cambridge Records*, p. 159.
41. *Dorchester Records*, pp. 3, 7.
42. *Watertown Records*, p. 2.
43. *Dorchester Records*, pp. 95, 99, 110, 177, 257.
44. *Boston Records*, pp. 97, 112.
45. *Dorchester Records*, p. 7.
46. Ibid., p. 290.
47. Ibid., pp. 292–93.
48. Ibid., p. 3.
49. Ibid., p. 83; *Boston Records*, p. 212.
50. *Dorchester Records*, p. 8.
51. *Boston Records*, p. 115.
52. Herbert B. Adams, *The Germanic Origin of New England Towns* (Baltimore: Johns Hopkins University Studies in Historical and Political Science, 1882), vol. 1, no. 2, p. 12. For an opposing view, consult Alfred Worcester, *The Origin of the New England Town Meeting* (Waltham, MA.: Waltham Historical Society, 1925).
53. Adams, *The Germanic Origin*, p. 18.
54. Ibid., pp. 27–28.
55. W. Eric Jackson, *Local Government in England and Wales* (Hardmonsworth, Middlesex: Penguin Books, 1959), pp. 23–25; Wallace Notestein, *The English People on the Eve of Colonization* (New York: Harper & Row, Publishers, 1954), pp. 240–49.
56. Shurtleff, *Records*, vol. 1, p. 74.
57. Notestein, *The English People*, p. 241; *Dorchester Records*, pp. 7, 47.
58. Sumner C. Powell, *Puritan Village* (Middletown, Conn.: Wesleyan University Press, 1963).
59. Ibid., p. 6.
60. Ibid., p. 139.

Chapter 3

The Massachusetts
Open Town Meeting

The town meeting is the distinguishing feature of town government in Massachusetts and is sanctioned by the constitution of the Commonwealth, which dates to 1780:

> The people have a right, in an orderly and peaceable manner, to assemble to consult upon the common good; give instructions to their representatives, and to request of the legislative body, by way of addresses, petitions, or remonstrances, redress of the wrongs done them, and of the grievances they suffer.[1]

The open town meeting, which developed as a primary assembly of freemen during the 1630s (see Chapter 2), remains fundamentally the same today as the local law-making body in 84 percent of the towns; its trappings have changed little. The development of the finance committee as a valuable adjunct represents the most important change in the town meeting structure in these towns (for town organization, see Appendix II).

Massachusetts currently has 312 towns and thirty-nine cities. Two hundred and sixty-two towns hold open town meetings, forty-two towns hold representative or limited town meetings, five towns have a town manager and a town council, and four towns have a mayor and a town council. The towns with a council in effect have become cities but have retained the term "town."

To collect data, a questionnaire was mailed in 1996 to each town with an open town meeting. Responses were received from 170 towns (65%), but not every respondent answered each question. Interviews also were conducted with a number of town clerks, town meeting moderators, and knowledgeable citizens, and public reports and newspaper accounts of numerous meetings were examined.

THE ANNUAL TOWN MEETING

Somnolent-appearing towns spring to life at annual town meeting time when town officers are elected and town business is transacted. Each town must hold its annual meeting in February, March, April, or May unless a special law or charter specifies a different month; the selectpersons may call special meetings when necessary.[2] Walpole, for example, holds its annual town meeting on the third Monday of January.[3] If a fixed meeting date falls on a legal holiday, the meeting is held the next day. A by-law enacted by the town meeting may specify the hour at which the annual meeting will be convened. Meetings may be held any place in the town and adjourned when necessary.

Traditionally, town meetings have been held in the town hall, but the population growth of many towns has necessitated the use of larger assembly halls such as a school auditorium or gymnasium. The attorney general of the commonwealth opined in 1961 that a town meeting may not be held in a regional school unless it is located in the town.[4] Ashburnham desired to hold town meetings in the Oakmont Regional High School auditorium but was prevented from so doing, as the auditorium is located on the Westminster side of the building, "which straddles the boundary between the two towns forming the district."[5] In 1971, however, the Supreme Judicial Court opined that a 1971 statute permitting the holding of the deliberative session of a town meeting outside the town but within the regional school district in which the town was a member did not violate the constitution provision regarding town meetings.[6] Election of town officers, however, must be held within the town.

Town meetings normally are called by the selectpersons, but may be called by the town clerk if all selectpersons vacate their offices for any reason. If there is no town clerk, a justice of the peace may call a town meeting.[7] The selectpersons must call a special meeting upon the written request of 200 voters or 20 percent of the registered voters.[8] Should the selectpersons unreasonably refuse to call a meeting, 100, or 10 percent of the registered voters, may submit a written application to a justice of the peace, who is authorized to call a meeting by issuing a warrant.[9]

The Warrant

Each town meeting is held in pursuance of a warrant or warning, which is the town meeting foundation stone, as it contains a listing of the articles for consideration by the town meeting. The warrant is drafted and issued by the selectpersons, who must give at least seven days' notice when calling the annual town meeting and fourteen days' notice when calling a special meeting.[10]

Since early towns were small, and freemen were required, subject to a fine, to attend all town meetings, there was no need to prepare a warrant listing the articles to be considered. With the dropping of the compulsory attendance requirement and the population growth of towns it became necessary to warn the voters of the matters to be considered at a town meeting in order to enable all voters interested in any or all matters to attend.

It is not uncommon for the selectpersons to list the more controversial articles first in the warrant for consideration early in the meeting when attendance is at its peak; routine articles sometimes are rushed over near the end of the meeting after many voters have left. This practice clearly is superior to the listing of polemical articles near the end of the warrant. The town meeting, however, may vote to consider articles out of the order in which they appear in the warrant.

A town meeting is not legal unless it is held in pursuance of a warrant issued by a majority of the selectpersons, the town clerk, or a justice of the peace.[11] Only articles included in the warrant may be considered by the town meeting; in other words, the warrant is the fixed agenda for the town meeting, and irrelevant motions may not be introduced.[12] The town meeting is not a continuing body, as it is dissolved upon the completion of action on the warrant; the meeting cannot be reconvened. However, a new town meeting can be called into existence by a new warrant.

The selectpersons may include in the warrant any article they wish to have considered by the town meeting and usually include articles requested by various town officers, boards, commissions, and committees. If there is no finance committee, the selectpersons must prepare and submit the town budget to the annual town meeting.[13] The initiative may be used by the voters in every town to insert articles in the warrant. The General Court on December 22, 1715, first authorized the use of the initiative in towns by requiring the selectpersons to insert in the warrant for calling a town meeting any matter accompanied by a petition signed by ten or more freeholders.[14] Selectpersons must insert in the annual meeting warrant all articles they have been requested to insert in writing by ten or more registered voters prior to the closing of the warrant and in a special town meeting warrant all articles they have been requested to insert "in writing by one hundred registered voters or by ten percent of the total number of registered voters of the town whichever number is the lesser."[15] However, the initiative seldom is used in most towns, as the selectpersons customarily include in the warrant any article requested verbally or in writing by a registered voter. In most instances the selectpersons include a requested article as worded by the voter(s), even though the wording may be improper. Should the selectpersons agree with the substance of the improperly worded article, they may insert a properly worded article immediately preceding the requested article; the adoption of the selectpersons' article obviates the necessity of acting upon the following article, and it usually is "passed over."

The Massachusetts Supreme Judicial Court has ruled that "the object of a warrant is to give previous notice to the inhabitants of the subjects to be acted on, and if this is done substantially it is sufficient."[16] The court later held that "warrants for town meetings are not to be construed with technical precision; it is enough if they give intelligible notice of the subjects to be acted on at the meeting."[17] A warrant article "to hear the report of any committee heretofore chosen, and pass any vote in relation to the same'' is adequate notice for a town meeting to vote funds recommended by a committee appointed at a previous town meeting under the provisions of a warrant that fully specified the business to be considered.[18] The Supreme Judicial Court also ruled that an article in the warrant ''to raise such sums as may be necessary to defray town charges for the ensuing year'' is sufficient notice to allow the town meeting to vote to raise funds for specific town purposes.[19] An article in the warrant for a Williamstown annual meeting ''to elect all necessary town officers for the ensuing year'' was held to be sufficient notice to authorize the town meeting to invest the collector of taxes ''with all the powers which a town treasurer has when appointed collector of taxes.''[20] At an adjourned session of a town meeting any article in the warrant may be reconsidered, provided the rights of other parties have not become vested under the votes passed at an earlier session.[21]

The procedure for notifying and warning the town of a forthcoming town meeting is formalized in law and tradition. The selectpersons direct the warrant to the constables or other specified persons, who give notice to the town meeting and make the return of the accomplishment of the directive according to the procedure specified in the town by-laws. In towns that lack by-laws, notice is given in the manner prescribed by a vote of the town meeting or the attorney general of the commonwealth.[22] In Oak Bluffs, for example, ''all Town Meetings, including the annual meeting, shall be notified by posting notice thereof in two or more public places in the Town at least seven days before the time of said meeting, and by publishing the same in some newspaper published in the county. Such notices shall contain the warrant in full which is to be acted upon in said meeting.''[23] The return of a constable upon the warrant for a town meeting certifying he posted the warrant according to law without specifying the manner of posting is sufficient.[24] The Supreme Judicial Court has ruled that a by-law specifying that notice of a town meeting be posted at the town hall was complied with by posting the notice at the building where the meeting was to be held, in view of the fact the town hall had been destroyed by fire.[25]

The Annual Report

The selectpersons are required by general law subject to a fifty-dollar fine to print, prior to the annual town meeting, the annual town report for the previous year containing the reports of town officers and boards, the jury list, and other matters required by law or town by-law to be included.[26] A copy must be sent to the state library; failure to do so results in the commonwealth's withholding from the town publications that are distributed to other towns.[27] Although the selectpersons must print the annual town report, they do not have to prepare it. The Adams annual report is compiled and edited by the Permanent Town Report Committee, authorized by a special town meeting held on June 24, 1963.

Several towns print the warrant for the forthcoming annual meeting in the annual report, which contains the action taken on the articles in the warrant for the previous year's annual meeting and warrant for each special town meeting, if any. This practice is very desirable, as it facilitates reference to previous action taken on warrant articles and pertinent information bearing on the articles contained in the reports of various town officials and boards.

Annual town reports often are difficult to read. Careful preparation and editing are prerequisites to the publication of readable annual reports. They should be written in a semi-popular style or contain an easy-to-read summary. Generous use should be made of charts, tables, maps, photographs, cartoons, and colors within the limits of reasonable cost. The 1964 Berlin annual report not only made use of bar and pie charts but also contained definitions of terms such as "overlay," "free cash," and "cherry sheet," which are confusing to the average town resident.[28] One of the most effective types of annual reports is the report issued as a newspaper supplement. It generally is written with an unusual clarity of expression and is distributed to nearly every home in the town.

The Pre–Town Meeting Meeting

Seventy-three of 170 (43%) surveyed towns reported that a pre–town meeting meeting was held where the warrant was explained by town officers, and questions were raised and answered. Attendance ranged from less than 1.0 percent to 4.5 percent of the registered voters. Several officers responded that attendance was only a few, a handful, or minuscule.

Reporting officers indicated they were disappointed that such a small number of voters attended these meetings, as they educate attendees prior to the business part of the annual town meeting relative to the issues and the reasons town officers and committees are advancing specific recommendations. One respondent wrote that "the majority of the townspeople have lived here less than fifteen years and one-third here less than five years. These new residents came from cities where there are no town meetings and it is difficult to educate them that they must take part in town government if they expect results."

Election of Town Officers

In the early towns, officers were elected first, and business was conducted immediately following the elections. Terms of office were indeterminate but generally were short, ranging from a few months to one year. Various methods of voting were utilized at early town meetings. The General Court first regulated the manner of voting in town elections on November 11, 1647, when it ordered that voting shall be done by "beanes and paper."[29]

The General Court on November 16, 1692, enacted the first act that generally regulated the election of town officers.[30] The annual town meeting for the election of officers was required to be held in March. Three, five, seven, or nine men were to be elected as selectmen and overseers of the poor; a town clerk, "a commissioner for assessments, constables, surveyors of highways, tythingmen, fence viewers, clerks of the market, sealers of leather, and other ordinary town officers'' also were to be elected. On January 15, 1743, the General Court approved an act stipulating that no person could participate in the election of officers and the conduct of business at a town meeting unless he was ''personally present at such meeting, and have a rateable estate in such town . . . besides the poll, amounting to the value of twenty pounds.''[31]

Although one-year terms for town officers are common today, the trend is toward longer terms. With certain exceptions, towns presently are required at the annual meeting when the term of any officer expires to elect by ballot from among the registered voters each of the following for a term of one or more years: a town clerk, town treasurer, one or more collectors of taxes, one or more auditors, one or more highway surveyors, one or more road commissioners, one or more sewer commissioners, a tree warden, one or more constables, three or more members of the school committee, and three or more members of the board of health if the town has created such a board.[32]

Voters also elect three or more selectpersons, one or more assessors, and three or more assistant assessors (if authorized by a town meeting) for terms not exceeding three years. The town meeting also is authorized to designate the town treasurer as collector of taxes. If a town has not established a board of health, the selectpersons act as the board of health. A town meeting also is authorized to provide for the appointment of the tree warden. All other town officers are appointed by the Board of Selectmen unless a town meeting has provided for another method of their selection.

The decisions relative to the terms and number of town officials and consolidations of offices are not made at each annual meeting. The town officials to be elected at a given annual meeting and their terms have been determined at previous town meetings. ''In any case where three or more members of a board are to be elected for terms of more than one year, as nearly one-third as may be shall be elected annually.''[33] Failure to elect selectpersons or assessors subjects the town to a fine of $1 to $500 as the county commissioners determine.[34]

The warrant for the annual town meeting warns the voters of the forthcoming election of town officers as well as the business to be considered. For example, the warrant for the 1964 Templeton annual town meeting reads, in part, as follows:

In the name of the Commonwealth of Massachusetts, you are directed to notify and warn the inhabitants of each of the several precincts of the Town of Templeton, County of Worcester, qualified to vote in Elections and Town places designated and appointed, by the Selectmen, to wit:
In Precinct No. 1—First Church Chapel Hall
In Precinct No. 2—Scout Hall
In Precinct No. 3—Otter River School
In Precinct No. 4—American Legion Hall
on Monday the second day of March, next, at 11 o'clock A.M. to bring in their votes to

the election officers, on one ballot. . . . The Polls will open at 11 o'clock A.M. and be closed at 7 o'clock P.M. And you are further directed to notify all the inhabitants of the Town of Templeton, qualified to vote in Elections and Town Affairs, to meet in the Narragansett Regional High School Auditorium in said Templeton on Saturday, March 7, next, at 1:30 P.M. then and there to act on the following articles.[35]

Towns, by by-law or charter, may designate the hour at which the annual meeting shall commence and the hours during which the polls may be open and, with the exceptions of the election of officers and matters required by law to be determined by ballot, stipulate the hour after which all business shall be considered or that all business shall be considered by adjournment to another day.[36] A town may schedule the election of town officers to be held within thirty-five days before or after the annual meeting at which business is transacted, provided the time and place(s) for the election are stated in the warrant for the annual meeting; the election is deemed to be part of the annual town meeting.[37] In the larger towns it is common practice to hold town elections on one day and consider all business at an adjourned session on another day. Agawam and Saugus are unusual in that town officers are elected in November.

Several different methods are utilized to nominate candidates for town offices. In all towns candidates for town offices can have their names placed upon the ballot by filing with the town clerk nomination papers signed by registered voters equal in number to 1 percent of the vote cast for governor in the town in the previous state election but no fewer than twenty nor more than fifty voters.[38] In a number of towns it is assumed that incumbents are running for re-election unless the town clerk receives a written communication to the contrary.

In towns with non-partisan elections nominations may be made by one of two caucus systems authorized by the general laws.[39] Each caucus system is basically the same. The caucus is called by the selectpersons and is called to order by the town clerk until a chairman is elected. The town clerk may not be elected clerk of the caucus or any other caucus officer. The chairman of the caucus is elected for only that caucus but often is elected chairman of caucuses held in subsequent years. His duties are somewhat comparable to those of the town meeting moderator. The town meeting "may determine whether nominations shall be made separately or partly or wholly on one ballot, and may within the limits defined by law, prescribe the day and hour when such caucuses shall be held and how long the polls shall be kept open, and make provision for the preparation and use of ballots."[40] In Wellesley, for example, an adjourned session of the annual town meeting on April 29, 1940, voted that caucuses shall be held at least twenty-five days prior to the town election commencing at 8:00 P.M., and the polls shall be kept open until 10:00 P.M. or later if the caucus so determines. One ballot prepared by the town clerk is given to each voter as he or she enters the hall.[41] Candidates nominated by caucus are so designated on the ballot and may benefit from this designation. Holden did away with the caucus because most candidates defeated in the caucus filed nomination petitions and ran in the town elections.

Towns that have partisan elections hold caucuses under provisions of the general laws.[42] Candidates may run in the caucus of each party. In Webster in 1961, for example, four Democrats entered both the Democratic and Republican caucuses; two Democrats were nominated by the Democratic caucus, and two were nominated by the Republican caucus.[43]

The arrangement of the names of candidates for town offices on the ballot is governed by general law. Candidates for re-election are listed first on the election ballot in alphabetical order by office followed by non-incumbents listed in alphabetical order by office.[44]

Towns divided into voting precincts may allow precinct voting for the election of town officers at the annual meeting and at special elections. The town clerk and the board of registrars are required to canvass the returns from the several precincts and declare immediately the results.[45] Absentee voting is allowed in towns that have accepted an enabling statute providing for absentee voting at regular town elections.[46]

Elections in most towns are non-partisan. Eighteen towns with open town meetings hold partisan elections: Canton, Clinton, Douglas, Dudley, Great Barrington, Hampden, Lenox, Maynard, Northfield, Palmer, Sheffield, Southbridge, Southwick, Stockbridge, Ware, Webster, West Stockbridge, and Wilbraham. Two towns with representative town meetings hold partisan elections: Lee and West Springfield. There has been talk in a few towns with non-partisan elections of adopting partisan elections, but no town has done so.

Citizen associations that recruit or endorse candidates for town officers are found in a few towns. Frequently, these associations prove to be temporary and die a natural death following one or two elections. Needham had a citizen association that played a somewhat unsuccessful role in one election and expired. In a few towns with non-partisan elections the citizen associations represent the Democratic and Republican parties under different names. A citizen association may gain dominance in town elections. To cite one example, the 1965 and 1966 slates of candidates selected by the Paxton Citizens Town Committee were unchallenged.

"Know Your Candidates Night" is sponsored by civic associations in many towns; these meetings most commonly are sponsored by the League of Women Voters. However, the sponsor may be the Chamber of Commerce, the Parent-Teacher Association, the Junior Chamber of Commerce, or a women's club. At these meetings candidates for town offices are introduced, are permitted to speak briefly, and answer questions raised by the audience.

Of 163 responding towns in 1996, only 6 (3.7%) had an electoral contest for each town office. Seventy-seven (47.2%) towns reported there was a candidate for each town office. These data suggest that citizen interest in serving in town government office is not great. However, recognition must be accorded to the fact that many town offices are minor ones, and one must remember that off-iceholding was compulsory in the early Massachusetts Bay towns.

Conduct of Business

All mundane matters, major or trivial, affecting the town may be brought before the town meeting to be debated and decided. Each article in the warrant is taken up and considered; the consideration may be no more than a motion and a vote "to pass over" the article.

At the typical town meeting debate tends to be practical rather than philo-sophical in nature. Its quality varies from the dull, shallow, specious, and su-perfluous to the didactic and the profound. A certain amount of levity often is interjected in the debates. Usually at least one voter will refer to what the tax rate was in 1963 or some other year and condemn excessive spending. On a zoning issue a voter may say, "You buy a piece of property and you cannot do what you want with it," and a second voter may accuse the planning board of "representing the people across the street instead of the whole town." However, debate in general is sensible.

Viva voce voting most commonly is used, but show of hands, standing votes, division of the meeting, a roll call, and written ballots may be used. A roll call seldom is demanded because it is too time-consuming in most towns. Secret ballots are used in voting on highly emotional issues to protect voters who fear recriminations if their votes were public. Such voting is slow and, depending upon the number of ballots cast, may take thirty or more minutes to cast the ballots and another fifteen or more minutes to count the ballots.

Articles are voted authorizing the town treasurer with the approval of the selectpersons to borrow funds in anticipation of tax revenue, the purchase of land, the selectpersons to employ counsel and defend the town against any suit brought against it, the creation of an unpaid committee to study the advisability of establishing a regional vocational school district, and the transfer of a street light from one pole to a second pole on the same street. Other articles are voted accepting the reports of committees and a street for plowing, fixing the salary and compensation of elective town officers, appropriating funds for vocational education and land damages resulting from street improvements, instructing the assessors to use a specified sum from free cash to reduce the tax rate, and changing the zone of a strip of land from commercial to residential. The town budget usually is the most important article adopted at the town meeting and varies from several thousand dollars in the smallest towns to millions of dollars in large towns.

Voters are authorized by general law to adjourn a town meeting from time to time, and any article included in the warrant may be acted upon at the ad-journed meeting.[47] In adjourning, a town meeting must fix a future time for the adjourned session to ensure all voters are informed of the meeting date and time.[48] An adjourned meeting may reconsider and revoke its approval at the first session of a warrant article, provided rights have not become vested.[49]

Annual town meetings in 1996 varied in length from one hour in several small towns to three hours on each of six days in Wayland (12,725), where the average number of nights over the past twenty-five years has been 4.8, and the average attendance has been 367. The vast majority of the 166 reporting towns do not have adjourned meetings or have them only on a very occasional basis. A moderator wrote that during the past ten years he had "managed the annual town meeting on one night on either two or three occasions." After the first night, he reported that the number of voters in attendance depended on the importance of the remaining warrant articles and that on occasion he did not have a quorum on the second night, which is a Tuesday. Somewhat surprisingly, he always had a quorum on the following Monday, when all business was concluded.

Five towns reported that no special town meetings are held, and the vast majority of the other towns reported holding only one or two such meetings. The length of special town meetings in 1996 ranged from ten minutes to four hours. Fifty-two (32%) of the 164 reporting towns indicated that 75 to 100 percent of the warrant articles were routine matters.

Certain actions of the open town meeting in Marblehead have been subject to referendum since 1954. Any vote appropriating

fifty thousand dollars or more as a special appropriation or establishing a new board or office or abolishing an old board or office or merging two or more boards or offices, or fixing the term of office of town officers, where such term is optional, or increasing or reducing the number of members of a board, or adopting a new by-law, or amending an existing by-law, shall not be operative until the expiration of five days, exclusive of Sundays and holidays, from the dissolution of the meeting, nor, if a petition for referendum thereon has been filed, until the question of ratification of such vote has been determined in the manner herein provided.[50]

A referendum must be held if petitions are signed by 300 registered voters, and the town meeting actions submitted to the voters for determination are reversed by majority vote, provided at least 20 percent of the registered voters so vote. In 1956, the voters in a referendum reversed by a vote of 3,873 to 2,141 the approval by the town meeting of an article providing for the re-valuation of property; a referendum on the same subject was held on March 21, 1966.[51] Prior to the adoption of a representative town meeting in 1948, Norwood voters were authorized by a 1939 special act to use the referendum.[52]

A presiding officer and procedural rules are essential at town meetings to protect the rights of individuals and minorities and also to facilitate the efficient conduct of business. Procedural rules for town meetings are contained in the general laws of the commonwealth and in many town by-laws. A town is authorized by general law to adopt by-laws for the regulation of the town meeting.[53]

The Moderator. The earliest town meetings were small and apparently did not have moderators, as the town records contain no references to them. The first order of business at an early town meeting was the election of a moderator for the meeting. The General Court in 1715 required each town to elect a moderator empowered to manage and regulate the meeting, and no one was permitted to speak without permission from the moderator.[54]

The moderator is the cynosure of the town meeting and its presiding officer, who is a person of great respect, parliamentary skill, and tact. Occasionally, a woman is elected moderator.

The moderator may be elected for each meeting as the first order of business at the meeting or for a term of one to three years by ballot with the use of the voting list at the meeting for the election of town officers.[55] In only a few towns is he or she elected for each meeting. Most moderators are elected to one-year terms with re-election to another one-year term nearly automatic. Prior to assuming office the moderator is sworn "to the faithful performance of his duties" by the town clerk.[56]

If the office becomes vacant for any reason, the town meeting elects a new moderator. A temporary moderator must be elected in the absence of the moderator. Until a moderator is elected, the town clerk presides at the meeting, but, if absent, the chairman of the Board of Selectmen presides or, in his or her absence, the senior selectperson.[57]

The moderator's duties are spelled out by statute and supplemented by by-laws and customs in many towns. Consequently, the practices of the moderator vary from town to town, as each has its own personality, which is reflected in the manner in which the town meeting is conducted; the moderator may follow the rule book closely, or he may conduct the meeting on a relatively informal basis as long as the meeting runs smoothly. If a motion is made that is not on the warrant, the moderator cannot accept it as an official motion but may accept it as an unofficial motion to take the sense of the meeting, provided no voter objects to the procedure.

A town meeting may be held in more than one building, provided the buildings have been equipped with a common public-address system that enables all registered voters in each building to hear and participate in the proceedings.[58] The moderator may appoint an assistant moderator to preside in each of the other buildings who possesses all the powers of the moderator with one exception: he or she may not recognize a citizen seeking the floor without first obtaining permission from the moderator.[59] The use of more than two buildings is unusual. However, four separate halls were used by the 1965 Marblehead annual town meeting because the warrant contained several highly controversial articles.

If the moderator determines that there are inadequate places for all voters who wish to participate in the town meeting or that voters in attendance are not afforded an opportunity to participate for any reason, he or she may recess the meeting until later in the day or, upon consultation with the selectpersons present, adjourn the meeting for up to fourteen days when facilities to accommodate all voters who wish to attend and participate can be made available.[60]

At the time specified in the warrant for the start of the meeting the moderator raps a gavel and states that "the meeting will come to order." The moderator in some towns, most commonly ones with many new voters, explains at the beginning of the meeting the basic procedural rules, which is a sound practice facilitating the smooth conduct of the meeting. Town meeting rules and definitions are printed in the Marshfield, Massachusetts, warrant calling each town meeting (see Appendix I). Should the town clerk be absent or the office vacant, the first business conducted is the election by ballot of a temporary town clerk.[61] The clerk reads the warrant and the return of the service thereof unless it is moved and carried that the reading be dispensed with. The moderator commonly requests unanimous consent to refer to articles by subject matter instead of reading them in their entirety. Articles are considered in the order in which they appear in the warrant unless the meeting votes to consider articles out of order. In Wayland, for example, an article may be considered out of order by a two-thirds vote of the meeting.[62]

The moderator as presiding officer of the town meeting is in charge of the proceedings, decides all points of law, publicly declares all votes, and in open meeting may administer the oath of office to any town officer elected thereat.[63] The Supreme Judicial Court, however, ruled in 1980 that the town meeting possesses the ultimate power to decide meeting procedures.[64] If seven or more registered voters immediately challenge a vote declared by the moderator, he or she verifies it either by dividing or polling the voters unless the by-laws provide for a different method of verification.[65] The moderator must accept the vote of any individual whose name appears on the voting list or who presents a certificate issued by the registrars of voters certifying he or she is a registered voter.[66]

No one may address a town meeting without the permission of the moderator, and at his or her request every person must be silent. An individual who continues to act in a disorderly manner after a warning from the moderator may be ordered to leave the meeting and may be ejected from the meeting and confined by a constable until the meeting has adjourned.[67]

A moderator may address the town meeting during the course of debate, but it is preferable for the moderator to enter the debate only if he or she steps down as presiding officer and allows a temporary moderator to preside. A moderator may vote in any open town meeting provided he or she is a registered voter of the town, but his or her vote is not needed except to break a tie or defeat a motion by creating a tie. In general, moderators do not exercise their right to vote.

Aside from conducting the meeting one of the duties commonly assigned to the moderator by the town meeting is the appointment of various committees.

In certain towns, the town meeting votes to authorize the moderator and se-lectpersons jointly to appoint study committees.

Statutory provisions dealing with the moderator's powers and duties com-monly are supplemented by town by-laws. In Oxford, the moderator may require that all motions submitted for consideration be in writing; citizens must stand while speaking and address the moderator; motions to lay on the table or to take from the table are non-debatable; no action shall be taken at a special town meeting on the report of any committee previously appointed unless voters are notified in the warrant calling the meeting; and *Demeter's Manual of Parlia-mentary Law and Procedure* must be used to settle disputes involving parlia-mentary procedure.[68]

The Kingston by-laws stipulate that all motions involving the expenditure of funds must be submitted in writing and the moderator may direct other motions to be submitted in writing; speakers recognized by the moderator must confine their remarks to the question under consideration and must avoid personalities; all committees shall be appointed by the moderator unless the meeting otherwise directs; *Robert's Rules of Order* is to be used to settle parliamentary questions where applicable to the town meeting; and the moderator "may speak to points of order in preference to all other persons."[69]

The Berlin by-laws stipulate that non-voters may not be admitted to the floor of the hall except newspaper reporters and guests at the discretion of the mod-erator, who determines the boundaries of the floor of the hall, may entertain a motion to consider an article out of order, and may refuse to entertain frivolous motions; a motion may not be made to dissolve a meeting until every article has been acted upon; the order of precedence of various motions and the method of taking votes are specified; no person may speak more than twice on a question except to answer an inquiry without obtaining leave of the meeting; and all committees shall be appointed by the moderator unless the meeting otherwise directs.[70]

The attorney general of the commonwealth approved a by-law adopted by the 1963 Spencer annual town meeting that stipulates that a handbook prepared by a committee of the Massachusetts Moderators' Association shall be used to settle disputes involving parliamentary procedures.[71] The use of this handbook as a guide for town meeting procedures is preferable to the use of *Cushing's Manual of Parliamentary Practice* and *Robert's Rules of Order*, which were not de-signed specifically to apply to town meetings. Furthermore, the Supreme Judicial Court has questioned the applicability of *Robert's Rules of Order* to town meet-ings.

Coming directly to § 68 of Robert's Rules of Order Revised, we are at once struck by its dubious application of town meeting government. The phrase "regular business meeting" would be an inept description of a town meeting, whether annual or special. The phrase "previous regular business meeting" would be even more inept. The two phrases in the same sentence must refer to the same type of meeting. Even by forced construction, the phrase "previous regular business meeting" would run counter to statute and to settled law.[72]

The Supreme Judicial Court has noted that town meeting procedures generally conform to the customary rules of parliamentary procedure, yet a town meeting is not required to conform to the strict rules of parliamentary procedure.[73] Although the rules of parliamentary procedure for legislative bodies require the same vote for the adoption of a motion to rescind as the original measure required, the rules do not apply to a town meeting.[74] At an adjourned session of a town meeting, a reconsideration of a vote taken in the first session of the meeting revokes the vote, and it ceases to have any effect.[75]

Role of the Town Clerk. The elected town clerk normally is the second most important individual at the town meeting and sits at a table near the moderator on the stage or at the head of the hall. He or she records the transactions of the town meeting as declared by the moderator and is required to count and enter in the records the votes on articles that by statute require a two-thirds vote for passage.[76] The clerk records all unanimous votes on such articles in the records as unanimous, and a count is not taken. A town clerk may correct a mistake in his or her records, but the Supreme Judicial Court has ruled that the town clerk's records are the official records of the proceedings of the town meeting and may not be changed or oral evidence utilized to correct omissions.[77]

Town by-laws often spell out the duties of the town clerk with respect to the town meeting. For instance, the Leicester clerk following a vote to adjourn a meeting to another day must post in a public place in each precinct and on his or her bulletin board in the entry of the town hall "a statement of the day and hour to which the adjournment was voted and of the business remaining to come before the meeting."[78] In addition, he or she must notify in writing all committee members appointed or elected at the meeting

stating the business upon which they are to act and the names of the persons composing the committee, and also to notify all officers, boards, and committees of all votes passed . . . in any way affecting them; and further after each Annual Meeting to post and maintain on the bulletin board in the Town Hall a corrected list of all elected and appointed officers of the Town.[79]

Role of the Town Counsel. The town counsel, an attorney specializing in municipal law, customarily is present at all town meetings in most towns to provide legal advice in response to questions from the floor directed to him or her through the moderator. In many towns the counsel prepares for the selectpersons most warrant articles and many of the motions, affirmative and negative, to be made at the town meetings. Henry W. Hardy has written:

Many a town meeting bogs down when a point of order is raised that a motion is "not within the scope of the article." It behooves the town counsel, therefore, so to phrase the articles as to permit a reasonable latitude for town meeting action. He should take particular care in drafting articles relating to by-laws, borrowing, and land acquisition, for votes under these articles are bound to come under close scrutiny later by, among others, the attorney general, counsel for lending banks and conveyancers.[80]

Many legal problems arise at town meetings; articles inserted by voter petition legally may be defective, and the moderator in many towns confers on complex legal question with the counsel, who may be asked to give a legal opinion on an article prior to a vote's being taken. On exceptionally complex legal questions the moderator may declare a recess to confer privately with the counsel.

Three experts on town meetings warn the moderator that the town counsel usually prepares articles inserted in the warrant by the selectpersons at the request of boards and officers and the motions to be made after conferring with the attorney general or a bond counsel, and, consequently, the moderator should be wary of publicly disagreeing with motions prepared by the counsel. If the moderator ''is troubled by a motion prepared by town counsel he would do well to declare a recess and consult him privately. The face he saves may be his own.''[81]

The dissolution of the meeting does not end the town counsel's work in connection with the meeting. If the meeting has so voted, he or she must examine titles to property, initiate eminent domain proceedings, draw up deeds, prepare petitions for submission to the General Court, prepare contracts, and meet with state officials and town committees.[82]

Role of the Finance Committee. The finance committee performs a watchdog advisory function for the town meeting. Any town may provide for the appointment or election of an advisory, appropriations, or finance committee, and all towns with valuations exceeding $1 million for the purpose of apportioning the state tax must provide for the appointment or election of such a committee.[83] Approximately three-fourths of the boards are appointed. The finance committee, by by-law, may continue in office for a maximum term of three years with the duties of studying any or all town questions, reporting on same, and submitting at the annual town meeting a budget unless a by-law charges the selectpersons with the duty of its submission.[84] Forty-four (26.6%) finance committees in 1996 limited their study and report to articles appropriating money; the committees in other towns study and report on all articles.

The finance committee's recommendations distributed to the voters prior to the town meeting are advisory only and not binding in any manner. Its recommendation on an article commonly is offered as a motion by a member of the committee. The Supreme Judicial Court has opined that the failure of the finance committee to hold a public hearing as authorized by town by-law on the question of raising funds for a proposed building did not invalidate the vote on the article in the warrant on the question.[85]

The committee is principally an advisory body to the town meeting but has the power in most towns to transfer funds between accounts. ''To provide for extraordinary or unforeseen expenditures,'' the annual town meeting may establish a reserve fund by appropriating ''a sum not exceeding five percent of the tax levy for the preceding year.''[86] Direct drafts may not be made against the reserve fund, but the finance committee may vote transfers from the fund, and the selectpersons are authorized to vote such transfers if the town does not have a finance committee.

Can funds be transferred from the reserve fund to finance an operation for which the town meeting had made no appropriation? The general laws contain no such prohibition; the law simply stipulates that the purpose must be ''extraordinary or unforeseen.'' Funds transferred from the reserve fund cannot be re-transferred to the fund.

The establishment of a reserve or contingency fund has obviated the need to hold special town meetings near the end of the year for the sole purpose of transferring funds. The wisdom of establishing a reserve fund is indisputable; the expense of holding a sparsely attended special town meeting to act on prosaic articles routinely transferring funds is avoided, and supervision of town finances is placed in the hands of a committee in close contact with town finances throughout the year.

Role of the Planning Board. Each town with a population exceeding 10,000 must, and other towns may, create a planning board ''which shall make careful studies of the resources, possibilities and needs of the town, particularly with respect to conditions injurious to the public health or otherwise in and about rented dwellings, and make plans for the development of the municipality, with special reference to proper housing of its inhabitants.''[87]

The number of members of the board is determined by the town meeting, which also decides whether the members are to be elected or appointed. The board prepares a long-range master plan, typically with the assistance of a professional planner, for presentation at the town meeting and also makes recommendations for zoning changes. Land use issues tend to be divisive ones, particularly if a developer is seeking permission to construct a large shopping mall or housing development, and generate considerable debate at town meetings.

Other Town Meeting Officers. The warrant for a town meeting prepared by the selectpersons is directed to the constables of the town or other specified persons ''who give notice of such meeting in the manner prescribed by the by-laws, or, if there are no by-laws, by a vote of the town, or in a manner approved by the attorney general.''[88] The constable also acts as a sergeant-at-arms at the town meeting; the moderator is authorized to direct a constable to remove a disorderly person from a town meeting and confine that person until the meeting is adjourned.[89]

The Board of Selectmen or the town clerk appoints checkers whose duty is to ensure that only registered voters are allowed to enter the town meeting floor. When a vote on an article must be counted, the moderator of the larger town meetings appoints tellers to help take the count; the tellers in a number of towns are sworn to perform their duties faithfully. The moderator may appoint tellers either prior to, or during, a meeting and obviously should not appoint as a teller a voter who has a personal interest in the debate or wishes to participate in the debate on a highly controversial and important issue.

In towns that have adopted precinct voting a warden under the supervision of the town clerk is in charge of each voting precinct. Larger town meetings utilize high school students as page boys to deliver messages, run errands, set up chairs, and pass the portable microphone to citizens recognized as speakers by the moderator.

Quorum Requirement. The general laws of the commonwealth neither establish, nor require towns to establish, a quorum for town meetings. A quorum is the minimum number of registered voters specified by the by-laws of the town who must be present at a town meeting for legal action to be taken on warrant articles. A number of voters less than a quorum is authorized to adjourn a town meeting, and this action is the only legal one that can be taken.[90]

A survey by the author of 158 towns in 1964 revealed that 36 (23%) towns had no quorum requirement for the annual town meeting. Most of these towns had a relatively small population. However, included in the list were Acton (10,188), Barnstable (15,609), Concord (14,516), Grafton (11,571), Lynnfield (9,821), Orange (6,206), Sharon (11,341), Spencer (8,514), Wakefield (25,571), Westport (8,200), and Williamstown (7,042). Several towns established the quorum requirement in terms of a percentage of the registered voters: 2 percent in Dudley; 4 percent in Hinsdale and Westborough; and 10 percent in Petersham, Plainfield, and Rawley. The clerk of a town with a population slightly less than 1,000 that has no quorum requirement reported that "we insisted on at least twenty-five" be present at town meetings.

A 1996 survey of 169 towns revealed 30 (18%) towns had no quorum requirement for the annual business meeting, 28 (17%) had no quorum requirement for special town meetings, and the remaining towns had a low quorum ranging from 9 voters in New Salem (800) to 300 in Hingham (20,052). The quorum for a special town meeting ranged from 5 in Ashland (15,022) to 250 in Hardwick (11,564) and Medfield (11,650). New Salem has a quorum of 9 for each type of meeting by custom and not by by-law. The 1997 Hopkington annual town meeting dismissed article 33, which would have authorized the Board of Selectmen to petition the General Court for a special act stipulating that any article providing for an appropriation of $1 million or more would be voted on by referendum and, by unanimous voice vote, approved a by-laws amendment providing that the quorum for any town meeting to appropriate money is 100 voters.

A moderator in a town with a quorum reported that towns lacking a quorum experience good attendance because voters must be concerned that a small number of participants could make decisions for the towns. He added that his town meeting did not accept the recommendation of the town clerk that the quorum be reduced to 10, although the town meeting twenty-five years earlier reduced the quorum from 300 to 175 and subsequently to 100.

The moderator should determine whether a quorum is present prior to calling the town meeting to order and state the presence of a quorum in calling the meeting to order. A voter at any time has the right to challenge the presence of a quorum. If a quorum call is demanded after action has been taken on a particular article, and less than a quorum is present, the action taken on the article remains in force, and the only action that can be taken is to adjourn the meeting until a later date.

The fact that quorum requirements are set low does not prevent quorum problems. It is not unusual for special town meetings to be adjourned for the lack of a quorum. The town clerk and other town officials occasionally have to "beat the bushes" to round up the necessary number of voters. At least one town attempts to solve the problem by purposely starting the meeting late. Day sessions of the annual town meeting may be sparsely attended, as many working persons are not free to attend until evening. New Ashford at one time held afternoon and evening sessions of the annual town meeting but dropped the afternoon session because of poor attendance.

Northborough selectpersons in 1964 refused to insert an article in the warrant for a forthcoming town meeting to increase the quorum requirement from fifty voters to 10 percent of the registered voters because of the difficulty of attracting fifty voters to a special town meeting, which was delayed one-half hour while fire department members were called to meet the quorum requirement.

Role of Select Committees. Town meeting government traditionally has been citizen government and still relies heavily upon citizen committees of the town meeting elected by the voters or appointed by the moderator or the selectpersons.

A select committee may be created by the passage of an article calling for the creation of the committee or as a result of a subsidiary motion to refer a subject being debated to a study committee. By-law revision, re-valuation of real property, school construction, aerial ladder truck, representative town meeting, sewage disposal plant, library, clerical help, town administration, a public works department, and regional planning are examples of subjects studied by select committees.

Although the moderator customarily is authorized to appoint committee members, three attorneys specializing in town government wrote that

it is not clear whether a town moderator has the power to appoint a chairman. Many do, and in any event the moderator may charge one of the members with the duty of bringing the committee together and organizing it. This may amount to a tactful way of designating the chairman without causing the members of the committee to feel that they have been deprived of the opportunity of choosing their own chairman. No doubt the vote instructing the moderator to appoint the committee could instruct him to appoint the chairman, but in practice it seldom does.[91]

The moderator's role with respect to a committee ends upon the appointment of its members; he or she possesses no supervisory powers over the committee but fills vacancies as they occur.

Committee procedures usually are informal, depending primarily upon the chairman. The number of meetings held by select committees and the amount of work conducted by committees vary considerably.

Role of Interest Groups. Organized economic pressure groups play a legitimate role in bringing their views before the town meeting. Local taxpayers' associations have been declining in number, and the existing ones generally are not very active. They seek to improve the efficiency of town government and keep taxes as low as possible. Examples of their activities include mailing a form letter to each voter prior to the town meeting and representatives of the association attending finance committee meetings.

Stories circulate relative to town and school employees and their families packing town meetings to pressure adoption of articles beneficial to them. While these employees and their families are among the most faithful attendees of town meetings, there is little evidence they pack and control a meeting (see Chapter 10).

The League of Women Voters is the most common type of non-economic citizen group found in towns and undertakes studies of town problems, issues public statements, and educates the citizenry by conducting public meetings, including "Pre-town Meeting Meetings" and "Meet the Candidates Nights."

Other non-economic citizens' groups are found in a few towns but often fail to establish firm roots. In 1965, for example, the Westford Independent Citizens' Council was organized to promote efficient government and citizen participation in town affairs and provide information to citizens.

Ad hoc citizen committees spring to life when highly controversial issues such as fluoridation of the water supply and certain construction projects are proposed in a town, but these committees are ephemeral in nature. In Wayland, for example, a "committee opposing overhead high tension wires" was organized to oppose a Boston Edison Company plan to run a high-voltage transmission line through marshland.[92]

Role of Factions. The relative absence of organized pressure groups in Massachusetts towns does not mean that conflict is absent. Factions or cliques with changing membership are found in most towns. The town meeting is the arbiter of any factional disputes that may exist. At one time or other a split between a faction favoring conservatism and a faction favoring innovation is not unusual. In certain towns the factional split is socio-economic: the split is between the white-collar and blue-collar workers, representing, to a certain extent, the haves and the have-nots. Rising income levels have tended to obliterate the sharp distinction between the haves and the have-nots, yet it still exists in a less noticeable form. Rapidly growing towns experience factionalism in the form of a division between the natives and the newcomers, with the more parsimonious natives generally favoring the status quo, and the newcomers demanding changes, especially in the form of new and improved town services, which push the town property tax rate upward.

Length of residence in a town usually influences a candidate's chance of winning a town election. Newcomers in many towns challenge the incumbent natives in town elections, more successfully as the influx of newcomers continues. However, newcomers often work outside the town during the day and are not able to establish as many close contacts with the citizens as can the natives. Further, the voters often prefer as town officers individuals employed in the town, as they are more accessible than those employed outside the town.

In the smaller towns factionalism may reveal itself in the form of family connection, with one family grouping pitted against another or against the rest of the town. In other towns the leadership of a prominent family may be accepted. Intermarriage between large, established town families over a period of years substantially increases their political power if they choose to exercise it.

The open town meeting is not a perfect instrument for adjusting factional differences but functions as adequately as any substitute.

Non-voters. Town by-laws usually stipulate that non-voters, "strangers," may be allowed to attend a town meeting with the approval of the moderator or the town meeting. The gallery or a section in the rear of the hall is set aside for non-voters, who may not enter within the bounds of the town meeting floor. The Kingston by-laws, for example, stipulate that the checklist is to be "used in admitting voters to a town meeting, except that non-voters may be admitted to a defined and separate portion thereof, and non-voters may address the meeting if the meeting so voted."[93] Most by-laws are silent on the question whether non-voters may address the meeting.

Town Meeting Attendance

A number of town officers reported their towns did not keep data on town meeting attendance, and several indicated they would collect such data in the future. Other town officers not reporting attendance data wrote they were reluctant to estimate the attendance.

The 138 reporting towns had an average unweighted attendance of 13.72 percent of the registered voters at the business part of the 1996 annual town meeting and a weighted average attendance of 11.89 percent. The aggregate data, however, mask the wide range of attendance at town meetings in each population class, as revealed by Table 3.1.

Data for the annual town meetings in 1966, 1976, 1986, and 1996 generally reveal a decline in attendance of registered voters. However, attendance varies by year in accordance with the number of major unresolved issues on the warrant. A town in the 1,000–4,000 population range reported attendance in 1986 was 9.5 percent and in 1996 was 19.0 percent. A town of approximately 12,000 population witnessed an increase in attendance from 10 percent in 1996 to 25 percent in 1996. A town under 500 population had a decline in attendance from

Table 3.1

Massachusetts Annual Town Meeting Business Attendance (Percent of Registered Voters, 1996)

Population Range	Number of Towns	Average Attendance	Attendance Range
499 and under	5	44.50	10 to 60
500-999	9	20.67	5 to 48
1,000-1,999	12	16.58	5 to 25
2,000-4,999	26	12.57	3 to 47
5,000-7,499	34	7.31	2 to 25
7,500-9,999	10	9.60	2 to 33
10,000-14,999	26	6.54	1 to 23
15,000-19,999	5	9.60	1 to 22
20,000-24,999	8	6.80	2 to 22
25,000 and over	3	3.00	3

45 percent in 1976 to 30 percent in 1996, and a second town in this population class reported the following attendance percentages: 32 in 1966, 50 in 1976, 17 in 1986, and 30 in 1996.

A town in the 500–999 population range had attendance percentages of 65 in 1966, 49 in 1976, 51 in 1986, and 48 in 1996. A town in the 1,000–1,999 population class had attendance percentages of 15 in 1966, 10 in 1976, 12 in 1986, and 5 in 1996. With respect to the 2,000–4,999 population group, one town had attendance percentages of 40 in 1966, 30 in 1976, 10 in 1986, and 7 in 1996. A town in the 5,000–7,500 population class witnessed an attendance percentage drop from 20 in 1966 and 1976 to 15 in 1986 and 8 in 1996. Similarly, a town in the 7,500–9,999 population range experienced an attendance percentage decrease from 20 in 1966, to 15 in 1976, to 10 in 1986 and 1996.

Attendance in the larger towns, as a percentage of registered voters, generally remained constant over the 1966 to 1996 time period, although one growing town with a population in excess of 25,000 experienced a drop from 15 in 1966 and 1976 to 10 in 1986 and 3 in 1996.

It is important to highlight the fact the number of registered voters in the typical town exceeds the number of year-round residents for two reasons and depresses the town meeting attendance figures as a percentage of the registered voters. First, many Massachusetts towns attract a large number of seasonal, particularly summer, residents who are town registered voters but spend part of the year, including the time of the annual town meeting, in other states where the climate is warmer. Second, an unknown number of registered voters reside in adjoining states, and the National Voter Registration Act of 1993 prevents the purging of voters who may have moved from the town from the checklist for failure to vote for four years in an era when population mobility is common.[94] Nevertheless, taking account of these factors leads one to conclude that voter turnout at the annual business meeting is very low except in the small towns.

The amount of debate at town meetings varies considerably from town to town and from year to year depending, in part, on local customs and traditions, the length of the warrant, and the number of major unresolved issues brought to the meeting. A 1996 survey revealed that the percentage of voters who spoke on a controversial issue varies from less than 1 percent in a town such as Westwood (14,000) to 50 to 60 percent in several small towns such as Otis (1,073). Relatively few people spoke in most towns, and one clerk wrote that it is the "same twelve or fifteen people who speak on most issues."

Questionnaire recipients were requested to answer yes or no to the following question: Do people generally believe that certain interest groups pack the town meeting? One hundred and thirty-nine (87.4%) of the 159 respondents checked yes, and 20 (12.5%) checked no. The former identified principally public school supporters (parents and teachers), volunteer firemen, and town employees who attend town meetings in large numbers. Several towns also cited conservation and environmental groups, development groups, members of the National Rifle Association, public library supporters, senior citizens, and taxpayer groups. One respondent wrote he would not consider the groups "exactly interest groups, but relatives, friends, neighbors with similar views." A second respondent referred to "local small town family groups not political groups."

Many respondents who believed that interest groups packed the town meeting indicated that these groups can exert great influence, but not always. They also responded that members of an interest group typically depart the meeting immediately following action on the warrant article they were interested in.

A moderator wrote that

the word pack is pejorative. When school related articles are on the warrant people with children are more likely to attend. Likewise, older residents come out for senior projects. People trying to bring out the vote usually stir up opposition as well. I do not believe that any one group is capable of "packing" the meeting, but concern over this issue brings out voters.

A second moderator gave three examples of groups that people believe pack the meeting and added, "I do not believe they do though anyone can come to any meeting and no one is excluded. So 'packing the meeting' simply means the speaker was on the short end of the vote."

Only 11 (6.5%) of questionnaire respondents checked no as an answer to the question, "Do long-term residents have views different from those of new residents?" One respondent wrote that the newcomers lack historical perspective, a second respondent indicated that long-term residents were more conservative, and a third respondent who checked no wrote that "residents, old or new, like the low tax rate. People expect town services without an increase in tax." Most commonly, respondents referred to the interest of newcomers in schools, and one referred to long-term residents who have raised their children and resent the higher tax bills necessary to support schools.[95] He added that older residents are more interested in protecting the environment and maintenance of the "old time ambiance of the town." A moderator wrote that many long-term residents have specific interests in matters concerning senior citizens, but they support issues of interest to younger voters, particularly school budgets. He noted that new residents "seem more concerned about protecting the status quo 'character' of the town."

Town Meeting Decision-Making

Participants in a town meeting are guided in their decision-making by the recommendations of town officers and committees. The finance committee and the planning board in particular exercise great influence when the voters assemble to perform their legislative duties.

One hundred and twenty-seven (76%) of 167 surveyed town officers reported that their finance committees made recommendations on all warrant articles. One hundred and forty-seven respondents (88%) answered the question whether the committee's recommendations were followed always, most of the time, seldom, or never. Committee recommendations always were followed in 21 (14%) towns, most of the time in 131 (88%) towns, and seldom in 2 (1%) towns. No town reported that its town meeting never followed the committee's recommendations.

Similar data were reported relative to the influence of the town planning board. Although no town officer reported that the town meeting always followed the recommendations of the town planning board, 98 percent of the 170 responding town officers checked that the recommendations were followed most of the time. Only four (1%) towns reported that the board's recommendations seldom were followed and no town officer reported that the town meeting never followed the board's recommendations.

Surveyed town officers were requested to rate the quality of town meeting debate in terms of getting explanations of budget items, exploring pros and cons of proposals, and neighbors influencing neighbors' opinions on town issues. Of 157 responding town officers, 39 (25%) rated the quality of debate as excellent, 90 (57%) selected good, 25 (16%) checked fair, and only 3 (2%) selected poor. Several respondents wrote that attendees today are more informed and interested than in the past and want more questions answered in detail. One town clerk reported that "the quality of debate has always been excellent and right to the point." A town moderator explained that "the quality of debate is good in content, but a few of the older, talented debaters who were knowledgeable about town meeting procedures have been lost. However, we do not lack thoughtful and intelligent debate." A town clerk who judged debate quality as poor added that "it is getting worse."

Does debate change the outcome of the vote on warrant articles? A town clerk responded in the negative by pointing out that "ninety percent of 'selling' your position, pro or con, is done prior to town meeting. If the various town committees have reached consensus, with support from the finance committee, it is highly unlikely there will be changes on town meeting floor.''

Questionnaire recipients also were requested to judge the quality of decisions made at town meetings as excellent, good, fair, or poor. Twenty-eight (17%) of 161 reporting town officers rated the quality of town meeting decisions as excellent, 110 (68%) checked good, 22 (14%) towns selected fair, and only one town (.6%) checked poor. Nine respondents who judged the quality of decisions to be good judged the quality of debate as excellent.

THE SPECIAL TOWN MEETING

Selectpersons may call a special town meeting at any time, provided at least seven days' notice is given, and must include in the warrant all subjects requested in writing by 100 registered voters or 10 percent of the registered voters, whichever number is the lesser.[96]

A special town meeting must be called by the selectpersons within forty-five days when requested to do so in writing by 200 registered voters or 20 percent of the registered voters, whichever number is the lesser, and insert in the warrant all articles requested in the petition.[97] If the selectpersons unreasonably refuse to call a town meeting, a justice of the peace may issue a warrant for a town meeting if requested to call one in writing by 100 registered voters or 10 percent of the registered voters.[98]

Any number of town meetings for distinct purposes may be called by the same warrant.[99] An important matter can be considered in the first meeting scheduled, and other business may be taken up in the second meeting scheduled for later the same evening, when attendance is apt to be less. Action taken at the first meeting cannot be reconsidered by the second meeting. However, it is more common for two separate warrants to be issued calling two distinct special meetings for the same evening. Northborough, for example, scheduled one meeting to begin at 7:30 P.M. and a second meeting to begin at 7:35 P.M. on June 22, 1964. The moderator called the first meeting to order at 7:30 P.M., and a motion was made and carried to recess the meeting to take up the articles on the warrant of the second town meeting scheduled for 7:35 P.M. The second meeting was called to order, and after the conclusion of its business it was adjourned, and the first meeting reconvened. The typical reason for two meetings on the same evening is a development requiring relatively prompt town meeting action that arose after the warrant for a special town meeting had been closed. A second warrant is issued calling a second town meeting for the same evening, provided the required warning can be given; for this reason Northborough held two special town meetings the same evening.

Special town meetings are held in a number of towns during the last month or two of the calendar year for the purpose of transferring funds from certain accounts to depleted accounts. In other towns the need to hold special town meetings for this purpose has been obviated by establishing a reserve account and authorizing the finance committee in its discretion to transfer funds from the reserve account to depleted accounts; such a policy is a sound one, as it provides the necessary fiscal flexibility by authorizing an informed citizen committee, which continually has been exercising oversight over town finance, to transfer funds and thereby avoid the expense of holding a special town meeting that few citizens would attend.

Only 1 (0.6%) of the surveyed 166 towns reported that voters by petition frequently called special town meetings. Eighty (48%) reported such meetings occasionally are called by voters, and 67 (40%) indicated voters never had called a special town meeting. Other towns reported such meetings were convened very infrequently or very seldom. One town officer reported that voters have ''threatened but never used'' their authority to call a special town meeting.

The small attendance at the average special town meeting argues against the calling of such a meeting unless it is essential to hold one, or a large turnout of voters can be predicted. However, there is much merit in calling a special town meeting to consider an important and highly controversial issue that could be considered at the annual town meeting. The annual meeting warrant in most towns is of such length that an important and highly controversial issue may not receive adequate consideration, or action may be postponed.

BY-LAWS

By-laws are town laws enacted by the town meeting and, if not repugnant to law, have the same validity as statutes enacted by the General Court.[100] Any by-law approved by a town meeting and proof of compliance with procedural requirements for the adoption of by-laws must be submitted by the town clerk to the attorney general of the commonwealth for approval; a by-law so submitted becomes effective when approved by the attorney general or after ninety days without action by the attorney general.[101] The penalty for a breach of a by-law is determined by the town but may not exceed $300 for each offense.[102] The Supreme Judicial Court has opined that every presumption is in favor of the validity of a by-law.[103] A ''by-law is more than a mere rule of parliamentary procedure. It is a protective measure designed to safeguard the financial interests of taxpayers and of the town. . . . A by-law . . . cannot be overridden at the behest of a majority of the voters present, in the absence of an article in the warrant under which such action can be taken.''[104]

In the past there were a relatively large number of towns without by-laws. A three-member commission appointed by the governor prepared in 1920 a code of by-laws for towns as a model for towns without by-laws.[105] In 1940, the Massachusetts Federation of Taxpayers Association, Incorporated, published a set of model by-laws to assist towns in updating their by-laws.[106]

Town by-laws often are out of print or in need of updating. Many town clerks are apologetic about the condition of the town by-laws and indicate a need for their revision by pointing to archaic provisions. Ashfield, for example, has one framed copy of its town by-laws, which have not been amended since their adoption in 1849. Berlin has solved this problem by adopting a by-law requiring the selectpersons to publish by-laws at least once every five years.[107]

By-laws usually are printed as a separate pamphlet, and paper supplements often are printed as new by-laws are adopted, or old ones are amended. A few towns approach the publication of their by-laws in a different manner. Milton prints its by-laws in the annual town report, a practice to be commended, as it is an inexpensive manner of making the by-laws readily available. It may not be essential to include the by-laws in each annual town report, but including them in the annual report every two or three years would be desirable. A case can be made for incorporating the by-laws and the warrant for the forthcoming annual town meeting in the annual town report, as the provisions of the by-laws commonly regulate phases of town meetings.

Nowell binds its by-laws in a plastic cover and sells the pamphlet; by-laws subsequently enacted are mailed to the purchasers for insertion, thereby keeping the by-laws up to date. Groton publishes a municipal manual for its citizens containing the by-laws of the town, state legislative acts accepted, and other pertinent information bound in a three-ring binder, which facilitates adding or deleting pages.

SPECIAL DISTRICTS

One of the least-known phases of local government in Massachusetts is special district government within towns. Towns vary considerably in terms of geographical area, population, and population concentrations. It is not uncommon for a town to have two or more population clusters of unincorporated villages that require or desire services not needed elsewhere in the town. A governmental mechanism for the provision of services in one section of a town is the improvement district. A town meeting may authorize an unincorporated village with a population of 1,000 or more to organize an improvement district under a name approved by the meeting ''for the purpose of erecting and maintaining street lamps, establishing and maintaining libraries, building and maintaining sidewalks, or for employing and paying police officers.''[108] Each district must have a prudential committee and a clerk and may elect a treasurer and other officers; each district officer holds office for one year or until a successor is qualified. A district is authorized to adopt by-laws to govern the calling of meetings and specify the duties of its officers.

Other special districts such as fire and water districts are created by special acts of the General Court, which take effect when approved by a specified number, usually two-thirds, of the voters of the territory of the proposed district. For example, the General Court enacted a statute in 1933 to take effect when accepted by two-thirds of the voters within the territory of the district creating the West Boylston Water District of West Boylston as a corporate body, specifying the activities it may engage in, authorizing it to borrow money and hold district meetings providing for three-year terms, and authorizing the district to adopt by-laws.[109]

The government of a special district is basically the same as that of a town in terms of organization and procedures. The annual meeting of a special district is called by the issuance of a warrant by the prudential committee or governing board notifying the inhabitants of the district where and when the meeting will be held and the articles to be acted upon; warrants are short and frequently contain only six to ten articles. Special meetings of the district may be called at the discretion of the governing board. Meetings of special districts are conducted in the same manner as town meetings. Fire, water, light, and improvement districts are authorized to elect by ballot at any annual election of district officers a moderator to preside at all district meetings held during the year.[110] Until a moderator or temporary moderator is elected, the district clerk presides, and in his or her absence the chairman of the prudential committee presides.[111] The moderator of a district meeting performs the same functions as the moderator of a town meeting, and the town meeting moderator may be elected moderator of the special district meeting. The annual meeting of a special district utilizes select committees in the same manner as they are utilized by the annual town meeting. Attendance at meetings of a special district is less than at a town meeting, as the district covers only a portion of the town, and the number of important issues to be resolved is small. The governing board performs functions similar to those performed by town selectpersons. The by-laws or rules and regulations of a special district are similar in nature to town by-laws.

An annual meeting of a water district, for example, will consider articles in the warrant relating to the election of district officers, appropriation of funds for salaries and operating expenses, borrowing money in anticipation of revenue, extension of water mains, creation of a stabilization fund, and installation of an automatic valve at the pumping station to stabilize water pressure. The annual meeting of a fire district will consider articles in the warrant relating to the election of district officers, appropriation of funds for salaries and operating expenses, borrowing money in anticipation of revenue, entering into a contract with a water company for water service, purchase of a new fire apparatus, transfer of money from the stabilization fund to the new apparatus fund, sale of a pumper, and purchase of land as a site for a new fire station.

SUMMARY

The annual open town meeting is convened in 262 towns by the issuance of the warrant by the selectpersons notifying residents of the towns that elections will be held to select town officers, and decisions will be made on warrant articles. In many respects, the town meeting continues to function as it did in the seventeenth century, with the most noticeable difference that women today are also participants. Forty-four percent of surveyed town officers reported that their towns held a pre–town meeting meeting where town officers explain the warrant and answer questions, but attendance is very small.

Proceedings of the annual and special town meetings are under the control of the elected town moderator, who possesses broad discretion in conducting the proceedings subject to being overridden by a vote of town meeting participants. Such an occurrence is extremely rare.

The finance committee and the planning board play key advisory roles at town meetings, and their recommendations seldom are rejected by the assembled voters. In particular, these two bodies help to offset the influence of pressure groups at town meetings where attendance frequently is low, except in the small towns (see Chapter 10). The unweighted average attendance at the 1996 annual meeting in 136 towns was only 13.72 percent of the registered voters. Eighty-seven percent of the town officers responding to a 1996 survey reported that people generally believe that certain interest groups pack the town meeting. A similar percentage indicated that long-term residents generally have different views from those of new residents.

Forty-two of the larger Massachusetts towns have abandoned the open town meeting, in favor of the representative town meeting, which is the subject of Chapter 9. In addition, nine towns during the past twenty-five years have adopted the town council form of government while retaining the name "town."

The New Hampshire open town meeting, the subject of Chapter 4, is similar in terms of organization and procedures to the Massachusetts open town meeting.

NOTES

1. Commonwealth of Massachusetts, *Constitution of the Commonwealth of Massachusetts*, Part the First, art. XIX.

2. *Massachusetts General Laws*, chap. 39, § 9.

3. *Massachusetts Acts of 1924*, chap. 377, § 1.

4. Commonwealth of Massachusetts, *Opinion of Edward J. McCormack, Attorney General*, July 17, 1961.

5. Commonwealth of Massachusetts, *Report Submitted by the Legislative Research Council Relative to Town Meetings in Regional Schools* (Boston: December 27, 1961), p. 18.

6. *Opinion of the Justices*, 358 Mass. 838, 267 N.E.2d 113 (1971). See also *Massachusetts Laws of 1971*, chap. 88.

7. *Massachusetts General Laws*, chap. 39, § 11.

8. Ibid., § 10.

9. Ibid., § 12.

10. Ibid., § 10.

11. *Reynolds v. Inhabitants of New Salem*, 47 Mass. 340 (1843).

12. *Massachusetts General Laws*, chap. 39, § 10.

13. Ibid., § 16.

14. *The Acts and Resolves of the Province of the Massachusetts Bay* (Boston: Wright

and Potter, 1874), vol. 2, p. 30. See also Joseph F. Zimmerman, *Participatory Democracy: Populism Revived* (New York: Praeger Publishers, 1986), pp. 68–104.

15. *Massachusetts General Laws*, chap. 39, § 10.

16. *Torrey v. Inhabitants of Millbury*, 38 Mass. 64 (1838).

17. *Kittredge v. Inhabitants of North Brookfield*, 138 Mass. 286 (1885).

18. *Fuller v. Inhabitants of Groton*, 77 Mass. 340 (1858).

19. *Westhampton v. Searle*, 127 Mass. 502 (1879).

20. *Sherman v. Torrey*, 99 Mass. 472 (1868).

21. *Reed v. Inhabitants of Acton*, 117 Mass. 384 (1875).

22. *Massachusetts General Laws*, chap. 39, § 10.

23. Oak Bluffs, Mass., *By-Laws of the Town of Oak Bluffs, Massachusetts*, chap. III, § I.

24. *Rand v. Wilder*, 65 Mass. 294 (1853).

25. *Commonwealth v. Sullivan*, 165 Mass. 183 (1896).

26. *Massachusetts General Laws*, chap. 40, § 49.

27. Ibid., § 50.

28. Berlin, Mass., *Annual Report of the Several Official Boards of the Town of Berlin, Massachusetts*, 1964, pp. 5, 144–45.

29. Nathaniel B. Shurtleff, ed., *Records of the Governor and Company of the Massachusetts Bay in New England* (Boston: From the Press of William White, Printer to the Commonwealth, 1853), vol. 2, p. 220.

30. *The Acts and Resolves, Public and Private of the Province of the Massachusetts Bay* (Boston: Wright and Potter, 1869), vol. 1, p. 65.

31. *The Acts and Resolves of the Province of the Massachusetts Bay* (Boston: Wright and Potter, 1869), vol. 3, p. 47.

32. *Massachusetts General Laws*, chap. 41, § 1.

33. Ibid.

34. Ibid., § 4.

35. *Annual Reports of the Town Officers and Committees of the Town of Templeton, Massachusetts for the Year Ending December 31, 1963*, pp. 166–67.

36. *Massachusetts General Laws*, chap. 39, § 9.

37. Ibid., § 39A. See also *Opinion of the Justices*, 358 Mass. 838, 167 N.E.2d 113 (1971).

38. *Massachusetts General Laws*, chap. 53, § 6.

39. Ibid., §§ 117, 121.

40. Ibid., § 121.

41. Letter from Mrs. Mary C. Ditano, town clerk of Wellesley, Mass., dated August 14, 1964.

42. *Massachusetts General Laws*, chap. 54, § 42.

43. Howard S. Knowles, "How Massachusetts Towns Choose Their Officers," *Sunday Telegram* (Worcester), February 12, 1961, p. B-1.

44. *Massachusetts General Laws*, chap. 54, § 42.

45. Ibid., chap. 39, § 21.

46. Ibid., chap. 54, § 103A.

47. Ibid., chap. 39, § 9.

48. *Reed v. Inhabitants of Acton*, 117 Mass. 384 (1875).

49. *Adams v. Cook*, 245 Mass. 543, 139 N.E. 803 (1929).

50. *Massachusetts Acts of 1954*, chap. 405.

51. *Boston Sunday Herald*, February 6, 1966, p. 11.

52. *Massachusetts Acts of 1939*, chap. 79.

53. *Massachusetts General Laws*, chap. 39, § 15.

54. *The Acts and Resolves of the Province of the Massachusetts Bay*, vol. 2, p. 30.

55. *Massachusetts General Laws*, chap. 39, § 14.

56. Ibid., chap. 41, § 107.

57. Ibid., chap. 39, § 14.

58. Ibid., § 10.

59. Ibid., § 14.

60. Ibid., § 10.

61. Ibid., chap. 41, § 14.

62. Wayland, Mass., *By-Laws of the Town of Wayland, Massachusetts*, art. 2, § 3.

63. *Massachusetts General Laws*, chap. 39, § 15.

64. *MacKeen v. Town of Canton*, 379 Mass. 514, 399 N.E.2d 22 (1980).

65. *Massachusetts General Laws*, chap. 39, § 15.

66. Ibid., § 18.

67. Ibid., § 17.

68. Oxford, Mass., *By-Laws of the Town of Oxford, Massachusetts*, art. 2, §§ 4–11.

69. Kingston, Mass., *By-Laws, Rules and Regulations of the Town of Kingston, Massachusetts*, art. II, §§ 2-2-3, 2-2-4, 2-2-6, 2-2-9, 2-2-10.

70. Berlin, Mass., *By-Laws of the Town of Berlin, Massachusetts*, art. II, §§ 4–10.

71. Richard B. Johnson, Benjamin A. Trustman, and Charles Y. Wadsworth, *Town Meeting Time* (Boston: Little, Brown and Company, 1962). See also Geoffrey Bolton, *A Handbook for Town Moderators*, 2nd ed. (Boston: Massachusetts Federation of Taxpayers Associations, 1954).

72. *Blomquist v. Town of Arlington*, 338 Mass. 598 (1959).

73. *Wood v. Town of Milton*, 197 Mass. 531 (1908).

74. *Adams v. Cook*, 245 Mass. 543 (1923).

75. *Withington v. Inhabitants of the Town of Harvard*, 62 Mass. 66 (1851).

76. *Massachusetts General Laws*, chap. 39, § 15.

77. *Taylor v. Henry*, 19 Mass. 397 (1824).

78. Leicester, Mass., *Revised By-Laws of the Town of Leicester, Massachusetts*, chap. 2, § 6.

79. Ibid., chap. 3, § 2.

80. Henry W. Hardy, *The Role of the Town Counsel* (Amherst: Bureau of Government Research, University of Massachusetts, 1960), p. 11.

81. Johnson, Trustman, and Wadsworth, *Town Meeting Time*, p. 30.

82. Hardy, *Town Counsel*, p. 10.

83. *Massachusetts General Laws*, chap. 39, § 16.

84. Ibid.

85. *Young v. Town of Westport*, 302 Mass. 597 (1939).

86. *Massachusetts General Laws*, chap. 40, § 6.

87. Ibid., chap. 41, § 70.

88. Ibid., chap. 39, § 10.

89. Ibid., § 17.

90. Ibid., § 13. The Supreme Judicial Court has ruled that parol evidence cannot be received by a court to prove a quorum was not present in the contradiction of the written

record that a quorum was present. *DelPrete v. Board of Selectmen of Rockland*, 351 Mass. 344, 220 N.E.2d 912 (1966).

91. Johnson, Trustman, and Wadsworth, *Town Meeting Time*, pp. 36–38.

92. John A. Long, "N. E. Town Fights for Landscape," *Christian Science Monitor*, February 13, 1965, p. 2.

93. Kingston, Mass., *By-Laws*, art. II, § 1.

94. *National Voter Registration Act of 1993*, 107 Stat. 77, 42 U.S.C. §§ 1973gg to 1974e.

95. For a newspaper account of this type of division in a town, see Anthony Flint, "Petersham Lost," *Boston Globe*, September 17, 1996, pp. B1, B3.

96. *Massachusetts General Laws*, chap. 39, §§ 9–10.

97. Ibid., § 10.

98. Ibid., § 12.

99. Ibid., § 10.

100. Ibid., chap. 40, § 21.

101. Ibid., § 32.

102. Ibid., § 21.

103. *Brown v. Town of Carlisle*, 336 Mass. 147 (1957).

104. *Loring v. Inhabitants of Town of Westwood*, 237 Mass. 545 (1921).

105. Commonwealth of Massachusetts, *Report of the Commission to Complete the Work of Revising and Codifying the Laws Relating to Towns*, Senate Number 2, 1920, pp. 38–42.

106. "Model By-Laws for Massachusetts Towns" (Boston: Massachusetts Federation of Taxpayers Association, 1940).

107. Berlin, Mass., *By-Laws of the Town of Berlin*, art. I, § 3.

108. *Massachusetts General Laws*, chap. 40, § 44.

109. *Massachusetts Acts of 1933*, chap. 352.

110. *Massachusetts General Laws*, chap. 39, § 14.

111. Ibid.

Chapter 4

The New Hampshire
Open Town Meeting

The territory of present-day New Hampshire was included within the boundaries of the November 3, 1620, patent of James I to the Council of Plymouth in the county of Devon, which exercised granted powers until its dissolution in 1635.[1] New Hampshire's first settlements date to Dover and Portsmouth in 1623, which were established primarily as fisheries and without title to the land. The Plymouth charter allowed its council to delegate its powers, and Captain John Mason was granted the territory of New Hampshire in 1629, but no government was established.

The first government was established by Exeter residents in 1639, and their lead was followed in 1641 by Dover and Portsmouth residents. In the same year, New Hampshire voluntarily was united with the Massachusetts Bay Colony and remained a part of the colony until 1679, when Charles II separated New Hampshire from Massachusetts.[2] Francis N. Thorpe explained:

Two causes moved in the direction of the union and the establishment of a separate province, one being the promotion of the interests involved in the Masonian title, and the other the policy in the Home Government and the desire of a small minority of royalists in the New England colonies to counteract and restrain the growing influence of the Puritan or Home Rule Party.[3]

A new provincial government was established by the Crown in 1680. By 1689, however, New Hampshire was without a colonial government, as none was provided by the home government. The General Court of the Massachusetts Bay Colony in 1690 ordered the reunion of New Hampshire with the colony, which continued until 1692, when the Province of New Hampshire again was established as a separate government.[4]

Currently, there are 221 towns in New Hampshire, ranging in population from 39 in Hart's Location and 69 in Ellsworth to approximately 23,000 in Merrimack and 30,000 in Salem. The traditional open town meeting is utilized by 181 (81%) of the towns. No town operates with a representative town meeting (RTM), but Derry (32,000) and Durham (11,500) abandoned the open town meeting as a decision-making body completely in favor of a town council. The Durham charter provides for a discussion town meeting, which lacks legislative authority.

Bedford (13,052) and Hooksett (8,896) each adopted a charter providing for a budget town meeting and vesting all other legislative powers in the town council. Newmarket (7,308) voters approved a similar charter in 1991 but in 1996 accepted a state statute authorizing the adoption of the town budget by referendum in place of its adoption by assembled voters. In 1996, Londonderry (20,392) voters decided to act on future proposed bond issues by official ballot (OB), which also is known as the Australian or secret ballot. In 1996, voters in twenty-seven towns approved a warrant article providing for the use of the official ballot to decide all warrant articles commencing in 1997, a subject examined in detail in a subsequent section. Eight additional towns adopted the official ballot in 1998, effective in 1999. Hooksett voters in 1996 adopted the official ballot relative to the town budget, and the town no longer holds a decision-making assembled town meeting.

Hanover operates under a town charter enacted by the 1963 New Hampshire General Court (state legislature) and accepted by the town voters that declares that they are the legislative body of the town and authorizes them to delegate any or all of their powers to the Board of Selectmen with the exceptions of the enactment or amendment of a zoning ordinance or abandonment of a public highway.[5] The 1964 annual town meeting delegated powers to the board, including the power to enact ordinances. On average, one new ordinance is enacted annually, and other ordinances are amended on an as-needed basis.[6]

New Hampshire has thirteen cities, ranging in population from 8,342 in Franklin to 101,039 in Manchester. Lebanon in 1957 was the last town to abandon the town meeting in favor of a city charter. Seven village districts and all school districts are governed by district meetings conducted in essentially the same manner as town meetings, except in school districts that have adopted the official ballot described in a subsequent section. In addition, there are twenty-five unincorporated areas known as grants, locations, and purchases covering 6 percent of the territory of the state.

To collect data, a questionnaire was mailed to each town with an open town meeting or official ballot town meeting. Completed questionnaires were returned by ninety-six (43%) towns, but not every respondent answered each question. Interviews also were conducted with a small number of town clerks, town meeting moderators, and knowledgeable citizens, and newspaper accounts of numerous town meetings were examined.

THE ANNUAL TOWN MEETING

Procedures in towns with open town meetings in New Hampshire are generally similar to those in Massachusetts. Each town holds an annual meeting on the second Tuesday in March unless the town has adopted an optional fiscal year, in which case the town meeting may vote to hold the annual meeting on the second Tuesday in May.[7] The meeting is held in pursuance of a warrant or warning, issued by the Board of Selectmen, which is the foundation stone of the meeting, as the warrant provides for the election of town officers and contains a list of articles for consideration by the attending voters (see Appendix III for the warrant calling the Fitzwilliam 1997 annual meeting).

Twenty-five or more voters, or 2 percent of registered voters if at least ten, by petition submitted to the selectpersons "not later than the fifth Tuesday" prior to the date of the annual meeting may add articles to the warrant.[8] Similarly, fifty voters or one-fourth of the voters, whichever is fewer, by petition may add articles to the warrant for a special town meeting. In towns with a population of 10,000 or more, the petitions must be signed by 5 percent of the registered voters to add an article to a special town meeting warrant.[9]

The New Hampshire Supreme Court has held that the inclusion of a petitioned article in the warrant is a right of voters and that failure to include such an article subjects the selectpersons to a criminal penalty.[10] On the other hand, the court has ruled that the selectpersons are not required to include a petitioned article in the warrant, which cannot have legal effect because of a conflicting statutory provision.[11] Typically, selectpersons add suggested articles to the warrant without a petition.

Commencing in the 1970s, national and regional interest groups utilized town meetings to obtain publicity for their respective cause by persuading the required number of voters in a town to sign a petition to place a non-binding question on the town meeting warrant. The issue was the Panama Canal Treaty in 1978; transportation, storage, and disposal of nuclear materials in 1979 and 1983; acid rain and El Salvador in 1983; and campaign finance reform in 1996. The acid rain resolution, for example, was approved by 197 town meetings in 1983.[12]

A town meeting legally can take action only on warrant articles but is free to amend articles, provided the subject matter is not changed. Selectpersons may include two or three articles on a given subject in the warrant in order to give voters a choice of policy options.

The subject matter of all business to be acted upon at the deliberative assembly must be "stated distinctly" in the warrant, and the meeting is free to act on details implied in the subject matter even if they are not specifically listed in the warrant.[13] It is not uncommon to find an article at the end of the warrant "to transact any other business which may legally come before the meeting," but actions taken by a town meeting on this article would be invalid.

Selectpersons must sign and address the warrant to registered voters and post a copy at the town meeting place and a copy in at least one other public place in the town a minimum of fourteen days prior to the meeting.[14] The New Hampshire Supreme Court in 1860 interpreted the vague statutory "at one other public place" to mean "places where the inhabitants must frequently meet or resort or, have occasion to be, so that a notice posted there for that reason would be likely to meet public view and attract attention."[15] The court in 1850 ruled that the posting required was not met by placing a copy of the warrant on the inside of the meetinghouse door when the door was locked until the day of the meeting.[16] In 1944, the court held that the posting and meeting days are not included in the required fourteen days' advance of meeting posting.[17]

The selectpersons or the town constable acting at the direction of the selectpersons must provide the town clerk with a certificate of service of the warrant.[18] Should the selectpersons neglect or unreasonably refuse to issue a warrant or insert a petitioned article in the warrant, a superior court justice, on the written application of twenty-five or more registered voters or one-sixth of such voters, may issue a warrant for the meeting or order the insertion of a petitioned article in the warrant.[19]

The Annual Report and Pre–Town Meeting Meeting

Each town publishes an annual town report containing information on the organization of the town, election results from the previous annual meeting, reports of committees and departments, minutes of the preceding business part of the annual town meeting, independent auditor's report on town finances, and the warrant for the forthcoming annual town meeting, among other information.

Of great interest to readers of the report are the comparative fiscal data on annual expenditures during the preceding fiscal year, the budgeted amounts for the current fiscal year, and the budget to be presented at the forthcoming town meeting. The report also may contain the recommendations of the municipal budget committee or the Board of Selectmen if there is no committee.

Fifty-five (75%) of the seventy-three responding towns hold a pre–town meeting meeting where warrant budget articles and other articles in certain towns are explained, and questions are raised by citizens and answered by town officers. In common with Massachusetts towns, attendance typically is very low at these meetings and ranges from a fraction of 1 percent to 10 percent of the registered voters if there are major issues contained in warrant articles. One town in the 500 to 999 population range reported a turnout of 75 percent of the voters at the 1996 meeting.

Election of Town Officers

The warrant for the annual town meeting must warn voters of the election of named town officers; the day, place, and time of the election; and propositions to be voted on by ballot.[20] Election of town officers and the business meeting traditionally occurred on the same day. Since 1969, however, towns have the option of a "bifurcated" town meeting with election of town officers and other actions required by the General Court, such as zoning amendments, taken by official (Australian) ballot at the first session of the town meeting, and other business conducted on another day set by the selectpersons.[21] This option can be adopted only by town meeting voters in towns that use the official ballot. A single warrant warns the voters of the forthcoming election and articles to be considered by assembled voters.

If a town has not voted at a previous town meeting to adopt the official ballot system or has rescinded such adoption, voters must elect town officers by means of the unofficial ballot system, and a majority vote is required to elect each officer.[22] Under this system, the town clerk provides the moderator with pieces of white paper of uniform size, which at the discretion of the clerk may have the names of candidates printed thereon, to be utilized as ballots.[23] Nomination of candidates is by motion at the town meeting if the voters have not adopted the partisan ballot system.[24] Ballots are counted by the moderator in open meeting, and the candidate receiving the majority of the votes for an office is declared elected by the moderator.

No town has partisan elections, but should a town adopt such elections, voting at a party's caucus must be by ballot.[25] Nominations by a party are limited to parties that at the preceding state election polled at least 3 percent of the total vote for governor.[26] The New Hampshire statutes authorize a town to adopt the non-partisan official ballot system or to repeal its adoption.[27] Should a town with a population of 4,500 adopt partisan elections and subsequently desire to consider adoption of non-partisan elections, the plurality rule determines the winner of elections in towns using the non-partisan ballot system.

Towns that have adopted the official ballot system are required to provide for absentee voting for town officers.[28] Registered voters may apply for absentee ballots if they are members of the armed services, cannot appear in public on election day because of religious beliefs, or are disabled.

Questionnaire recipients were requested to indicate whether all offices were contested and whether there was a candidate for each office. Of sixty-seven responding towns, only four (6%) checked that all offices were contested. Of sixty-one responding towns, twenty-nine (48%) reported that there was at least one candidate for each office. In other words, there was no candidate for one or more offices in 52 percent of the reporting towns.

Conduct of Business

The New Hampshire Supreme Court in 1962 opined that the open town meeting is not a continuing body, and hence, one meeting lacks authority to adopt by-laws or standing rules governing the proceedings of subsequent town meetings.[29] Each town is free to establish a quorum requirement for the conduct of business at annual or special town meetings. Only three responding towns reported a quorum requirement for the conduct of business at the annual town meeting, and the requirement was low, only six voters in Ellsworth (69). For a special town meeting, Clarksville (250) has a quorum of 10 percent of the registered voters, whereas the quorum is fifty voters in Littleton (5,800), 50 percent of the registered voters in Newfields (1,000), two-thirds of the registered voters in Randolph (370), and 4 percent of registered voters in Wales.

The average length of the business part of the 1996 annual town meeting, according to respondents, was approximately three to four hours. The length varied from one hour in Clarksville to eighteen hours in Washington (684), where there is a tradition to discuss an issue until there is a consensus before a vote is taken. Relative to Washington, Ronald Jager reported:

The principle of the secret ballot and the principle of uncurtailed debate are treated in this town with a piety reserved for few other things. Punctuating the long meeting with a frequent "paper ballot," as it is called here, relieves tedium, rearranges the seating, fosters sociability, extends the market for coffee and sandwiches.[30]

An interviewed, experienced former town moderator stated that his meeting was over in ninety minutes, in contrast to a nearby town, which would have three to four recessed meetings due to the inexperience of a moderator. A second interviewed, experienced town moderator would not let anyone speak twice until everyone desiring to speak had spoken. In consequence, a voter occasionally would make a statement in the form of a question, but this tactic was not abused. He observed that years ago participants debated almost everything. As time went on, voters recognized that highways and welfare were expenses they must pay and did not debate them. He added: "The smaller the proposed expenditure, the more they debated. They apparently could understand from personal experience a $500 article for Old Home Day, but not large proposed appropriations."

The Moderator

The business part of the annual town meeting is conducted in a manner similar to that of the Massachusetts annual town meeting, and a wide variety of matters is included in the warrant articles. In even-numbered years, the moderator is elected by ballot at the town meeting by a plurality vote.[31] The moderator continues in office until the conclusion of the annual town meeting two years following his or her election or until a successor is qualified. The moderator is ineligible to hold simultaneously the office of selectperson, treasurer, trustee of trust funds, collector of taxes, auditor, or highway agent.[32]

Should the moderator be absent from a town meeting or unable to perform his or her duties, a moderator *pro tempore* is elected by the town meeting.[33] Vacancies in the office of moderator are filled by appointment by the board of supervisors of the checklist (voting list) or the selectpersons if no board exists.[34] The moderator is authorized by state law to appoint an assistant moderator who has the powers of the moderator "subject to the control of the moderator."[35] In addition, the moderator may appoint an assistant moderator for each additional polling place.[36]

The moderator's duties are to "preside in the town meetings, regulate the business thereof, decide questions of order, and made a public declaration of every vote passed, and . . . prescribe rules of proceedings; but such rules may be altered by the town."[37] Town by-laws often assign additional duties to the moderator.

The New Hampshire Supreme Court in 1876 ruled the moderator is not held to strict adherence to parliamentary rules.[38] However, the moderator lacks broad discretion relative to procedures when he or she counts votes, as he or she is required to perform this duty in a ministerial capacity.[39] Reversible procedural decisions of the moderator can be reversed only by a vote of the meeting at which the ruling in question is made.[40]

A vote, other than by ballot, on a warrant article declared by the moderator may be questioned immediately by seven or more voters, and the moderator is required to have a new vote by secret ballot.[41] Any town meeting vote, with three exceptions, may be reconsidered at the same meeting or a subsequent meeting. The first exception is a third-party contractual obligation that relied upon the vote.[42] Second, a state statute stipulates that the vote on issuance of bonds or notes exceeding $100,000 cannot be reconsidered at the same session and can be reconsidered only at an adjourned session.[43] Third, another state statute authorizes a town meeting after any affirmative vote on a warrant article to vote to restrict reconsideration of the prior vote.[44] If later in the meeting a motion is approved to reconsider the vote on the article, the reconsideration cannot take place until an adjourned session is held at least one week later. The vote to restrict reconsideration cannot be reconsidered.

In a town with a population exceeding 500, five voters at a town meeting may request in writing prior to a *viva voce* vote or division vote that voting be by secret ballot.[45] Voting by secret ballot does not necessarily involve using voting booths, as a number of moderators hand out "tear-off" ballots at the door when voters enter via the checklist. When a secret ballot vote is taken on an article, a voter tears off the strip of paper labeled "Question A" (or other letter), marks his or her vote, and folds and deposits the strip in the circulating ballot box, which may be a shoe box. Furthermore, upon request of five voters, the moderator must conduct a recount of any secret ballot vote immediately following the public announcement of the vote, provided the vote margin is less than 10 percent of the votes cast.[46]

In the early 1970s, the Hooksett moderator decided that appropriation articles should be decided by secret ballot because he believed that a significant number of voters felt they were intimidated when voting in public. Ballot voting gave them greater freedom in making decisions without fear of intimidation, and the count of ballots is supervised by ballot inspectors, which removes any doubt about the moderator's decision based on shouts of yeas and nays when *viva voce* voting is employed.

Ten voters may file a request for a recount of ballots with the town clerk within seven days of the conclusion of the meeting, on any question that appeared on the official or non-partisan ballot at the meeting.[47] A ten-dollar filing fee must be paid.

A town moderator who completed a questionnaire explained that one of the duties of the moderator is to ensure that voters understand each article they will be voting on. He calls upon the sponsor(s) of each article for an explanation before taking a vote on the article. An interviewed, very experienced former moderator stressed that a moderator should be perceived as impartial and fair. He added that "once you are perceived to have integrity, you are not challengeable. Once you have established this perception, a moderator can channel debate the way he wants the debate to go." He also noted that not every voter can speak as long as he or she wants, but every voter can speak. As moderator, he always handled all articles by voice vote.

Role of the Budget Committee

A town meeting may establish a municipal budget committee to provide prudent advice relative to the appropriation of town funds. The enabling statutes stipulate that such a committee "is intended to have budgetary authority analogous to that of a legislative appropriations committee."[48]

If a town has a municipal budget committee, total appropriations approved at the annual town meeting may not exceed the committee's recommended expenditures by more than 10 percent.[49] Although the committee must submit budget items requested by the selectpersons to the town meeting, the committee does not have to recommend their approval. Similarly, the committee determines whether to recommend the approval of any petitioned appropriation article.

Committee-recommended appropriations cannot deliberately avoid the possibility of the annual meeting's increasing appropriations by 10 percent, as authorized by law, by determining the total amount necessary for the forthcoming year and recommending only 90 percent of the amount.[50]

Towns are subject to a state-imposed net indebtedness limit of 1.75 percent of their assessed valuation of property as equalized by the State Department of Revenue Administration.[51] Bonds and notes issued for specified purposes, such as sewage treatment facilities and waterworks, are excluded from the debt limit.

Town meeting participants in general rely heavily for advice on the budget committee, composed of fellow citizens who study in detail town finances. Seven reporting towns lack such a committee, but the selectpersons make recommendations on petitioned warrant articles in two of these towns. Thirty-eight (64%) of the fifty-nine towns with committees reported the committee made recommendations on all warrant articles, and twenty-one (36%) responded that the committee offered advice only on appropriation articles.

Of fifty-eight town officers who answered the question, the committee's recommendations were followed always in four (6.9%) towns, most of the time in fifty-two (89.7%) towns, and seldom in only two (3.4%) towns. It is reasonable to assume that a number of town voters rationalize that their participation in the town meeting is not essential because the budget committee's recommendations, which protect their interests, will be approved by attendees.

Role of the Planning Board

Each town with an open town meeting may create a planning board with five or seven members and authorize selection of the members by one of two methods.[52] First, the selectpersons can be authorized to appoint four or six residents and designate one selectpersons as an *ex officio* member. Second, the town meeting can provide for the election of the members of the board. A town meeting also is authorized to abolish the town planning board.[53]

The *New Hampshire Statutes Annotated* spells out the duties of the planning board.[54] Its principal duty is to prepare and amend as needed a master plan to guide the town's development. The board is authorized to conduct investigations and prepare maps and reports. The board also is responsible for recommending the erection of public buildings and their financing and may recommend changes in the zoning ordinance or zoning map to the town meeting.

Only two reporting towns lack a planning board. The other reporting towns responded that their respective planning boards wield great influence on zoning, building code amendments, and historic district ordinance amendments decisions made by the town meeting. The board's recommendations were followed always in six (9.1%) towns, most of the time in fifty-eight (87.9%) towns, and seldom in only two (3.0%) towns.

Armed with the facts, the board generally experiences little difficulty in convincing voters to accept most of its recommendations. Nevertheless, a particularly controversial land use issue occasionally is brought to the town meeting for resolution, and participation in the meeting by registered voters increases substantially.

Town Meeting Attendance

Only sixty respondents reported attendance data relative to the business part of the 1996 annual town meeting. Several town officers left the attendance section of the questionnaire blank, and others reported they did not keep track of attendance. Bedford, Hooksett, and Newmarket, which had only a budget town meeting, reported that 2.00 percent, 3.75 percent, and 5.20 percent of the registered voters, respectively, participated in the 1996 meeting. Hooksett voters in 1996 adopted the official ballot, described in a subsequent section, and voters commencing in 1997 no longer will appropriate funds at an assembled town meeting. Similarly, Newmarket voters in 1996 adopted a state statute amending

Table 4.1
New Hampshire Annual Town Meeting Business Attendance (Percent of Registered Voters, 1996)

Population Range	Number of Towns	Average Attendance	Attendance Range
499 and under	8	38.00	25 to 50
500-999	11	33.36	12 to 50
1,000-1,999	13	18.15	3 to 54
2,000-4,999	15	18.40	3 to 60
5,000-7,499	5	17.60	10 to 30
7,500-9,999	2	12.50	5 to 20
10,000-14,999	4	8.00	2 to 20
15,000 and over	2	14.00	3 to 25

its charter to provide for the use of the official ballot to vote on the proposed budget.[55] In 1997, 16 percent of the eligible voters went to the polls in Newmarket to vote on the proposed town budget and candidates for town offices.

Table 4.1 reveals that there generally is a direct correlation between the size of a New Hampshire town and town meeting attendance by registered voters, with small towns having the largest turnout of voters. Data on attendance at the 1996 annual business meeting differed from data produced by a limited 1982 survey, when one town (over 15,000 population) reported 5.00 percent attendance, three towns (10,000–14,999) reported 11.80 percent, five towns (5,000–9,000) reported 15.00 percent, and five towns (2,500–4,999) reported 22.60 percent.[56]

The sixty reporting towns had an unweighted average attendance of 20.00 percent of the registered voters participating in the business part of the 1996 annual town meeting and a weighted average attendance of 22.60 percent. It is important to recognize that voters enter and leave the meeting during its duration, and the number in attendance at the beginning of the meeting typically is significantly larger than the number present when the last article is considered. For example, approximately 270 registered voters were present at the 1994 Peterborough town meeting when it was convened on a Saturday morning, but fewer than 100 voters were present when the thirty-seventh and final warrant article was decided.[57]

Forty respondents reported comparative data on attendance at the business part of the 1996 annual town meeting (see Table 4.2). Attendance in many towns remained substantially below attendance during an earlier period in this history of the open town meeting. The 1640 Exeter town meeting approved the levying of a fine on absentees, and the 1652 town meeting imposed a two-shilling fine on any freeman who was more than one-half hour late in arriving at the scheduled time for a town meeting.[58]

In examining attendance figures, one should keep in mind the written comment of a town clerk who reported that "weather can be a factor or a particularly controversial issue.'' The annual town meeting must be held on the second Tuesday in March or the second Tuesday in May. Snowstorms are relatively common in New Hampshire in early March. Attendance also is influenced by the civic culture of the town.

Furthermore, controversial issues are not contained every year in the warrant for the annual town meeting. If the warrant articles are routine ones, as they frequently are, voters may conclude that their attendance at the business part of the annual meeting is not essential. Data provided by town clerks reveal that participation in the first part of the annual town meeting is considerably higher than participation in the business part of the meeting. One clerk reported that 862 residents voted to elect officers, and 500 attended the business part of the 1996 annual meeting. The same clerk reported that 866 residents voted, but only 150 attended the annual business meeting in 1986.

The number of registered voters in the typical town exceeds the number of year-round residents for three reasons and depresses the figure for town meeting attendance as a percentage of the registered voters. New Hampshire attracts a large number of seasonal, particularly summer, residents who are registered voters but spend part of the year, including the time of the March annual meeting, in other states where the climate is warmer. Second, an unknown number of registered voters reside in adjoining states but maintain a New Hampshire address for purposes of insuring their motor vehicles since the insurance rates are substantially lower in New Hampshire. Third, the National Voter Registration Act of 1993 prevents the purging of voters who may have moved from the checklist for failure to vote until two federal elections have been held.[59] Taking these factors into account nevertheless leads to the conclusion that voter turnout at the annual business meeting is very low except in the small towns.

Respondents indicated that the percentage of town meeting participants who speak on a controversial issue varies from less than 1 percent to 85 percent. As one would anticipate, a higher percentage of attendees speaks in the smaller towns. The number of voters who speak also is influenced greatly by the presence of controversial articles in the warrant.

Questionnaire recipients were requested to indicate whether a perception exists in their respective town that special interest groups pack the town meeting. Thirty-eight (54%) of the seventy town respondents answered in the affirmative, and thirty-two (46%) replied in the negative. In common with the other New England states, firemen, schoolteachers, parents of pupils, senior citizens, and town employees and their families were faithful attendees at the annual and special town meetings.

In contrast to the early New Hampshire towns, citizens today tend to be mobile, and it is not uncommon to have a substantial number of registered voters who are relatively new residents of the town. Not surprisingly, the views of long-term residents and recently arrived residents tend to differ. Sixty-one (91%) respondents indicated that long-term residents held views on certain warrant articles that differed from the views of new residents. Only six respondents (9%)

Table 4.2
New Hampshire Annual Town Meeting Business Attendance (Percent of Registered Voters, 1966–1996)

Town	1996 Population	1966	1976	1986	1996
Alton	4,200	-	10.00	10.00	10.00
Ashland	1,972	18.00	18.00	18.00	18.00
Belmont	6,600	13.00	15.00	10.00	10.00
Benton	320	-	30.00	40.00	42.00
Bradford	1,500	-	20.00	20.00	20.00
Brentwood	3,000	-	35.00	15.00	10.00
Clarksville	265	60.00	50.00	35.00	25.00
Columbia	691	8.00	10.00	10.00	12.00
Conway	8,300	20.00	20.00	20.00	20.00
Danville	3,400	-	10.00	10.00	10.00
Derry	32,000	23.00	26.00	25.00	No town meeting
Effingham	900	-	-	35.00	41.00
Ellsworth	69	100.00	50.00	40.00	50.00
Exeter	12,950	2.44	2.55	3.62	21.00
Hampton	12,500	-	-	5.00	5.00
Hancock	1,600	20.00	15.00	10.00	10.00
Hart's Location	39	-	-	50.00	50.00
Holderness	1,700	-	10.00	10.00	10.00
Langdon	600	-	-	20.00	18.00

Town	Population			
Lincoln	1,200	-	3.00	3.00
Litchfield	6,300	-	4.00	13.40
Marlow	649	-	33.00	43.00
Monroe	730	50.00	50.00	50.00
Mont Vernon	1,854	20.00	20.00	20.00
Nelson	535	26.00	29.00	25.00
New London	3,320	-	21.30	8.30
Northfield	4,300	-	20.00	5.00
Northumberland	2,500	-	60.00	60.00
Orford	1,022	-	22.00	22.00
Pelham	10,000	5.00	5.00	5.00
Rollinsford	2,645	-	24.00	25.00
Rumney	1,429	-	15.00	15.00
Salem	30,000	3.00	3.00	3.00
Salisbury	1,100	33.00	33.00	33.00
Sandown	4,700	-	13.00	3.00
Shelburne	435	-	25.00	25.00
South Hampton	800	-	20.00	20.00
Stoddard	625	68.00	60.00	55.00
Sutton	1,447	-	15.00	10.00
Swanzey	6,289	10.00	10.00	5.00

reported that the views of the two groups did not differ. One respondent wrote that many new residents are strong supporters of traditional town meeting governance.

Quality of Debate and Decisions

Questionnaire recipients were requested to rate the quality of debate at the annual town meeting—in terms of explanations of budget items, exploring pros and cons of proposals, and neighbors influencing neighbors' opinions on town issues—as one of the following: excellent, good, fair, or poor.

Seventy-one town officers rated the quality of debate. Thirteen (18%) rated the quality as excellent, thirty-nine (55%) selected good, sixteen (23%) checked fair, and only three (4%) considered the debate quality to be poor.

Questionnaire recipients were requested to make a similar rating of the overall quality of town meeting decisions. Sixty-eight town officers responded. Sixteen (24%) rated the quality as excellent, forty-seven (69%) selected good, four (6%) checked fair, and only one (1%) believed the quality of decisions was poor.

The ratings of debate quality and decision quality in the same town were not always the same. Two respondents rated debate quality as only good but decision quality as excellent. Two town respondents rated the debate as poor but the decisions as good. Similarly, one respondent checked poor for debate and fair for decisions.

THE SPECIAL TOWN MEETING

The selectpersons may call a special town meeting "when, in their opinion, there shall be occasion therefor."[60] A special town meeting can appropriate money or reduce or rescind appropriations previously authorized only if the vote to do so is by secret ballot, and the number of ballots cast equals or exceeds 50 percent of the registered voters on the town checklist entitled to vote at the preceding annual or biennial election.[61] Only on extremely rare occasions can the Board of Selectmen count on a 50 percent turnout of voters on the checklist if a special town meeting is called. Forty-four (65%) of the survey respondents reported their towns did not hold a special town meeting in 1996. Other towns held one or, at most, two special town meetings in 1996.

However, permission of the Superior Court is required if the special town meeting is to appropriate funds.[62] State law makes two exceptions relative to authorization of expenditures by a special town meeting. No court permission is needed for the selectpersons to call such a meeting to authorize the expenditure of federal funds allocated to the town because of a major disaster as certified by the governor or to appropriate the town's matching share of the federal funds.[63] The New Hampshire Supreme Court has held at a special town meeting, called in an emergency with permission of the Superior Court, that bonds may be authorized by a two-thirds vote of participants who vote regardless of the total number of voters present.[64] A few towns seeking permission to hold a special town meeting to appropriate funds to implement collective bargaining agreements have been refused permission by the Superior Court.[65] In a related development, the New Hampshire Supreme Court in 1996 ruled that a school district could not hold a special school district meeting to allow voters to consider a collective bargaining agreement, because the achievement of a collective bargaining agreement, is not an emergency under the circumstances of the case justifying the calling of a special meeting.[66] Hence, it is still possible that a district may be able to obtain permission to hold a special meeting to vote on a collective bargaining agreement.

In an unusual action, the New Hampshire Supreme Court on July 24, 1997, overturned the decision of Belknap County Superior Court judge James Barry denying the town of Belmont permission to hold a special town meeting to consider purchasing land on Lake Winnisquam for a town beach.[67] Judge Barry found that no emergency existed and that no irreparable harm to the town would be caused if the meeting was not held. On appeal, the town successfully argued that the town had signed a purchase agreement with a firm to acquire the land, which was the only waterfront property in the town on the market. The purchase had been recommended by the town budget committee.

Registered voters are authorized by state law to direct the selectpersons to call a special town meeting by petition. Such a meeting can be held sixty or more days prior to the annual town meeting upon the petition of fifty or more voters or one-quarter of the registered voters, whichever is fewer.[68] Should the selectpersons refuse to call the meeting, twenty-five voters or one-sixth of the registered voters, whichever is fewer, may petition the Superior Court for the issuance of a warrant calling the special town meeting.[69]

The New Hampshire Supreme Court has opined that although selectpersons may exercise a degree of judgment in deciding whether to call a special town meeting when petitioned by the voters, the selectpersons do not have complete discretion to frustrate the attempt of voters to call a special meeting.[70] The court, however, has held that the selectpersons are not required to call a petitioned special meeting if the warrant article is illegal, that is, if the article conflicts with a statutory provision.

Special town meetings last from fifteen minutes to three hours, depending on the issue. Attendance at these meetings on average is significantly lower than attendance at the business part of the annual town meeting.

THE OFFICIAL BALLOT REFERENDUM SYSTEM

The Granite State Taxpayers Association, with representation in forty-three towns, was distressed by the low voter attendance (5% to 10%) at school district meetings, which vote to appropriate funds that consume 65 percent to 75 percent of all town property tax revenue. The district meetings approve contracts with teachers' unions and approve all school spending. The association estimated that at least 60 percent of district meeting participants were teachers and other school district employees and their families and friends.

The official ballot (OB) referendum bill (SB 2) was introduced in the General Court and originally was intended to apply only to school district meetings. Pressure grew for inclusion of town meetings, and the bill was amended and enacted in 1995 to include both types of meetings.[71] A three-fifths vote of town meeting participants is required to adopt or repeal the OB acceptance statute. In sum, the statute authorizes a referendum form of school district meeting and town meeting. The first session of the annual town meeting is devoted to discussion and possible amendment of the articles contained in the warrant issued by the selectpersons. One month later, in April, the voters go to the polls to vote, via the referendum, on the warrant articles (see Appendix IV).

A member of a taxpayer association wrote to the author in 1996 explaining the reason he supported enactment of the statute:

Many of us have sought more accountability, better schools, more expertise from our school boards and less reliance on Superintendents. Many have been concerned for the devious manipulation of facts and figures by the administration and the inability of 95% of the Superintendents to manage schools like a business. . . . If we accept the values of tradition, such as the town meeting form of governing, then it should be strengthened when its status is in jeopardy. The problem is simply people don't, won't, can't participate in sufficient numbers to allow representative local government to function as intended. To get people more involved, to participate in major decisions that affect them, we felt the use of an OB will be a good place to start.

He also reported that fear of retaliation is a second major problem at the traditional school district and town meetings. Specifically, he noted ''the fear of intimidation and the economic reprisals for standing up and opposing the fire chief or the police chief, or the school budget. Most businessmen simply stay away rather than risk loss of customers. The C of C will have less than .5% of their membership in attendance and those there say nothing.''

Opponents of the OB referendum statute feared it will destroy traditional lawmaking by assembled voters if the statute is adopted by town and school district voters. Voters participating in twenty-seven town meetings and thirty-four school district meetings in 1996 adopted the statute, effective in 1997, and eight additional town meetings adopted the statute in 1997, effective in 1998.[72] Supporters of traditional town meeting government reject the argument that the official ballot is needed to eliminate the fear of intimidation and economic reprisal, because voters currently have the ability to vote on controversial warrant articles by secret ballot if five voters sign and present a petition to the moderator for a secret ballot.

One group of traditional meeting supporters expressed their view of the OB referendum system in the following terms:

Much of this vitality is the result of the dialogues and discussions (sometimes heated) that we have during school district and town meeting time. . . . Ideas are exchanged, adjusted, and affirmed in an open democratic manner.

We believe that a voter who will take the time to attend a town meeting has a vital interest in and is better informed about town and school affairs than the voter who is willing to cast a ballot but who has not attended the meeting and listened to deliberations. If town meetings require too much of a commitment now, this proposed process expects the informed voter to attend budget hearings in February, the deliberative session in March, and then spend 25 minutes in the voting booth reading the articles in April. If the articles fail to gain approval, another deliberative session and another chance to cast votes [will be held] sometime in mid-June.[73]

Voters in none of the few official ballot referendum towns with a 1997 article repealing the system approved the article. Canaan (3,132) voters, by a margin of 435 to 365 (54%), favored the repeal, but the repeal proponents failed to secure the required supermajority vote. In addition, voters in six OB referendum towns rejected the repeal. Several 1997 town meetings rejected articles calling for adoption of the OB system, including Ackworth, Alexandria, Alton, Chichester, Carroll, Gilmanton, Swanzey, and Walpole.

The warrant for the 1998 town meeting in thirteen SB2 towns contained an article proposing the repeal of the system. The article was defeated in each town, although 52.9 percent of Wakefield voters and 52.4 percent of Allentown voters favored the repeal, which required a 60.0 percent affirmative vote.

Returns from the twenty-seven official ballot referendum towns in 1997 reveal attendance at the deliberative session averaged 4.3 percent with a range of .7 percent of the voters on the checklist in Hampstead (7,750) to 14.5 percent in Dorchester (395). Public hearing attendance, excluding town officers required to be present, averaged .82 percent and varied from zero in two towns to 3.4 percent in Charlestown. Absentee ballots cast in twenty-five reporting towns averaged 1.60 percent of the total ballots cast and varied from .24 percent in Goffstown to 5.7 percent in Hampton.

Ballots cast ranged from 17.3 percent of the registered voters in Plaistow (7,384) to 57.6 percent in Grafton (1,000). The unweighted average of ballots cast in the twenty-seven towns was 38.1 percent of the registered voters, and the weighted average was only 27.7 percent. In traditional New Hampshire open meeting towns, the unweighted average voter participation rate in 1996 was 19.7 percent, and the weighted average (number of ballots cast in SB2 towns divided by twenty-seven) was 16.82 percent.

The number of warrant articles varied from twelve in Alstead to sixty-one in Conway (8,900). The length of the warrant ballot ranged from two pages in Dorchester and Hampstead to thirteen pages in Atkinson (5,685). Returns from twenty-two towns reveal that seven (32%) posted a copy of the warrant to each household or registered voter prior to the deliberative session. Of twenty-seven replying towns, the deliberative session reduced one or more budget items to zero in fourteen (53%) towns and sharply reduced items in five (19%) additional towns. Seven of twenty-three official ballot-reporting towns posted the amended warrant to each voter, and Merrimack and Newton (3,527) published the amended warrant in a newspaper.

Eight of the twenty-four reporting towns indicated that recommendations of the budget committee were included in the amended warrant. Similarly, eight towns checked that the budget committee's recommendations were included in the official ballot articles. No town officer reported that all budget recommendations were followed, but ten of fifteen reporting town officers wrote that most recommendations were adopted by the voters. Budgets were approved by voters in twenty-one (78%) of the twenty-seven towns, and no town officer replied that absentee ballots affected the outcome of the vote on the budget.

Returns from thirty-five OB referendum towns in 1998 reveal that attendance at the deliberative session averaged 3.3 percent, a decrease from 4.3 percent in 1997, and ranged from .5 percent in Hampton to 8.4 percent in Grafton.

Ballots cast varied from 21.5 percent of the 9,584 registered voters in Exeter to 65.0 percent of the 189 voters in Orange. The unweighted average of ballots cast in the 35 towns was 36.1 percent, and the weighted average was 31.1 percent.

The number of warrant articles varied from thirteen in Barrington and Winchester to fifty-six in Seabrook. The warrant ballot length ranged from two pages in Bennington, Littletown, and Weare to thirty-three pages in Hudson. The deliberative session reduced budget items to zero in eleven towns and reduced other items in an additional four towns. The town budget was approved in twenty-seven (77.1%) of the thirty-three towns. All recommendations of the budget committee were adopted in twelve towns, most of its recommendations were followed in sixteen towns, only a few recommendations were adopted in three towns, and all recommendations were rejected in four towns.

The participation rate relative to voting on the business articles was increased to a very minor extent by the fact that voters could cast absentee ballots on such articles for the first time, provided they were disabled or elderly or anticipated being absent from the town on election day. Previously, such ballots were limited to electing town officers. One hundred absentee ballots, for example, were cast in 1997 in Milford, which was double the number typically cast at each town election in the recent past.

Citizens' reactions to the system were mixed, depending on the length of the warrant and the amount of information provided by town officers in advance of the voting date. A significant percentage of the voters failed to vote on each article in a long warrant. Faced with a seventy-six-article combined town and school district ballot, many Charlestown residents in 1997 reported they started "checking 'no' because the process was taking too long."[74]

Very few voters attended the deliberative town meetings where articles were explained, and a number of town officers doubted that the voters understood all the articles they were voting on. Exit interviews in several towns confirmed that voters had difficulty understanding the language of certain articles.

Most OB voters did not recognize the importance of the deliberative session of the town meeting where warrant articles are discussed and can be amended. The few participants in this session in several towns amended the proposed spending articles by lowering drastically the amounts or reducing the amounts to zero. When voters went to the polls, they discovered that they had only two choices—approve or reject each article. The Superior Court of Hillsborough County, Northern District, in 1997 upheld the authority of voters attending the deliberative session of the town meeting to amend a warrant article "because the subject matter remained the same," even though the amendment changed substantially the article's intent.[75]

Milford mailed a voter information bulletin containing the warrant to each household with a registered voter prior to the March 11, 1997, deliberative session. A second bulletin containing the amended town and school districts' warrants was posted to each registered voter prior to the April 8, 1997, referendum on the warrant articles. The recommendations of the budget committee and the Board of Selectmen on warrant articles were included in the first mailing, but not in the second mailing, which contained the ballots for the town and school district. Previously, the warrant for each meeting was posted in public buildings, and few read the warrant prior to the town meeting. Many Milford voters used "cheat sheets" on which they wrote in advance how they would vote on warrant articles. In general, Milford voters were very satisfied with the system, although several admitted they failed to vote on a number of articles because they did not understand them. Conway made similar mailings of informational materials in advance of the deliberative and voting sessions of the town meeting.

Complaints were registered by a number of voters relative to the non-inclusion of budget committee recommendations on the official ballot. Responding to the complaint and recognizing the need to provide guidance to voters, the 1997 General Court amended the OB statute to require that committee recommendations be printed on the official ballot relative to appropriations articles.[76] Numerous committees in the past have made recommendations on all warrant articles.

Vice President Fran Chapman of the Granite State Taxpayers Association surveyed official ballot towns and school districts after the 1997 annual meetings. He found "there were long ballots, some as high as 65 articles and people were evidently very prepared and informed and selectively voted on the articles."[77] Chapman concluded:

Special interest groups, such as unions will lose much of the influence they have wielded over the public, but can counter that with stronger selling efforts. All in all, for a few extra bucks per voter, the voters are going to get what they want—the right to vote on budgets.[78]

Exeter town manager George N. Olson in 1998 emphasized the importance of SB2 town and school district officers' actively seeking voter support of their proposals well in advance of referendum day:

> If you are a selectman or school board member . . . and you expect the public to follow your lead, get ready to approach town meeting with an eye to promotion and not the weather . . . if local officials are not ready to promote their initiatives in every way possible, then their initiatives will likely fail.[79]

Olson announced his town will prepare for the 1999 SB2 town meeting by requesting the local newspaper to publish a specimen warrant ballot voters can take to the polls, utilizing the community television channel to share the selectpersons' position on warrant articles with viewers, directing department heads to write at least one article for the local newspaper explaining the warrant articles pertinent to their respective department, and providing all fraternal and social organizations with a list of town government speakers who will review the warrant.[80]

The 1996 General Court was aware that the OB system is *terra incognito* and a dramatic change in the nature of the town meeting that might not operate smoothly. In consequence, a statute was enacted creating a joint legislative committee to study OB procedures, including adoption of the system.[81] Questions being studied include:

1. If a town meeting rejects adoption of the OB system, how long must the town wait prior to voting again on the question of adoption?
2. Should multiple articles be allowed on the same subject or issue?
3. Should the deliberative session be authorized to amend appropriations articles to zero?
4. Should the deliberative session be authorized to amend petitioned articles?
5. Should the recommendations of the budget committee and/or selectpersons on non-appropriation articles be printed on the ballot?
6. Should OB voters be allowed to spend more than ten minutes in the voting booth?

SUMMARY

Traditional town meeting democracy remains in 181 New Hampshire towns that conduct an annual town meeting and occasionally a special town meeting. The selectpersons, the plural executive of a town unless there is a town manager, are charged by state law with preparing and posting the warrant warning voters of the forthcoming election of town officers and containing articles to be acted upon by the business part of the meeting.

The town meeting, annual or special, is under the control of the elected town meeting moderator, who possesses broad discretion relative to the conduct of the meeting, subject to possible reversal by vote of the meeting. Although *viva voce* voting is utilized for most warrant articles, voting must be by secret ballot if requested in writing by five voters.

Voters at a town meeting rely heavily upon two committees—the budget committee and the planning board. The former possesses persuasive power because the state statutes stipulate that the total appropriations approved by the voters at the annual meeting may not exceed the committee's recommendations by more than 10 percent. Recommendations of the committees, according to survey respondents, were followed always or most of the time by 96.6 percent of the town meetings. Similarly, the recommendations of the planning board were followed always or most of the time in 96.0 percent of the town meetings. Whether town meeting attendees are representative of town voters at large is examined in Chapter 10.

Critics of the open town meeting find support for their belief that the meeting is an unrepresentative legislative assembly in attendance statistics. Surveys reveal an unweighted average attendance of 20 percent of the registered voters at the 1996 annual meetings and a weighted average attendance of nearly 23 percent. Attendance at the annual town meeting in any town typically varies from year to year depending on the number of major, controversial issues contained in the warrant. Furthermore, attendance nearly always is higher at the commencement of the meeting than at the conclusion of the meeting. Whether town meeting attendees are representative of town voters at large is examined in Chapter 10.

Town officials who completed a questionnaire do not accept the judgment of the critics of the open town meeting. Nearly three-quarters of the respondents rated the quality of the town meeting debate in terms of informing attendees as excellent or good. Of greater importance is the judgment of 93 percent of the respondents that the quality of the decisions made by participant voters was excellent or good.

Only two towns have abandoned the town meeting completely in favor of a town council as the legislative body, and only Durham has retained the town meeting for discussion purposes and lodged law-making authority in the town council. Three additional towns have retained the town meeting only for budget purposes, but two of these towns vote on the proposed budget by referendum. In contrast, twenty-one Rhode Island towns have abandoned the town meeting completely, and the remaining ten towns retain it only for financial matters.

The official ballot adopted by twenty-seven town meetings in 1996 and eight town meetings in 1997 may generate pressures in these towns to abandon the town meeting in favor of a town council, especially if attendance at the discussion town meeting continues to be minuscule.

Chapter 5 examines the operation of the open town meeting in another northern New England state—Vermont—and compares its experience with town meeting government in the twin state of New Hampshire.

NOTES

1. Francis N. Thorpe, ed., *The Federal and State Constitutions, Colonial Charters, and Other Organic Laws* (Washington, D.C.: Government Printing Office, 1909), vol. 4, p. 2513.

2. Ibid., p. 2521.

3. Ibid., p. 2523.

4. Ibid., p. 2527.

5. *New Hampshire Laws of 1963*, chap. 374, § 7.

6. Letter to author from town of Hanover administrative assistant Jean G. Ulman dated September 5, 1996.

7. *New Hampshire Revised Statutes Annotated*, §§ 39.1, 31:94-a.

8. Ibid., § 39:3.

9. Ibid.

10. *Woodside v. Selectmen of Derry*, 116 N.H. 606, 366 A.2d 210 (1976).

11. *Levasseur v. Selectmen of Hudson*, 116 N.H. 340, 358 A.2d 665 (1976).

12. "Acid Rain Resolution Passed at 197 N.H. Town Meetings," *Keene (N.H.) Shopper News*, May 25, 1983, p. 5.

13. *Town of Pittsburg v. Danforth*, 56 N.H. 272 (1875).

14. *New Hampshire Revised Statutes Annotated*, § 39:5.

15. *Russell v. Dyer*, 40 N.H. 173 (1860).

16. *Osgood v. Blake*, 21 N.H. 550 (1850).

17. *Drowne v. Lovering*, 93 N.H. 3 (1944).

18. *New Hampshire Revised Statutes Annotated*, § 39:7.

19. Ibid., § 39:9.

20. Ibid., § 669:2.

21. Ibid., § 39:2-a.

22. Ibid., § 669:11.

23. Ibid., §§ 669:55–669:57.

24. Ibid., § 669:54.

25. Ibid., § 669:43.

26. Ibid., § 669:37.

27. Ibid., § 669:13.

28. Ibid., § 669:26.

29. *Town of Exeter v. Kennick*, 104 N.H. 168, 45 A.2d 638 (1963). For a set of traditional rules of fairness employed by a number of moderators, see H. Bernard Waugh, Jr., *Town Meeting & School Meeting Handbook* (Concord: New Hampshire Municipal Association, 1995), pp. 28–35.

30. Ronald Jager, *Last House on the Road: Excursions into a Rural Past* (Boston: Beacon Press, 1994), p. 229.

31. *New Hampshire Revised Statutes Annotated*, § 40:1.

32. Ibid., § 669:7.

33. Ibid., § 40:3.

34. Ibid., § 669:62.

35. Ibid., § 40:3-a.

36. Ibid., § 658:14.

37. Ibid., § 40:4.

38. *Hill v. Goodwin*, 56 N.H. 170, 262 A.2d 609 (1970).

39. *Pierce v. Langdon*, 110 N.H. 170, 262 A.2d 609 (1970).

40. *Town of Exeter v. Kenick*, 104 N.H. 168, 45 A.2d 638 (1962).

41. *New Hampshire Revised Statutes Annotated*, § 40:4-b.

42. *Preston v. Gilliam*, 104 N.H. 279, 184 A.2d 462 (1962); *Byron v. Timberlane School District*, 113 N.H. 449, 309 A.2d 609 (1973).

43. *New Hampshire Revised Statutes Annotated*, § 33:8-a.

44. Ibid., § 40:10.

45. Ibid., § 40:4-a(a).

46. Ibid., § 40:4-a(b).

47. Ibid., § 669:30–33.

48. Ibid., § 32:1.

49. Ibid., § 32:18.

50. *Baker v. Hudson School District*, 110 N.H. 389, 269 A.2d 128 (1970).

51. *New Hampshire Revised Statutes Annotated*, §§ 33:4-a, 33:4-b.

52. Ibid., § 673:2(II).

53. Ibid., § 673:18.

54. Ibid., § 674:1.

55. *New Hampshire Laws of 1995*, chap. 53; *New Hampshire Revised Statutes Annotated*, § 49-D3(a).

56. Joseph F. Zimmerman, "The New England Town Meeting: Pure Democracy in Action?" *The Municipal Year Book 1984* (Washington, D.C.: International City Management Association, 1984), p. 103.

57. Eric Aldrich, "Peterborough Buys Police Station, Trims Spending," *Keene (N.H.) Sentinel*, March 14, 1994, p. 3.

58. Lewis Soule, "The New Hampshire Town Meeting," unpublished paper provided by deputy New Hampshire secretary of state Robert Ambrose, n.d., p. 14.

59. *National Voter Registration Act of 1993*, 107 Stat. 77, 42 U.S.C. §§ 1973gg to 1974e.

60. *New Hampshire Revised Statutes Annotated*, § 39:1.

61. Ibid., § 31:5-a.

62. Ibid., § 31:5.

63. Ibid., § 31:5-a.

64. *Opinion of the Justices*, 86 N.H. 604, 171 A.2d 443 (1934).

65. Waugh, *Town Meeting & School Meeting Handbook*, p. 5.

66. *Appeal of Mascoma Valley Regional School District*, 141 N.H. 98, 667 A.2d 679 (1996).

67. Roger Amsden, "High Court OK's Special Belmont Meeting on Town Beach Purchase," *Union Leader* (Manchester, N.H.), July 25, 1997, p. A5.

68. *New Hampshire Revised Statutes Annotated*, § 39:3.

69. Ibid., § 39:9.

70. *Winchester Taxpayers' Association v. Selectmen*, 118 N.H. 144, 383 A.2d 1125 (1978).

71. *New Hampshire Laws of 1995*, chap. 164; *New Hampshire Revised Statutes Annotated*, § 40:13.

72. Letter to author from Andrea M. Reid of the New Hampshire Municipal Services Division dated February 20, 1997.

73. Allen MacNeil et al., "Official Ballot Bill Tears Away at the Wrong Thing," *The Citizen* (Laconia, N.H.), March 2, 1996, p. 2.

74. "Big Vote, Long Vote," *Keene (N.H.) Sentinel*, April 9, 1997, p. 5.

75. *Tucker, et al. v. Town of Goffstown, et al.*, New Hampshire Superior Court of Hillsborough County, Northern District, docket no. 97-E-2103, March 26, 1997.

76. *New Hampshire Laws of 1997*, chap. 318; *New Hampshire Revised Statutes Annotated*, § 40:13 VI.

77. Letter to author from Vice President Fran Chapman of the Granite State Taxpayers Association dated May 10, 1997.

78. Ibid.

79. George N. Olson, "President's Corner," *New Hampshire Town and City*, May 1998, p. 5.

80. Ibid.

81. *New Hampshire Laws of 1996*, chap. 176, § 3.

Chapter 5

The Vermont
Open Town Meeting

The first European to visit Vermont was French explorer Samuel de Champlain in the seventeenth century. The territory, however, was not settled until Fort Dummer was built in 1724 near the location of the current village of Brattleboro. Vermont originally was claimed by Massachusetts, New Hampshire, and New York. Nine years after the 1740 settlement of boundary disputes with Massachusetts, Governor Benning Wentworth of New Hampshire issued a charter for the town of Bennington.[1] Within the next five years, he issued an additional fourteen charters for towns in Vermont.

Lieutenant Governor Colden of New York in 1763 proclaimed that the territory of Vermont belonged to New York and commenced to issue charters for towns in the Connecticut River Valley. The vast majority of the settlers of Vermont, who emigrated principally from Connecticut, resisted the claims of New York, organized a Council of Safety led by Ethan Allen and Seth Warner, and commenced to term the territory New Connecticut.[2]

Meeting in Windsor on July 2–8, 1777, delegates to a constitutional convention drafted and proclaimed a constitution of Vermont to be in effect. The constitution was ratified by the legislature in 1779 and again in 1782. The Preamble referred to the dispute between New Hampshire and Vermont in the following terms:

And whereas the Territory, which now comprehends the State of Vermont, did antecedently of right belong to the government of New Hampshire, and the former Governor, thereof, viz. his excellency Benning Wentworth, Esq. granted many charters of lands and corporations within this State to the present inhabitants and others. And whereas the late Lieutenant-Governor Colden, of New York, with others, did, in violation, of the tenth command, covet those very lands: and by a false representation, to the Court of Great-

Britain, (. . . the inhabitants were desirous of being annexed to that government) obtained jurisdiction of those very identical lands, *ex parte*, which ever was and is disagreeable to the inhabitants.[3]

Massachusetts agreed to the independence of Vermont in 1781, and the following year New Hampshire reached a similar agreement with Vermont. By 1790, New York was in need of support in the U.S. Senate, decided New York's interests were similar to those of its neighbor, and approached the Republic of Vermont.[4] An agreement was reached that cleared the way for the admission of Vermont to the Union as the fourteenth state in 1791.[5] Interestingly, the last boundary dispute between New Hampshire and Vermont was not settled until 1933, when the U.S. Supreme Court decreed the western bank of the Connecticut River as the official boundary line.[6]

Currently, there are 237 towns in Vermont, and 180 have a population under 2,500. Three towns have a population under 100: Victory (52), Granby (88), and Searsburg (93). The largest towns are Colchester (15,973), Bennington (16,192), and Essex (17,608). There also are nine cities ranging in population from Vergennes (2,264) to Burlington (39,435), "five unorganized towns, three gores, one grant, and forty-five incorporated villages."[7]

Towns, which decided they wished to be governed by special provisions in place of many state statutes, have town charters enacted by the state legislature and accepted by town voters. There has been a slow growth in the number of charter towns since Springfield was chartered by special act of the state legislature in 1947, to sixteen in 1983 and the current twenty-seven.

The Board of Selectpersons or a petition signed by 5 percent of the voters can propose the adoption of a town charter.[8] At least two public hearings must be held on the proposal, which subsequently is placed in the warning for the next annual town meeting, where voting is by Australian (official) ballot. If approved by the voters, the charter becomes effective when ratified by the Vermont General Assembly.

The Vermont General Assembly has authorized any municipality (city or town) to use the Australian (official) ballot to elect officers and act by referendum on the proposed municipal budget and/or other questions.[9] All towns hold a traditional open meeting with nine exceptions: Brattleboro adopted a representative town meeting (RTM) in 1959 (see Chapter 9), and Bennington, Poultney, Pownal, Rutland, Shelburne, Shrewsbury, West Rutland, and Winooski act on all warning articles at the polls by Australian referendum ballot.[10]

Under the official ballot (OB) referendum system, an informational town meeting must be held to discuss the warning during the ten days preceding the voting by Australian ballot. These towns hold the meeting either on the Monday night preceding the first Tuesday in March, when town meetings are held, or on the preceding Saturday. In common with New Hampshire OB referendum towns, voter turnout at the informational meeting is low and ranges from approximately 2.4 percent to 5.9 percent. In contrast to New Hampshire OB referendum towns, voters at the informational town meeting in Vermont may not amend the warning. Voter turnout at the polls to elect town officers, adopt the town budget, and act on all other warning articles averages slightly in excess of one-third of the voters on the checklist.

Four additional towns employ the Australian ballot to act by referendum on most warning (warrant) articles. Brandon uses this ballot for all but three to five minor articles, and Castleton and Clarendon decide all articles except five by this ballot. Fairhaven holds only a budget town meeting, and voters act on all other articles at the polls. The minor articles handled in three of these towns include: Shall the town act on all town officers' reports? Shall the town authorize the treasurer to collect taxes? Shall the town authorize the selectpersons to borrow in anticipation of taxes?

A 1997 survey by the Vermont League of Cities and Towns found that the Australian ballot is employed by 154 (65%) towns to elect officers, 67 (28%) towns to decide one or more public questions, and 42 (18%) towns to act on the proposed town budget.[11]

To collect data on the operation of the Vermont open town meetings, a questionnaire was posted to each town with such a meeting. Returns from 107 towns (44%) were received, but not every respondent answered each question.

THE ANNUAL TOWN MEETING

Town meeting procedures in Vermont are generally similar to those in Massachusetts and New Hampshire. Each town meeting is held in pursuance of a warning or warrant, issued by the Board of Selectpersons, which must include the date and time of the election of town officers, location of polling places, and specific articles of business to be acted upon.[12] The warning also must include any article requested by a petition signed by 5 percent of the town's registered voters and filed with the town clerk at least forty days prior to the day of the meeting.[13] To ensure that there is no improper influence on town meeting participants, a state statute stipulates that "neither the warning, the notice, the official voter information cards, nor the ballot itself shall include any opinion or comment by any town body or officer or other person on any matter to be voted on."[14] Traditionally, the annual town meeting was held on the first Tuesday in March. Currently, approximately four-fifths of the towns hold their annual meetings on this date, approximately 6 percent hold their meetings on the preceding Saturday, 9 percent schedule their meetings on the preceding evening, and six towns by charter have selected a different date.

The warning must be posted between thirty and forty days prior to the meeting in a minimum of two public places in the town in addition to a posting in or near the town clerk's office and must be published in a newspaper of general circulation in the town a minimum of five days prior to the meeting unless the warning is published in the annual town report, which is mailed to voters at least ten days prior to the meeting.[15]

The Annual Report and Pre–Town Meeting Meeting

The annual report published by a town contains information on the organization of the town, appointed and elected officials, reports of the Board of Selectpersons and other town officers and boards, statement of revenues and expenditures for the preceding year and proposed expenditures, reserve funds, and delinquent taxes and may contain minutes of the preceding annual town meeting and the warning for the annual town and school district meetings.

Voters particularly focus their attention on the comparative fiscal data relative to annual town expenditures during the preceding fiscal year, amounts proposed for the forthcoming fiscal year, and recommendations of the budget committee if there is such a committee.

Forty-five of 106 (43%) responding towns held a 1996 pre–town meeting meeting where warrant budget articles and other articles in certain towns were explained, and questions were raised by voters and answered by town officials. In common with Massachusetts and New Hampshire towns, attendance usually is very low at these meetings and ranged in 1996 from 1 percent in a town with a population of approximately 2,500 to 65 percent in a town with a population of approximately 600.

Election of Town Officers and Referenda

The annual meeting warning must notify voters that town officers will be elected at the town meeting. Traditionally, they were elected on the same day that warning articles were decided, but today many towns have a bifurcated town meeting with officials elected on one day, and voters assembling on another day to act on the articles. A state statute specifically stipulates that a town resident may refuse to accept appointment or election to any town office.[16]

Towns are mandated by state law to elect at the annual town meeting the following officers unless their selection is provided otherwise by law:

1. A moderator;
2. A town clerk for a term of one year unless the town votes that a town clerk shall be elected for a term of three years . . . ;
3. A town treasurer for a term of one year unless a town votes that a town treasurer shall be elected for a term of three years . . . ;
4. One selectman for a term of three years who shall be elected by ballot;
5. One lister for a term of three years who shall be elected by ballot;
6. One auditor for a term of three years who shall be elected by ballot;
7. A first constable, and if needed a second constable unless the town has voted to authorize the selectmen to appoint constables . . . ;
8. A collector of current taxes, if the town so orders;
9. A collector of delinquent taxes, if the town so orders;

10. One or more grand jurors;

11. A town agent to prosecute and defend suits in which the town school district is interested;

12. A trustee of public funds if the town has so ordered;

13. A trustee of public money, but only in towns that retain possession of a portion of the surplus funds of the United States received under the Act of 1836;

14. A cemetery commissioner if the town has so ordered;

15. One or more patrolmen to patrol town highways under the direction of the selectmen, if the town so orders;

16. One or two road commissioners who shall be elected by ballot if the town has so ordered; otherwise they shall be appointed by the selectmen . . . ;

17. Three water commissioners who shall be elected by ballot if the town has so ordered; otherwise they shall be appointed by the selectmen.[17]

Candidates for office in towns utilizing the Australian ballot must be nominated by petitions containing the signatures of a minimum of thirty registered voters or 1 percent of the town's registered voters, whichever is less, filed with the town clerk by the sixth Monday prior to the annual meeting election.[18] By the following Wednesday, a candidate must file a written consent to the printing of his or her name on the ballot. Only one person may be nominated by a petition. Only the town of Mendon (1,056) reported that elections were partisan. However, a town clerk wrote that "elections supposedly are nonpartisan."

A candidate nominated by petition must receive a plurality of the votes cast to be elected, but a write-in candidate must receive a minimum of 1 percent of the votes cast or votes equal to 1 percent of the town's registered voters, whichever is less.[19] If there is a tie vote, a runoff election is held between fifteen and twenty-two days after the issuance of the warning for such election.

Town officers traditionally were elected by *viva voce* voting at the annual town meeting prior to action the same day on the warning's business articles. Today, *viva voce* voting is utilized in many small towns, but officers in 154 towns (65%) are elected by the Australian ballot, which also is employed in 66 (28%) towns to decide referenda questions and in 44 (19%) towns to act on the town budget.[20] Four towns—Brattleboro, Milton, Windsor, and Middlebury—have charter provisions allowing voters to petition for a special election to determine whether a named town officer(s) should be removed from office.[21]

Questionnaire recipients were requested to indicate whether all offices were contested and whether there was a candidate for each office. Of 100 reporting towns, only 6 (6%) checked that all offices were contested. Of 91 reporting towns, 55 (60%) indicated that there was at least one candidate for each office. In other words, there were no candidates for one or more office in 45 percent of the towns. It is important to recognize that many town offices are minor ones dating to the colonial period and involve few or no duties during the course of any given year.

Figure 5.1
Official Special Town Meeting Ballot, Town of Arlington, Vermont

---

OFFICIAL SPECIAL
TOWN MEETING BALLOT
MARCH 5, 1996

INSTRUCTIONS TO VOTERS: To vote for an article printed on the ballot mark an (X) in one of the squares at the right of the article. Mark an (X) in the square marked **YES** if you want it to pass or mark (X) in the square marked **NO** if you do not want it to pass.

NON-BINDING ADVISORY REFERENDUM

ARTICLE 29. Shall the Selectmen of the Town of Arlington approve the sale of Four (4) parcels of land comprising a total of Three Thousand Four Hundred Fifty-Three (3,453), plus or minus, acres of land in the Town of Arlington to the United States for inclusion in the National Forest.

    YES ☐

    NO ☐

As explained in a subsequent section, ordinances enacted by the Board of Selectpersons can be challenged by means of the protest referendum, and the question of repealing an ordinance can appear on the ballot. Questions involving the issuance of bonds by the town and proposed zoning changes also can be placed on the ballot. Occasionally, a non-binding referendum question is placed on the ballot by town officers (see Figure 5.1).

A relatively recent development is the use of town meetings by national and regional interest groups as "straw polls," which attract widespread media coverage. By petitions, voters may insert a non-binding international, national, or regional question in the town meeting warning. The proposed Panama Canal treaties appeared in many warnings in 1978, and similar questions dealing with El Salvador, a nuclear arms freeze, and transportation of nuclear wastes were contained in numerous warnings in 1982 and 1983. Voters in 178 towns at their 1983 annual meetings endorsed a nuclear arms freeze proposal.[22] Acid rain was a prominent warning issue in 1984 and 1985. In 1989, voters in fifty-four towns ratified an article supporting the death penalty, which had not been used in Vermont during the preceding thirty-five years.[23]

These "straw polls" generated considerable debate in Vermont relative to whether the town meeting is the appropriate forum to entertain such questions and induced many Vermonters to write letters to the editors of various Vermont, regional, and national newspapers. In response to a letter entitled "Wrong Place for a World Issue," U.S. Senator Patrick J. Leahy of Vermont in 1982 wrote he was disappointed that the letter writer "sees the voter as someone who delegates to the elected the job of doing the nation's thinking. Town meetings have never worked that way, and neither does American democracy."[24] He added he could not think of a "more appropriate forum for sending such an important message than a gathering like a Vermont town meeting. And what topic could be more germane to any town meeting than its own survival?"[25]

The debate continued the next year. Jeffrey Good, who had lived in Vermont for four of the previous six years, maintained in 1983 that Vermonters "don't want to New Hampshireize Vermont" by placing the El Salvador issue in town meeting warnings and emphasized that "local and outside activists and network executives must recognize the fragility of this most stubbornly Yankee of traditions and resist the urge to dilute it, to create still more illusion."[26]

A different perspective on "straw polls" was in 1984 provided by Professor Frank M. Bryan of the University of Vermont, a longtime student of Vermont town meetings:

We would like to govern ourselves locally, privately, away from the video madness of national communications systems and the manipulations of special-interest groups. Town meeting is not a hot commodity. It should not be exploited, but if the present trends continue, town meetings may become nothing more than springtime forums for those who champion whatever causes are current—and a great national treasure will be lost.[27]

A bill was introduced in the 1983 Vermont state legislature that, if enacted, would make it more difficult to place issues by petitions on town meeting ballots.[28] Supporters of the bill argued that too much time is wasted at town meetings debating global and national issues, and local issues receive inadequate consideration. The bill's opponents countered that its enactment would lead to less discussion of international and national issues that affect town citizens. The bill also was opposed by Vermont secretary of state James Douglas because its enactment would make it difficult for registered voters in cities to collect voter signatures equal to the required 10 percent of the registered voters. The bill was not enacted.

Conduct of Business

Each town is free to establish a quorum for the annual meeting and the same or different quorum for a special town meeting. Eighty-eight (95%) of ninety-three responding towns indicated that there was no quorum requirement for the annual town meeting. Five (6%) of eighty-eight reporting towns have a quorum for special town meetings.

The average length of the 1996 annual meeting in 106 towns, according to

questionnaire respondents, was approximately four hours. The length varied
from thirty minutes to eight hours. This finding is consistent with the finding of
Bryan that the average length of 1,215 meetings between 1970 and 1994 was
three hours and fifty-five minutes of deliberative time.[29] Most 1996 special town
meetings lasted one hour, although two towns had special meetings lasting three
hours.

The business part of the traditional annual town meeting is conducted in a
manner similar to that of the Massachusetts and New Hampshire annual town
meetings, and a broad array of issues are brought to the town meeting for resolution. The first order of business at the annual meeting is the election of a
moderator. The Vermont statutes stipulate:

The moderator shall be the presiding officer of municipal meetings, shall decide questions
of order and shall make public declaration of votes taken, except in elections using the
Australian ballot system. When a vote declared by him is immediately questioned by
one voter, he shall divide the meeting, and if requested by seven voters, shall cause the
vote to be taken by paper ballot, unless the town has provided some other procedure in
such cases. Robert's Rules or some other rules or order shall govern all municipal meetings, except in elections using the Australian ballot system.[30]

The Vermont Supreme Court held in 1968 that it is not the duty of the moderator
of a town meeting to invite open discussion at meetings, as his duties are to
decide questions of law and to make public declaration of votes.[31]

State law mandates that each town shall appropriate funds deemed "necessary
for the interest of its inhabitants and for the prosecution and defense of the
common rights."[32] The town meeting must "express in its vote the specific
amounts, or the rate on a dollar of the grant list, to be appropriated for laying
out and repairing highways and for other necessary town expenses."[33] The Vermont League of Cities and Towns recommends that a specific amount be voted
for each purpose because the amount of funds to be raised based on the Grant
List (of property) will not be known until it is prepared approximately two
months after the annual meeting, and the amount may differ from the amount
needed to balance the budget.[34]

In 1996, the Vermont Supreme Court ruled that an annual town budget approved on a reconsideration vote may not be reconsidered a second time by the
town meeting.[35] The court opined:

There is necessarily a tension between the democratic principles supported by allowing
reconsideration and the need for finality if the district is to deliver educational services
upon which its families depend. . . . An endless cycle of votes and reconsiderations . . .
give no weight to the need for finality. . . . Inevitably, as the process drags on . . . , the
rights of innocent third parties, led by the children to be educated . . . are inextricably
involved.[36]

In its opinion, the court made a distinction between the preceding ruling and its decision in a 1967 case, when the court allowed a second reconsideration.[37] The earlier case did not involve a budget and dealt with authorization for issuance of bonds and the proposed purchase of a different site, an option to purchase, and a higher purchase price. Because of these important differences between the action taken by assembled voters on the original consideration and the first reconsideration, a second reconsideration was held to be proper.

Questionnaire recipients in 1996 were requested to indicate whether their respective town meeting had rejected a town budget or a school budget. Seven (11%) of sixty-one reporting towns reported a town budget had been rejected, and fifty-three towns (88%) indicated a school budget had been rejected. The town of Benson (837) had thirteen votes before a school budget was adopted. Castleton (4,302) had four votes on adopting a school budget in 1996, and Northfield (5,647) voters rejected the proposed school budget in 1993, 1994, 1995, and 1996.

The number of warning articles to be acted upon by assembled voters varies considerably from town to town. There may be relatively few articles other than appropriation ones in the very small towns. Growing towns, on the other hand, tend to have a relatively long warning. As noted, article 1 always provides for the election of a moderator, and a separate article provides for the election of other town officers. The warning typically contains an article asking, "What action will the Town take in regard to the printed report of the Town officials for the year ending December 31, 19—?"

Other articles may ask voters to decide (1) if a discount should be allowed on town taxes paid by a specified date, (2) the amounts to be appropriated for highways and other purposes, (3) whether the selectpersons should be empowered to borrow funds on the credit of the town, and (4) whether certain animals should be regulated and open burning should be banned.

The warning may contain articles inserted by voter petitions. Of ninety-eight questionnaire respondents, thirty (31%) reported that citizens frequently initiate articles, sixty-three (64%) indicated that such articles seldom are inserted in the warning, and five (5%) towns never have had such articles inserted in the warning.

The Vermont statutes authorize the Board of Selectpersons to enact ordinances subject to a thirty-day permissive referendum.[38] In other words, if voters file petitions containing verified signatures equal to 5 percent of the voters on the checklist within forty-four days of the enactment by the selectpersons of an ordinance, a referendum will be held on the question of repealing the ordinance. Unless challenged by petition, the issues decided by selectpersons' adopted ordinances do not come before the voters. Ninety-two town correspondents answered the question, How often does the Board of Selectpersons adopt ordinances? Two (2%) of the respondents answered often, sixty (66%) checked seldom, and thirty (32%) responded never.

The number of articles that come before the assembled voters also is reduced in towns by statutes mandating Australian ballot voting on all articles proposing issuance of bonds and in rural towns' adoption of zoning by-laws.[39] Furthermore, the number of articles to be decided in open meeting is reduced in sixty-seven towns that have adopted the Australian ballot for deciding certain warning articles in addition to electing town officers. Fifty-six (55%) of 102 reporting towns have adopted the Australian ballot for certain matters of business, and forty-six towns (45%) have not adopted such a ballot. Town correspondents wrote that the secret ballot had been adopted for such matters as proposed bond issues, zoning changes, and the high school budget in one town. One respondent stressed that his town adopted the Australian ballot only for the election of officers and "not for budget."

Role of the Budget Committee

Each town meeting may establish a town budget committee to provide advice with respect to appropriation of funds. In contrast to the other New England states where almost all towns have a budget or finance committee, only 17 (16%) of the 106 responding towns have a budget committee, although three additional towns reported that the Board of Selectpersons makes recommendations on budget items. However, the recommendations of the budget committee or any other town body may not appear in the warning or the official ballot.

The recommendations of the budget committee were followed always in three towns (17.6%), most of the time in thirteen towns (76.5%), and seldom in one town (5.9%). It is reasonable to assume that if such committees were established in other towns, the committees would be very influential in guiding the decisions made by town meeting participants.

Role of the Planning Commission

A town meeting at any time may create a town planning commission with three to nine voting members.[40] A majority of the members must be residents of the town, and the selectpersons of a rural town are nonvoting *ex officio* members of the commission. Members of a town planning commission either are appointed to a term of four years or are elected by the town meeting to terms of one to four years.[41] State statutes spell out the duties of the town planning commission, which include preparing and recommending land development proposals, various codes (plumbing, electrical, fire, and housing), and an annual capital budget and holding public meetings.[42]

A town planning commission prepares a long-range master plan for the future development of the town, drafts zoning regulations for consideration by the town meeting, and makes recommendations for zone changes. The proposed adoption of a zoning ordinance or changes in the zoning for particular parcels of land often generate considerable debate at the town meeting.

Twenty (19%) of the reporting 107 towns reported they lacked a planning

Table 5.1
Vermont Annual Town Meeting Business Attendance (Percent of Registered Voters, 1996)

Population Range	Number of Towns	Average Attendance	Attendance Range
499 and under	19	35.26	20-80
500-999	27	25.44	4-58
1,000-1,999	19	18.00	5-44
2,000-4,999	13	20.85	1-40
5,000-7,499	2	9.00	9
7,500-9,999	-	-	-
10,000-14,999	-	-	-
15,000-19,999	-	-	-
20,000-24,999	-	-	-
25,000 and over	-	-	-

commission. Of the seventy-nine town respondents who answered the question relative to whether the town meeting followed the recommendations of the planning commission, four (5%) reported the recommendations are always followed, seventy (90%) checked most of the time, three (3%) selected seldom, and three respondents (3%) reported never.

Town meeting participants appear to rely heavily on the planning commission for advice on land use issues, as 93 percent of surveyed towns reported the 1996 town meetings followed its recommendations always or most of the time. This finding is similar to the findings relative to the persuasiveness of planning boards in Massachusetts and New Hampshire, where assembled voters in the overwhelming number of open town meetings followed the advice of the town planning board.

Town Meeting Attendance

Eighty (80%) of the 99 open town meeting questionnaire respondents provided estimated data on attendance by registered voters at the business part of the annual town meeting. The other respondents either left the attendance section of the questionnaire blank or indicated that they do not keep attendance records. Excluded were the eight towns that use the Australian ballot to decide all warning articles, three towns that use this ballot for all but three to five minor articles, and Fairhaven, which uses this ballot to decide all articles except adoption of the town budget.

Table 5.1 reveals a general correlation between population size of a town and the percentage of registered voters who assembled to make decisions at the 1996 annual town meeting. Towns with a population of 499 and under had the highest average turnout of registered voters, and the two towns in the 5,000–7,499 population range had the lowest average turnout. Bryan reported that the average annual town meeting attendance in eighty-two towns in 1970–1971 was 25 percent, and the average annual attendance in seventy-nine towns in 1978 was 21 percent. No town in Bryan's sample had a population of 3,500 or over, and the average population was approximately 1,000.[43]

Data on attendance at the 1996 annual business meeting differed from data produced by a very limited 1982 survey, conducted by the author, when eight towns under 2,500 population reported an average attendance of 21.5 percent, and three towns in the 2,500 to 4,999 population range had an average attendance of 14.6 percent.[44]

The eighty reporting towns had an unweighted average of 21.7 percent of the registered voters participating in the business part of the 1996 annual town meeting and a weighted average attendance of 25.5 percent. To properly interpret these figures, one must recognize that voters enter and leave the meeting during its duration, and the number in attendance reaches its peak at or near the beginning of the meeting and often falls off sharply toward the end of the meeting. Other factors affecting attendance at the annual town meeting in any given year are weather conditions and presence or absence of controversial articles in the warning. In common with New Hampshire and Maine, Vermont is a tourist state, and an unknown number of registered voters reside in other states, particularly New York, but register their motor vehicles in Vermont for insurance purposes. Attendance figures on a percentage basis also are depressed by the number of registered voters who spend the winter and spring in southern states and the National Voter Registration Act of 1993, which does not allow an annual purging of the voter rolls to remove the names of individuals who have moved from the town.

Bryan and his students took attendance at 1,315 town meetings when it was highest between 1970 and 1996 and determined that the average participation rate for registered voters was 21.15 percent.[45] Figures 5.2 and 5.3, prepared by Bryan, reveal a secular decline in attendance of the towns in his study between 1970 and 1992 and a positive correlation between higher rates of voter participation and smaller towns.

Several respondents attributed the decline in attendance at the business part of the annual town meeting to the adoption of the Australian ballot since many articles are acted upon at the polls instead of the open meetings. One clerk reported a sharp drop-off in participation and noted that "we passed the Australian ballot because there were people with jobs who could not take the day off to attend or they would either lose money, get fired, etc." A second town clerk noted a similar decline following introduction of the Australian ballot for school budgets and wrote that only 34 of 1,920 voters attended the pre–town meeting informational meeting, and "seven of us had to be there because of our offices."

A third town clerk wrote:

Figure 5.2
Attendance at Vermont Town Meetings, 1970–1992

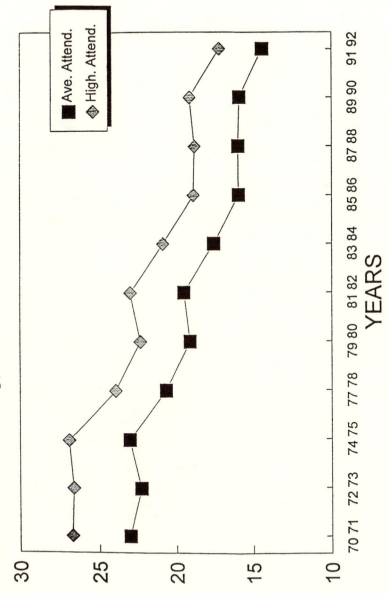

Source: Frank M. Bryan, *Real Democracy: What It Looks Like: How It Works* (work in progress).

Figure 5.3
Vermont Town Meeting Attendance by Town Size, 1970–1992

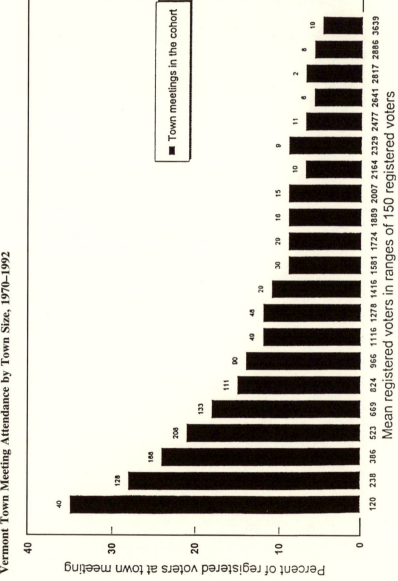

Source: Frank M. Bryan, *Real Democracy: What It Looks Like: How It Works* (work in progress).

People participate when there is an immediate result to their actions. Prior to the Australian ballot, nominations for office were made from the floor, right there in town hall. If you don't believe that brought people out for the vote . . . think again. Then the vote was taken (right then) and everyone knew the results!

I have never understood why states, like Vermont, who say they prize their town meeting format, don't make the first Tuesday in March a state holiday, so voters without penalty may attend their town meetings. Makes sense to me.

A fourth town clerk made a most interesting comment: "Newcomers like to attend town meetings while 'locals' have given up attending unless it's real controversial. They say it's futile and don't like to be laughed at or talked down to."

Town clerk Clyde A. Jenne of Hartland wrote,

I assume that because of our mobile society, people who did not grow up in the town meeting form of government and/or have moved here from the city council form of government don't know that they can truly participate in the meeting. There seems to be a lack of teaching of historical reasons for this form of government.

In the 1970s, Jane J. Mansbridge studied a Vermont town of approximately 350 population, which she termed Selby, and discovered about 25 percent of interviewed townspeople indicated they were disturbed by the "face-to-face" character of town meetings, which discouraged their attendance.[46]

Respondents indicated the percentage of town meeting voters who speak on a controversial issue ranges from 1 percent to "all of them, sometimes." The average verbal participation rate did not vary much by population grouping and ranged from 10 percent in towns with a population of 1,000–1,999 to 14 percent in towns with a population of 500–999 and 5,000–7,999. The accuracy of these estimates of the percent of participants who speak can be questioned. Bryan and his students observed 1,215 town meetings between 1970 and 1994 in 210 towns with populations under 4,500 and found that "7 percent of a town's eligible voters (37 percent of the attenders) will speak out at least once."[47]

Questionnaire recipients were requested to indicate whether a perception exists in their respective town that special interest groups mobilize their supporters to attend the town meeting. Forty-one (40%) of 103 respondents answered in the affirmative, and 62 (60%) answered in the negative. School supporters were identified as the group that most often packs the town meeting. A town clerk wrote that "our town has certain factions that want their views heard. It is like the North against the South. Unless the South has their views heard, the North rules." Another town clerk pointed out that "usually the minority group, which seems to change with each issue, accuses the other side of packing the meeting."

Vermont, in common with New Hampshire, has attracted a significant number of new residents in recent decades. Hence, it is not surprising that 89 (87%) of 102 questionnaire respondents reported that the views of long-term residents and the views of newer residents often differ on certain issues. One respondent wrote that "new residents want to change things," a second pointed out that "newcomers are less patient," a third noted that "most of the natives don't like change," and a fourth stated his belief that people who come to the town appreciate the small town and respect the long-term residents.

Quality of Debate and Decisions

Each recipient of a questionnaire was requested to rate the quality of debate at the annual town meeting—in terms of explanations of budget items, exploring pros and cons of proposals, and neighbors influencing neighbors' opinions on town issues—as one of the following: excellent, good, fair, or poor.

One hundred town officers rated the quality of debate. Eighteen (18%) rated the quality as excellent, sixty (60%) selected good, twenty (20%) checked fair, and only two (2%) considered the debate quality to be poor. Vermont town officers in general rated the quality of debate higher than the rating assigned by New Hampshire questionnaire respondents.

Comments on the quality of debate varied considerably. One officer reported that debates are "less heated today than they used to be." A second respondent wrote that "most debate is productive. Of course, the same few seem to enjoy the sound of their own voice." A third officer pointed out that "opinions on the correct answer to this question would vary widely between 'new' people and 'old' people" and added, "I think many people, most people, are decided before the meeting. Maybe I'm a cynic; I hope so." A fourth respondent wrote, "I see a lack of respect for others and superiority attitudes."

Questionnaire recipients also were requested to make a similar rating of the overall quality of town meeting decisions. Ratings were provided by 104 town officers. Eighteen (17%) considered the quality to be excellent, seventy-five (72%) selected good, and eleven (11%) selected fair; no respondent selected poor.

The respondent's ratings of the quality of debate and the quality of decisions in the same town occasionally diverged. Eight respondents who rated the quality of decisions as excellent judged the quality of debate to be good. Eleven survey recipients who evaluated the quality of decisions as good rated the quality of debate as fair. Relative to the two town respondents who rated debate quality as poor, one selected fair for decision quality, and the other checked good for decision quality. A town officer who judged debate quality to be fair assigned a rating of excellent to the decision quality.

THE SPECIAL TOWN MEETING

The Board of Selectpersons may call a special town meeting "when they deem it necessary and shall call a special meeting on the application of five percent of the voters."[48] The selectpersons may rescind a call for a special town meeting except one called in response to a petition of the registered voters.

In 1973, the Vermont Supreme Court ruled that the Board of Selectpersons was in violation of its statutory duty for its failure to call a special meeting, in response to a petition signed by more than 5 percent of the voters, to elect two additional selectpersons to comply with the annual town meeting vote to increase the number of such persons from three to five.[49] The court held in 1988 that the selectpersons did not have a duty to call a special town meeting, in response to a petition signed by more than 5 percent of the town's voters, for the purpose of rescinding an agreement entered into by the Board of Selectpersons since the agreement was legally binding if the selectpersons had the authority to enter into the agreement, and the agreement would be invalid if the selectpersons lacked the authority.[50]

Vermont towns are similar to New Hampshire towns in that special town meetings are not common. Forty-five (42%) Vermont towns and forty-four (62%) New Hampshire towns do not hold special town meetings. The majority of the remaining Vermont towns hold only one special town meeting annually. One town reported holding two special town meetings in the preceding five years, and another town held one special town meeting during the past decade. Only five towns (5%) reported that registered voters frequently call special town meetings. Twenty-three towns (22%) indicated that voters never have called a special town meeting, and the remaining seventy-eight (73%) towns occasionally held a special town meeting in response to a petition submitted by voters. Attendance at special town meetings tends to be lower than attendance at the annual meeting unless the warning for a special town meeting contains one or more controversial articles.

SUMMARY

Town meeting government continues to function in its traditional form in the bulk of the 237 towns. Only the town of Brattleboro has abandoned the open town meeting in favor of the representative town meeting, but eight towns have abandoned the assembled town meeting in favor of deciding warning articles by Australian ballot.

Changes have been occurring in the nature of the town meeting in many towns and particularly in the twenty-seven towns that have adopted town charters or the official ballot to act on all warning articles or the proposed town budget. The moderator continues as the presiding officer with broad discretion over the town meeting proceedings. *Viva voce* voting continues to be employed, but it has been replaced by the Australian ballot relative to certain items in a gradually increasing number of towns.

Voters participating in Vermont town meetings appear to place their faith in the town planning commission to provide guidance on land use issues, according to surveyed town officers. In sharp contrast to Massachusetts towns, only 16 percent of the responding Vermont towns have a budget committee. Voters in these towns rely heavily on the committee for advice relative to warrant articles.

The Vermont town meeting has been criticized as an unrepresentative institution because of the relatively low turnout of registered voters at most town meetings. Our survey data reveal an estimated unweighted average attendance of slightly more than one-fifth of the registered voters at the business part of the 1996 annual town meeting and an estimated weighted average of slightly more than one-fourth of the voters. Data collected by Bryan and his students at 1,315 town meetings when attendance was at its peak reveal that the rate of participation declined between 1970 and 1996.

A 1996 survey of town officials contradicts the critics of the Vermont town meeting. Town officials rated the quality of debate, with a few exceptions, as excellent or good and similarly rated the quality of decisions made as excellent or good.

Chapter 6 examines the operation of the open town meeting in the State of Maine, which entered the Union in 1820 after separation from the Commonwealth of Massachusetts.

NOTES

1. Andrew E. Nuquist and Edith W. Nuquist, *Vermont State Government and Administration* (Burlington: Government Research Center, University of Vermont, 1966), p. 2.

2. Ibid., pp. 3–4.

3. Francis N. Thorpe, *The Federal and State Constitutions, Colonial Charters, and Other Organic Laws* (Washington, D.C.: Government Printing Office, 1909), vol. 6, p. 3750.

4. Nuquist and Nuquist, *Vermont State Government and Administration*, p. 6. See also *Population and Local Government* (Montpelier: Vermont Secretary of State, 1990), p. 26.

5. 1 Stat. 191.

6. *Vermont v. New Hampshire*, 289 U.S. 593 (1933).

7. *Population and Local Government*, p. 25.

8. *Vermont Statutes Annotated*, tit. 17, § 2645.

9. *Vermont Act 30 of 1983*; *Vermont Statutes Annotated*, tit. 17, § 2680.

10. *Vermont Acts of 1959*, no. 302.

11. Data provided to author by Molly K. Duggan of the Vermont League of Cities and Towns in a letter dated August 20, 1997.

12. *Vermont Statutes Annotated*, tit. 17, § 2642.

13. Ibid.

14. Ibid., § 2666.

15. Ibid., § 1641.

16. Ibid., § 2654.

17. Ibid., § 2646.

18. Ibid., § 2681.

19. Ibid., § 2682.

20. Letter to author from Jana Bagwell of the Vermont League of Cities and Towns dated June 13, 1996; *1997 Municipal Census Report* (Montpelier: Vermont League of Cities and Towns, 1997), p. 5. See also *Vermont Statutes Annotated*, tit. 17, §§ 2682–88.

21. For details, consult Joseph F. Zimmerman, *The Recall: Tribunal of the People* (Westport, Conn.: Praeger Publishers, 1997).

22. "11 of 13 Vermont Towns Refuse to Join Hydropower Project," *The Keene (N.H.) Sentinel*, March 2, 1983, p. 9.

23. "54 Towns Support Death Penalty; Westminster, Rockingham Say No," *The Keene (N.H.) Sentinel*, March 8, 1989, p. 8.

24. Patrick J. Leahy, "America's Thinking Is a Citizen's Job," *New York Times*, April 10, 1982, p. 22.

25. Ibid.

26. Jeffrey Good, "Vermont Spoilers," *New York Times*, March 26, 1983, p. 23.

27. Frank M. Bryan, "Trouble in the Vermont Hills," *Newsweek*, March 5, 1984, p. 15.

28. "Vermonters Come Out against Revising State Election Laws," *The Keene (N.H.) Sentinel*, March 31, 1983, p. 15.

29. Frank M. Bryan, "Direct Democracy and Civic Competence," *The Good Society*, Fall 1995, p. 38.

30. *Vermont Statutes Annotated*, tit. 17, § 2658.

31. *Groton v. Union School District 21*, 127 Vt. 142, 241 A.2d 332 (1968).

32. *Vermont Statutes Annotated*, tit. 17, § 2664.

33. Ibid.

34. "The Warning for Town Meeting," *VLCT News*, December 1966, p. 1.

35. *Santi v. Roxbury Town School District*, 685 A.2d 301 at 304 (1996).

36. Ibid., at 304.

37. *Baird v. Town of Berlin*, 126 Vt. 348, 331 A.2d 110 (1967).

38. *Vermont Statutes Annotated*, tit. 24, §§ 1971–76.

39. Ibid., §§ 1758, 4404(d).

40. Ibid., §§ 4321–22.

41. Ibid., § 4323(a, c).

42. Ibid., § 4325.

43. Frank M. Bryan, "Town Meeting in Mass Society—What Role Remains?" paper presented at the annual meeting of the New England Political Science Association, Durham, N.H., April 6–7, 1979.

44. Joseph F. Zimmerman, "The New England Town Meeting: Pure Democracy in Action?" *The Municipal Year Book 1984* (Washington, D.C.: International City Management Association, 1984), p. 103.

45. Frank M. Bryan, *What If We Held a Democracy: Would Anyone Come?* (work in progress).

46. Jane J. Mansbridge, "Town Meeting Democracy," in Peter Collier, ed., *Dilemmas of Democracy* (New York: Harcourt Brace Jovanovich, 1976), p. 155.

47. Bryan, "Direct Democracy and Civic Competence," p. 38.

48. *Vermont Statutes Annotated*, tit. 17, § 2643(a).

49. *Welton v. Town of Brandon*, 132 Vt. 74, 313 A.2d 676 (1973).

50. *Kirchner v. Giebink*, 150 Vt. 172, 552 A.2d 372 (1988).

Chapter 6

The Maine
Open Town Meeting

King Henry IV of France in 1603 granted the first charter—the Charter of Acadia—for the settlement of Maine to Pierre du Gast, but no permanent settlements were established.[1] In 1622, King James I of Great Britain issued a charter for the province of Maine to Sir Ferdinando Gorges and John Mason.[2] The early settlers of Maine apparently established communities without legal authorization and governed themselves informally until 1639, when King Charles I selected Sir Ferdinado Gorges as overseer of the "Province or Countie of Maine," which included the land between the Kennebec and Piscataqua Rivers.[3] In 1651, the province of Maine was annexed by the Massachusetts Bay Colony and renamed the county of Yorkshire and became subject to the statutes enacted by the General Court of the colony. In consequence, towns in what today is Maine were operated subsequent to 1652 in the same manner as towns in the Massachusetts Bay Colony until 1820, when Maine entered the Union as a state.

Slavery was a dominant issue at the Constitutional Convention of 1787 in Philadelphia, and the ratified U.S. Constitution contained an important compromise between the northern free states and the southern slave states. The compromise provided that slaves could continue to be imported into the United States until the year 1808, but Congress was authorized to impose a tax of up to ten dollars on each imported slave.[4]

Whether western territories should be admitted to the Union as free states or slave states was a major issue during the early part of the nineteenth century. Since the U.S. Constitution provides for equal representation of each state in the Senate, neither the northern states nor the southern states wanted a territory admitted to the Union if the balance of power between the two regions in the Senate would be upset.[5] In 1820, Congress accepted the famous Missouri Compromise, providing that Missouri would be admitted to the Union as a slave state, and Maine would be detached from the commonwealth of Massachusetts and admitted to the Union as a free state.[6] There were 240 towns and no cities in Maine when it entered the Union, and the newly adopted state constitution recognized the legal status of towns incorporated by the Massachusetts General Court (legislature).[7]

Maine currently has 497 general purpose local governments—420 towns, 55 plantations, and 22 cities. Plantations are unique to Maine, although New Hampshire has several locations that are similar to a plantation and originally were designed as a temporary governmental form until the state legislature incorporated the plantation as a town. Plantations are governed by meetings of assembled voters, conducted in the same manner as town meetings, and elected officers. Plantations were organized by county commissioners and currently lack the home rule powers of cities and towns granted by the state constitution and statutes.

The state constitution stipulates:

The inhabitants of any municipality shall have the power to alter and amend their charters on all matters, not prohibited by the Constitution or general law, which are local and municipal in character. The Legislature shall prescribe the procedure by which the municipality shall so act.[8]

Only one Maine town—Sanford—has replaced the open town meeting with a representative town meeting (see Chapter 9), but thirteen towns have adopted charters creating a council with legislative powers, the position of town manager, and a financial town meeting.[9] An additional eighteen towns have adopted charters providing for a Board of Selectmen or a town council without legislative powers and an unlimited town meeting.[10] Six towns, including Mars Hill, with a population of 1,760, replaced the open town meeting completely with a town council because of poor attendance at town meetings. Ten towns, including Jay, have adopted the Australian (official) ballot to act on the proposed town budget via a referendum vote at the polls in place of a vote at an open town meeting. Gorham has a charter authorizing voters by petition to employ the referendum to reverse town council decisions and the initiative to enact ordinances and resolutions.

To collect data, a questionnaire was mailed to each town with an open town meeting. Completed questionnaires were returned by 154 (37%) towns, but not every respondent answered every question.

THE ANNUAL TOWN MEETING

Voters in Maine towns operating on a calendar fiscal year assemble in late March or early April to elect town officers and make decisions regarding the operations of the town. The annual town meeting is held in May or June if the town operates on a July 1 fiscal year. The type of business brought to the town meeting has changed since the early town meetings, where voters would authorize the building of a school and hiring a teacher and a minister and adopt by-laws providing for the regulation of animals. Roads and bridges initially were minor concerns but became major ones in Maine in the latter part of the eighteenth century.

Today's town meetings differ in many respects from meetings held early in the twentieth century. Walter Trundy, town clerk of Stockton Springs for sixty-nine years, described his first town meeting in 1908 in the following terms:

The meeting was held in what we called the old Meeting House. Everyone stood because there were no seats; wooden boxes filled with sawdust were scattered among the towns people for the tobacco chewers; the men wore buffalo coats, the cheapest available at the time; the meeting house was filled with smoke from men's pipes; and there were no women. Buffalo coats, tobacco spit, smoke . . . it was a pretty tough meeting.[11]

As one would anticipate, Maine town meeting procedures are similar to those in Massachusetts. Each annual town meeting is held in response to the warrant or warning, issued by the Board of Selectmen, notifying voters that town officers will be elected and decisions made relative to the other warrant articles. The warrant must specify the place and time of the meeting, contain distinct articles on business to be acted upon by the voters, and direct the town constable to post an attested copy "in some conspicuous public place in the town" a minimum of seven days in advance of the meeting unless the town has adopted a different notification system.[12]

The Maine Supreme Court has issued several opinions pertaining to the calling of a town meeting by warrant. In 1877, the court declared as unreasonable and void a town by-law mandating three months' notice for a town meeting.[13] Whether a separate article was required in a special town meeting warrant to pay each of several notes and orders to pay was decided in the negative by the court in 1887, when it ruled that one article was sufficient if it distinctly named all the notes and orders.[14] In 1923, the court held that an annual meeting warrant was not defective simply because it failed to note that the meeting hall was located in the town as the inhabitants were not misled by the warrant.[15] The court in 1985 opined that technical precision is not required in an annual town meeting warrant, whose sole function is to provide voters with a reasonably certain notice of the content of warrant articles.[16]

If there are no selectpersons in a town, a notary public may call a town meeting on the written application of three voters.[17] Similarly, if the selectpersons unreasonably refuse to call a town meeting, a notary public may call a meeting on the written petition of voters equal to 10 percent of the number of votes cast in the town in the preceding gubernatorial election, provided that there are at least ten signatures.[18]

Maine statutes authorize the filing of a written petition by voters equal to at least 10 percent of the total votes cast in the town at the gubernatorial election, but no less than ten voters, calling for the insertion of a particular article in the warrant for the next town meeting by the Board of Selectmen, which alternatively must call a special town meeting within sixty days for consideration of the article.[19] The Maine Supreme Court in 1991, however, upheld as a discretionary act the refusal of the Board of Selectmen of York to grant a petition for a special town meeting to consider an article that would rescind the previous town meeting approval of the construction of an elementary school.[20] The court decided that the decision to call a special town meeting to reconsider a previous town meeting vote was a discretionary act of the selectpersons that precluded mandamus relief.

The Annual Report and Pre–Town Meeting Meeting

In common with Massachusetts and New Hampshire towns, each Maine town is required by state law to publish an annual report, which typically lists all town officers, including members of boards and committees, financial reports, audits conducted by certified public accountants, reports of various officers such as the town clerk and the police chief, and in some towns a listing of property owners who have unpaid property taxes outstanding.[21]

Eighty (52%) of the 154 responding towns reported that a pre–town meeting meeting was held annually, which focused primarily on budget articles. As in Massachusetts and New Hampshire towns, attendance typically is very low at these meetings and ranges from a reported zero attendance to 58 percent of the registered voters. The average reported attendance was 8 percent. One town clerk reported the town is lucky if five voters attend. A town clerk described such a meeting as ''not required but necessary.''

Election of Town Officers

The warrant for the annual town meeting must warn voters of the election of named officers; the day, place, and time of the election; and propositions to be voted on by ballot. State law requires the annual election by ballot of a town meeting moderator, selectpersons, and members of the school committee but also authorizes a town meeting held ninety days in advance of the annual meeting to designate other town officers to be elected by ballot.[22] State law also stipulates that ''a town official may not be elected on a motion to cast one ballot.''[23]

Election is by plurality vote in towns with a population exceeding 4,000, whereas a majority vote is required in the smaller towns.[24] Each town is authorized to determine at a town meeting held at least ninety days prior to the annual town meeting whether three, five, or seven members will be elected to the Board of Selectmen and the Board of Overseers and their term of office.[25] If a town meeting does not establish the number of members of each board, state law stipulates that three members will be elected for a one-year term.[26] Additional state law provisions relate to the election or appointment of other town officers, boards, and commissions.

Historically, all nominations were made in open meeting, and attendees cast votes for the various nominees. The Maine state legislature in 1987 enacted a statute, which becomes effective only if accepted by a town meeting, providing for voting by the Australian (secret) ballot at town meetings and authorizing an alternative nomination procedure. A prospective candidate may file nomination papers for a specified office signed by (1) 3 to 10 voters in towns with a population of 200 or less, (2) 10 to 25 voters in towns with a population of 201 to 500, and (3) 25 to 100 voters in larger towns.[27]

Write-in voting is authorized at the annual town meeting, but a sticker bearing the name of a candidate may not be attached to a ballot in lieu of writing the name of a candidate.[28] Candidates also can be nominated by political caucuses.[29] Voting machines and absentee voting are allowed in towns that have accepted the authorizing statute.[30] The 1993 Maine state legislature authorized towns to establish the recall—a special election to remove a named town officer from office prior to expiration of his or her term—by enactment of an ordinance.[31] Previously, a town legally could provide for the recall only by adopting or amending a town charter.

Questionnaire recipients were requested to indicate whether all town offices were contested and whether there was a candidate for each office. Of 138 responding towns, only 16 (12%) indicated all offices were contested. Of the responding 131 towns, 90 (69%) reported there was at least one candidate for each office. In other words, there was no candidate for one or more offices in more than three-tenths of the towns.

Conduct of Business

Maine statutes require the town clerk to open the annual town meeting by calling for the election of the moderator by written, but not necessarily secret, ballots.[32] The moderator is elected only for the meeting, presides, supervises all voting, and may appoint a deputy moderator. The moderator may vote on all warrant articles.[33]

State law stipulates that all persons shall be silent at the moderator's command, and no one may speak prior to recognition by the moderator. A person who is not a town voter may speak at the meeting only with the consent of two-thirds of the voters in attendance.[34] The moderator is empowered to command order if a person is acting in a disorderly manner and may direct the constable to remove the person if he or she continues to act in a disorderly manner.

The declared vote of the moderator of any warrant article can be questioned immediately by a minimum of seven voters, and the moderator must poll the voters again or utilize a method approved by the meeting for resolving the uncertainty of the declared vote.[35] The town clerk is responsible for preparing ballots of uniform size and color that are blank except for two squares with "Yes" printed in one square and "No" printed in the other square.

Each town is free to determine whether there will be a quorum requirement at the annual town meeting and/or a special town meeting. Only 17 (13%) of 133 reporting towns have a quorum requirement for the annual town meeting. The requirement is generally low and is expressed as an absolute number, a majority of the registered voters, or, in one small town, 10 percent of the vote for governor in the preceding election. Another small town set one voter as the quorum requirement, and two other small towns set a majority of the registered voters as the requirement. Nineteen towns (14%) have a low quorum requirement for a special town meeting, including three towns that do not have a quorum requirement for the annual town meeting.

The length of the 1996 annual town meeting ranged from one to ten and one-half hours, with an average length of three hours. The town with the longest meeting held it over the course of two days. The length of special town meetings varied from ten minutes to five hours. Each of thirty-seven special town meetings was concluded within thirty minutes, and the average length was one hour. In 1836, the Maine Supreme Court ruled that a properly called town meeting possesses the incidental power to adjourn to a specific day and time.[36] A town clerk reported that the 1996 annual meeting was adjourned until "more retirees come back from Florida."

Warrant articles cover a wide variety of subjects. Many articles are routine ones and authorize payment of recurring expenditures. Other articles may be highly controversial if they involve large expenditures, and if the town has a well-organized taxpayers' association or a land use change authorizing a major new development. Environmental issues in particular can be debated hotly.

In most instances, decisions are made by a *viva voce* vote declared by the moderator. However, a town meeting may vote to accept a state statute authorizing the use of a secret (official) ballot to decide a warrant article inserted by petition of voters equal to 10 percent of the number of votes cast in the town at the previous gubernatorial election, but not less than ten voters.[37] If so petitioned, the Board of Selectmen must have the article placed on the next printed ballot or call a special town meeting to consider the article. A public hearing must be held on the article a minimum of ten days before the secret ballot or special town meeting vote on the article. The Maine Supreme Court in 1995 ruled that the statutory "next ballot printed" means the town ballot.[38]

Town voters may act on five specified subjects only by referendum using secret ballots regardless of whether the town has adopted the secret ballot acceptance statute. These subjects involve issuance of revenue bonds for revenue-producing facilities, sale of alcoholic beverages, municipal charters, school administrative districts, and school construction projects.[39] Furthermore, the Board of Selectmen may place referendum questions on the ballot that must be decided by secret ballot regardless of whether the town has adopted the official ballot statute.[40]

It is important to note that the Board of Selectmen is authorized by state law to enact ordinances relating to cable television and specified regulatory matters, including operation of motor vehicles and pedestrian traffic, general assistance, and use of surface waters.[41]

Role of the Budget Committee

A town meeting may vote to establish a budget committee to advise the meeting on the appropriation of funds at the annual town meeting and special town meetings. The recommendations of the budget committee relative to proposed town expenditures are required by state statute to be printed along with the recommendations of other town officers on the various warrant articles.[42] If a warrant article to appropriate funds is to be decided by secret referendum ballot, state law stipulates that the recommendations of the budget committee are to be printed instead of the recommendations of other town officers.[43]

The statutes are silent with respect to the establishment of such a committee, the number of members, and their duties. Each town meeting may use its home rule authority—by town charter provision, town ordinance, or town meeting vote—to establish the committee and define its duties and responsibilities. Eighteen budget committees and three finance committees have been established by charter provision.[44]

Eight (6%) town respondents of 137 reporting towns wrote that their respective town lacked a budget committee, but four of these respondents reported that the selectpersons made recommendations on warrant articles. Ninety towns (66%) reported that the committee or selectpersons made recommendations on all warrant articles, and forty-three (31%) towns indicated that the recommendations were limited to only appropriation articles.

Of the 130 town officers who answered the question, the committee's recommendations were followed always in 22 (17%) towns, most of the time in 104 (80%) towns, and seldom in only 4 (3%) towns. No respondent indicated that the town meeting never followed the committee's recommendations. A town clerk wrote that voter confidence in the budget committee had resulted in fewer questions being raised at town meetings.

The preceding findings that town meeting participants follow always or most of the time the recommendations of the budget committee comport with the findings of the acceptance of the budget or finance committee's recommendations by town meetings in the other New England states.

Role of the Planning Board

Each town is authorized by state law to establish a planning board responsible for preparation of a master plan, a zoning ordinance, and other recommendations to be presented to the town meeting.

Survey data reveal there is no planning board in 11 (8%) of 136 reporting

Table 6.1
Maine Annual Town Meeting Business Attendance (Percent of Registered Voters, 1996)

Population Range	Number of Towns	Average Attendance	Attendance Range
499 and under	38	36.20	10 to 90
500-999	35	20.30	5 to 30
1,000-1,999	34	12.52	2 to 82
2,000-4,999	12	6.60	1 to 25
5,000-7,499	-	-	-
7,500-9,999	1	9.30	9.3
10,000-14,999	-	-	-
15,000-19,999	1	13.00	13
20,000-24,999	-	-	-
25,000 and over	-	-	-

towns, and the selectpersons in one of the 11 towns act as the planning board. According to responses from officers in 126 towns, the recommendations of the planning board are followed always in 14 (11%) towns, most of the time in 105 (83%) towns, and seldom in 7 (6%) towns. These findings are not surprising, as town meeting voters placed great faith, with a few exceptions, in the planning board. As in the other New England states except Rhode Island, a very divisive land use issue occasionally is brought to the town meeting for resolution, tempers may flare, and the meeting may reject the recommendation of the planning board.

Town Meeting Attendance

One hundred and twenty-one towns reported attendance data at the business part of the 1996 annual town meeting. A number of respondents left the attendance section of the questionnaire blank, and others reported they did not keep track of attendance. One respondent wrote ''good question—must set up a system to track same.''

Table 6.1 reveals that there generally is a positive correlation between the size of a Maine town and the percentage of registered voters who attend the annual meeting, with the highest attendance in towns with a population under 500. Somewhat surprisingly, the two towns with a population exceeding 7,500 had an average attendance (11.1%) exceeding the average attendance (6.6%) of twelve towns in the 2,000 to 4,999 population range.

The 1996 business meeting attendance data differ from data produced by a limited 1982 survey, when one town in the 10,000–14,999 population range reported an average attendance of 20 percent, five towns in the 5,000–9,999 population range had an average attendance of 5.6 percent of the registered voters, twenty towns in the 1,500–4,999 population range had an average attendance of 16.4 percent, and 22 towns under 2,500 population had an average attendance of 24.6 percent.[45]

The 121 reporting towns had an unweighted average attendance of 16.32 percent of the registered voters participating in the business part of their 1996 annual town meetings and a weighted average attendance of 28.17 percent. Town meeting attendance is affected by two major factors in Maine. The first factor is the weather, which can be inclement in late March or early April, when town meetings are held. The second factor is the presence or absence of one or more controversial articles in the annual meeting warrant. If the articles are routine, attendance will be relatively low compared to a meeting that makes decisions on one or more controversial articles.

Several town respondents provided comparative data that in general revealed there has been a secular decline in the percentage of registered voters who attend town meetings. One town clerk attributed the drop in attendance, from 35 percent of the registered voters in 1966 to 10 percent in 1996, to the moving of the annual meeting "from March to June." A second town clerk noticed that there was a direct correlation between the population growth of the town and the decline in the percentage of registered voters who participate in the town meetings.

There were exceptions to the general decline in attendance because of the presence of unresolved issues in the warrant for the 1996 town meeting compared to the warrants issued ten to thirty years earlier. A town with a population under 500 had a turnout of 25 percent of the registered voters at the annual town meeting in 1976 and a turnout of 33 percent at the 1996 annual meeting. A second town in this population class witnessed an increase from 50 percent in 1976 to 70 percent in 1996 of the registered voters who attended the annual town meeting.

Maine, in common with New Hampshire and Vermont, is a major tourist state, and an unknown number of visitors purchase property and register as voters, although they spend a substantial portion of the year in other states, including the period of the town meetings. As noted, one clerk wrote that the annual town meeting in his town was adjourned in 1996 until more retired persons returned from Florida. Furthermore, the National Voter Registration Act of 1993 does not permit an annual purging of voters who have moved from the town from the voting rolls for failure to vote.[46] A town clerk wrote that "our voting list is in dire need of purging." Although the preceding factors overstate the number of registered voters in Maine towns, one cannot deny the fact that the turnout of voters at the average annual town meeting in Maine is relatively low.

According to 154 survey respondents, the percentage of town meeting participants who speak on a controversial issue at the annual meeting varies from 1 percent in twelve towns to 100 percent in a town with a population under 200. On average, 15.83 percent of the town meeting attendees spoke on a controversial warrant article. The town clerk of a small town reported that it is "usually the same two" who speak on controversial issues.

Recipients of questionnaires were requested to indicate whether a perception existed in their respective towns that special interest groups pack the annual open town meeting. Fifty-nine (42%) of the 139 responding towns answered yes to the question on packing of the town meeting, and eighty (58%) towns responded no. A town in the 2,000–4,999 population range reported that packing occurred only at special town meetings. Several respondents indicated that schoolteachers and parents of pupils, fire department members, large farmers, and town employees were regular in their attendance at annual town meetings, particularly when one or more articles would affect their respective interests. The clerk in one small town reported that shorefront property owners made it a point to attend the annual meeting to defend their interests against inland residents. A respondent in another town wrote "the belief [that packing] may be held by those who don't attend, but I have found it generally to not be so."

Questionnaire recipients also were requested to indicate whether long-term residents held different views on issues than newer residents. Of 142 reporting towns, 133 (94%) responded in the affirmative, and only 9 (6%) responded in the negative. A town clerk wrote that "some of the older residents feel that 'what was good for me is good enough for my grand kids.' "

Quality of Debate and Decisions

Survey questionnaire recipients were requested to rate the quality of debate at the 1996 annual town meeting—in terms of explanations of budget items, exploring pros and cons of proposals, and neighbors influencing neighbors' opinions on town issues—as one of the following: excellent, good, fair, or poor.

One hundred and forty-three town officers rated the quality of the debate. Nineteen (13%) rated the debate as excellent, ninety-one (64%) selected good, twenty-three (16%) checked fair, and ten (7%) considered the debate quality to be poor. Written comments on the quality of debate were diverse and included "improved, now debate, used to be just arguments"; "not as lively as in the past"; "more people are getting involved"; "quality has changed"; "they debate over smaller issues now"; "more informed debate"; "not quite as rowdy or lengthy as in the past at times"; "more people contribute and seem to be better informed"; and "lack of knowledge on warrant articles is reflected in debates."

A town clerk who rated debate as excellent noted there never was any debate years ago and added that "residents have become more aware of the changing times and status of government and they want to know where all monies go." A second town clerk explained: "If you have facts, they will listen. If not, forget trying to explain." He added that the quality of debate has changed because "more people are involved which is a learning process for all." A third clerk noted that "people seem to do their 'homework' more now." A fourth town respondent, who rated debate as fair, stressed there were "not enough comments from voters and some items go through which are not really agreed upon." A fifth respondent described debate as good and emphasized that today "everything seems to be debated."

Questionnaire recipients also were requested to make a similar rating of the overall quality of town meeting decisions. One hundred and forty-one town officers responded. Thirty-six (26%) judged the quality to be excellent, ninety-two (65%) selected good as the descriptor, ten (7%) rated the quality as fair, and three (2%) believed the quality to be poor. A town clerk who described the quality of decisions as fair wrote that the voters "generally rely too much on the Board of Selectmen." A second town clerk, who judged the quality of decisions to be only fair, emphasized that the voters "have a tendency to pass every article and then complain their taxes are too high. Taxes can't be cut if they're not willing to cut the budget." Rating the quality of decisions as good, a third respondent added, "it is amazing that out of all the controversy, confusion, and commentary pro & con that most if not all decisions are satisfactory to every one until the next time."

The ratings of debate quality and decisions quality in the same town were not always identical. Twenty-one of the respondents who judged the quality of decisions to be good rated the quality of debate as fair. Similarly, sixteen respondents who rated the quality of debate as fair rated the quality of decisions as good, and two town officers who judged debate to be of poor quality reported the quality of decisions as good.

THE SPECIAL TOWN MEETING

The Board of Selectmen may call a special town meeting as needed, and the warrant must "state in distinct articles the business to be acted on at the meeting. No other business may be acted upon."[47] In addition, the Board of Selectmen must place an article, petitioned for by voters equal to 10 percent of the votes cast in the town in the previous gubernatorial election, as a referendum item on the next scheduled town ballot or call a special town meeting to consider the article.[48] The Maine Supreme Court in 1887 opined that it is permissible for a warrant calling a special town meeting to include only one article proposing that the town pay several notes and orders, provided the article distinctly names all the notes and orders in lieu of a separate article for each note and each order.[49]

In common with New Hampshire, relatively few special town meetings are held in Maine. Thirteen (9%) of 141 reporting towns held no special town meeting in 1996. No town reported that voter-called special town meetings are held frequently. Sixty (44%) of 137 responding towns reported that voters occasionally call a special town meeting, seventy-six (55%) towns indicated that voters never call a special town meeting, and one (1%) town responded that voters seldom call a special town meeting.

Of the towns that hold special town meetings, fifty-eight (42%) reported that no routine matters are considered by the voters at such meetings. Three (2%) towns, however, have held special town meetings devoted exclusively to routine articles, two (1%) towns reported that 99 percent of the meetings are devoted to routine articles, and three (2%) towns devoted 95 percent of the meetings to such articles. In other towns a low percentage of the articles at a special town meeting were routine ones.

SUMMARY

The traditional open town meeting remains firmly entrenched in the state of Maine. One town among 475 towns and plantations has abandoned the open town meeting in favor of a representative town meeting, and thirteen towns hold an open town meeting limited to the appropriation of funds. Only a handful of towns have replaced the open town meeting completely with a town council exercising all legislative powers.

As in the other New England states, the conduct of the annual or special town meeting in Maine towns is under the control of the moderator, who possesses broad discretion in channeling debates and recognizing speakers. *Viva voce* voting continues to be the most common method of voting on warrant articles, but towns are free to accept a state statute authorizing the use of the secret ballot at town meetings.

Voters attending Maine town meetings place great confidence in two citizen bodies—the budget committee and the planning board—and accept their recommendations relative to the vast majority of the warrant articles. Only 3 percent of the reporting towns indicated the budget committee recommendations seldom were followed, and only 6 percent reported that the planning board's recommendations seldom were followed.

Critics of direct democracy find evidence to support their position in town meeting attendance statistics in Maine towns, where the unweighted average attendance at the 1996 annual town meeting was only 16.32 percent. Survey respondents, however, were convinced the open town meeting is not an unrepresentative legislative assembly. Ninety-one percent of 141 town officers judged the quality of town meeting decisions to be excellent or good, and only 2 percent believed the quality of the decisions to be poor.

Chapter 7 examines the operation of the open town meeting in a southern New England state—Connecticut—where authority has been delegated to the selectpersons in a number of towns to act on an increasing number of subjects in place of the open town meeting.

NOTES

1. Francis N. Thorpe, *The Federal and State Constitutions, Colonial Charters, and Other Organic Laws* (Washington, D.C.: Government Printing Office, 1909), vol. 3, pp. 1619–20.

2. Ibid., pp. 1621–25.

3. Ibid., pp. 1625–37.

4. *Constitution of the United States*, art. I, § 9.

5. Ibid., art. I, § 3.

6. 3 Stat. 544.

7. *Constitution of Maine*, art X, § 1 (1820).

8. *Constitution of Maine*, art. VIII, Part Second, § 1. The constitutional provision is implemented by *Maine Revised Statutes Annotted*, tit. 30-A, §§ 2101–9.

9. Geoffrey Herman, ''Municipal Charters: A Comparative Analysis of 75 Maine Charters,'' *Maine Townsman*, August 1992, p. 6.

10. Ibid.

11. Quoted in Kenneth L. Roberts, *Local Government in Maine* (Augusta: Maine Municipal Association, 1979), pp. 7–8.

12. *Maine Revised Statutes Annotated*, tit. 30-A, § 2523.

13. *Jones v. Inhabitants of Sanford*, 66 Me. 585 (1877).

14. *Brown v. Town of Winterport*, 79 Me. 305, 9 A. 844 (1887).

15. *Allen v. Hackett*, 123 Me. 106, 121 A. 906 (1923).

16. *State v. Town of Franklin*, 489 A.2d 525 (1985).

17. *Maine Revised Statutes Annotated*, tit. 30-A, § 2521 (3).

18. Ibid., § 2521 (4).

19. Ibid., § 2522.

20. *Dunston v. Town of York*, 590 A2d 526 (1991).

21. *Maine Revised Statutes Annotated*, tit. 30-A, § 2801.

22. Ibid., §§ 2525 (1)(A–C), and 2525 (2).

23. Ibid., § 2525 (3).

24. Ibid., § 2526 (1).

25. Ibid., § 2526 (4)(A).

26. Ibid., § 2526 (4)(A)(2).

27. Ibid., § 2528.

28. Ibid., § 2528 (4)(C).

29. Ibid., § 2528 (4)(B).

30. Ibid., §§ 2528–29.

31. Ibid., § 2602 (6)(A). See also Joseph F. Zimmerman, *The Recall: Tribunal of the People* (Westport, Conn.: Praeger Publishers, 1997).

32. *Maine Revised Statutes Annotated*, tit. 30-A, § 2524 (2)(A).

33. Ibid., § 2524 (1).

34. Ibid., § 2524 (3)(A).

35. Ibid., § 2524 (3)(B).

36. *Chamberlain v. Inhabitants of Dover*, 13 Me. 466, 29 Am. Dec. 517 (1836).

37. *Maine Revised Statutes Annotated*, tit. 30-A, § 2528 (1)(E)(5).

38. *Sweetall v. Town of Blue Hill*, 661 A.2d 159 (1995).

39. *Maine Revised Statutes Annotated*, tit. 30-A, §§ 161, 232, 1342 (2)(A), 5404 (1)(A), and 15904.

40. Ibid., § 2528 (5).

41. Ibid., §§ 2642, 3008–9, and 4305 (1).

42. Ibid., § 2528 (5)(B)(1).

43. Ibid., § 2061 (4).

44. Herman, ''Municipal Charters,'' p. 10.

45. Joseph F. Zimmerman, ''The New England Town Meeting: Pure Democracy in Action?'' *The Municipal Year Book 1984* (Washington, D.C.: International City Management Association, 1984), p. 103.

46. *National Voter Registration Act of 1993*, 107 Stat. 77, 42 U.S.C. §§ 1973gg to 1974e.

47. *Maine Revised Statutes Annotated*, tit. 30-A, § 2523.

48. Ibid., § 2528.

49. *Brown v. Town of Winterport*, 79 Me. 305, 9 A. 844 (1887).

The Connecticut
Open Town Meeting

The original patent of Connecticut was a March 19, 1631, grant by Robert, earl of Warwick and president of the Council of Plymouth, to William Viscount Say and Seal et al. to "all that part of New England . . . which lies and extends itself from a river there, called Harranganset river."[1] Connecticut first was settled in 1634 by immigrants from the Massachusetts Bay Colony who founded Wethersfield. Hartford and Windsor were founded the following year. Bruce C. Daniels maintained that the settlers of Connecticut were "Puritan zealots who hoped to continue the Massachusetts experiment in another geographic area."[2] Benjamin Trumbull reported that a principal reason for the migration of persons from the Massachusetts Bay Colony "was that they should be more out of the way and trouble of a general governor of New England, who, at this time, was an object of great fear in all the plantations."[3]

The three Connecticut river towns—Hartford, Windsor, and Wethersfield—each lacked a charter but united themselves in a General Court and surrendered most of their powers to it. Although the towns possessed relatively broad powers within the limits set by the General Court, the structure of the towns was uniform as the court decreed that towns had to create specified town offices and detailed their duties.[4] The town meeting was brought to Connecticut from the Massachusetts Bay Colony and functioned in a manner similar to that in the colony, where initially there was no separation of civil and ecclesiastical matters.

Major changes have occurred in town meeting government in Connecticut, where towns range in population from 630 in Union to 52,960 in Fairfield. The election of town officers no longer is part of the annual town meeting, as in the New England states north of Connecticut, since town elections are governed by state election laws. However, voters in five towns—Bristol, Milford, New Haven, Stratford, and Westport—are authorized by special acts of the Connecticut

General Assembly to employ the recall, a process involving the circulation of petitions calling for a special election to determine whether a named town officer(s) should be removed from office prior to the expiration of his or her term.[5] A number of other towns had home rule charter provisions authorizing the recall, but the Connecticut Supreme Court in 1985 invalidated three of these recall charter provisions on the ground they were unauthorized by the general statutes.[6]

The competence of the town meeting has been reduced by the adoption of home rule charters by voters in 108 (64%) of 169 towns. The 1957 General Assembly enacted a statute authorizing boroughs, cities, and towns to draft, adopt, and amend municipal charters, and the statute was supplemented by a voter-ratified constitutional home rule amendment effective July 1, 1969.[7] Municipalities also are authorized to revise a home rule ordinance enacted prior to October 1, 1982, provided it is not inconsistent with the state constitution and general statutes, and also to repeal such an ordinance by adoption of a charter.[8]

A town clerk reported in 1996 that his town has a charter providing for a town meeting, Board of Selectmen, and board of finance and added that "under our charter no one body has absolute authority. The town meeting may only consider and act upon the issues listed in the call of the meeting. Only a board of selectmen may issue a call of the meeting. Consequently, the board controls the topics of the meeting."

One hundred and six (63%) towns have the traditional selectpersons-town meeting-board of finance format, although the assembled voters in eight towns act only on the budget.[9] The open town meeting is authorized to act only on the proposed town budget at the annual meeting and proposed appropriations at special meetings in Bloomfield, Coventry, Killington, Monroe, and Watertown. The open town meeting in Farmington, Mansfield, and Windsor may vote only on proposed appropriations and articles proposing the repeal of town ordinances enacted by the Board of Selectmen. In fact, these towns never have utilized the latter power.

In fifty towns, the budget is approved by the town meeting in the form of a referendum using the Australian (secret) ballot. Glastonbury's charter has invested full legislative powers in the town council, and the annual town meeting is held solely for the purpose of providing advice to the council on the proposed budget. As explained in Chapter 4, the charter of Durham, New Hampshire, retains the town meeting for advisory purposes only. Seven Connecticut towns—Branford, Darien, Fairfield, Greenwich, Groton, Waterford, and Westport—have adopted the representative town meeting (RTM), which is examined in detail in Chapter 9. The state also has twenty-three cities ranging in population from 11,600 in Plymouth to 138,730 in Bridgeport.

To collect data, a questionnaire was mailed to each town with an open town meeting. Completed questionnaires were returned by 65 (61%) of 106 towns with a town meeting, but not every respondent answered each question. Interviews also were conducted with a small number of town officers, and newspaper accounts of town meetings were examined.

THE ANNUAL TOWN MEETING

Each town with an open town meeting is required by state law to hold an annual town meeting, which must act on the proposed town budget and may be adjourned from time to time unless the town has adopted the uniform fiscal year authorized by chapter 110 of the General Statutes.[10] Towns that have adopted the uniform fiscal year must fix at their respective annual town meeting the date for a special town meeting to act on the proposed town budget.[11] A 1973 statute, Public Act 73–412, deleted the requirement that the annual meeting be held on the first Monday in October.

The Board of Selectmen calls a town meeting by issuing a warning, which must be posted near the office of the town clerk and at other specified locations and published in a newspaper with a general circulation in the town at least five days prior to the holding of the meeting.[12] The five-day requirement includes the day of issuance and Sunday or a legal holiday but does not include the day of the meeting. Voters can determine the place of a town meeting and may meet outside the town should it lack an adequate facility, provided the meeting is held in "the nearest practical locations to the town."[13]

The annual town meeting is also the annual school district meeting and may act only on articles included in the warning issued by the Board of Selectmen.[14] There is no authorization for voters by petition to add items to those included in the selectpersons' call of the meeting. The Connecticut Supreme Court has ruled that action on an article "to do other business" is illegal since the article does not specify the subject matter.[15] Similarly, a vote taken on an article "to determine what is to be done" relative to a vote taken at a previous town meeting is invalid, according to the Connecticut Superior Court.[16] A warning for voters to assemble "for the purpose of obtaining information on a given subject" in the Supreme Court's judgment did not authorize the town meeting to employ a counsel and initiate court proceedings relative to the subject.[17] The Supreme Court, however, ruled in 1981 that the warning does not have to describe the proposed action in detail or with exactitude.[18]

Two hundred or 10 percent of a town's registered voters, whichever is less, may file a petition with the town clerk at least twenty-four hours in advance of a town meeting and request that any item(s) in the call of the meeting be submitted to the voters for their decision by paper ballots or voting machines not less than seven or more than fourteen days subsequent to the date of the meeting.[19] The Board of Selectmen is empowered to submit at its discretion any item that could come before a meeting to a referendum vote.

All registered voters may participate in a town meeting in Connecticut. In addition, any person liable for taxes assessed against him or her on an assessment of at least $1,000 by state law may vote at a town meeting unless the right to vote is restricted by a special act relating to the town enacted by the General Assembly.[20] Although this statutory provision has not been challenged in court, a similar Georgia law allowing nonresident real property owners of Savannah

Beach to vote was upheld in 1962 by the U.S. Supreme Court, which rejected the claim of city residents that the law resulted in the dilution of their votes and upheld the decision of the U.S. District Court, which opined that it was rational to "permit those persons owning property within the municipality, many of whom were summer residents therein, to have a voice in the management of its affairs."[21]

The Annual Report and Pre–Town Meeting Meeting

The Board of Selectmen in a town lacking a board of finance must publish an annual town report containing the reports of town officers and boards, a statement of receipts and expenditures, and other matters the selectpersons decide should be included.[22]

The board of finance is required by state law to hold a public hearing and present its proposed, itemized expenditures for the ensuing fiscal year at least two weeks prior to the annual town meeting. Subsequent to the public hearing, the board must hold a public meeting at which it must consider its estimates and any other matter brought to its attention and publish in a newspaper with a substantial circulation in the town a report in a form prescribed by the secretary of the Connecticut Office of Policy and Management.[23]

Forty-eight (75%) of the responding towns provided data on attendance of registered voters at the pre–town meeting meeting. Attendance ranged from 1 percent to 20 percent. One respondent wrote that the attendance in any given year "depends on how controversial the budget is."

Conduct of Business

The first order of business at the annual town meeting is the election of a moderator to preside at the meeting and at an adjourned meeting held in response to a petition of voters that specified items in the warning be decided by a referendum.[24] Should the moderator be unable to preside at the adjourned meeting, the town clerk is authorized by state law to preside or to appoint a registered voter to serve as moderator. The moderator is authorized to order the removal of any disorderly person from the town meeting. In contrast to the other New England states, the moderator is elected *ad hoc* at each meeting and is eligible to be elected at each subsequent meeting. It is not uncommon for the same person to be elected at each meeting as moderator for a period of years. One moderator reported in 1996 that he frequently had been elected to the post for the past thirty years but had missed a few meetings.

The moderator at a special town meeting often is a person who has knowledge of the topic to be acted upon by the assembled voters. Town officers in many towns attempt to predetermine who the moderator will be to ensure that he or she knows parliamentary rules and how to run the meeting. A town officer interviewed in 1996 said that "you can not leave it to chance that such a person will be present at a special town meeting."

Each town is free to establish a quorum requirement for the annual town meeting and for a special town meeting. Nine (15%) of sixty reporting towns had a quorum requirement for town meetings. The remaining towns lack such a requirement. In general, the quorum is low. A town with a population in excess of 6,500 had a quorum of seven at the annual meeting and a quorum of three at special town meetings.

The average length of the 1996 annual town meeting, according to respondents, was forty-five minutes, and the range was five minutes to two hours. Special town meetings on average lasted approximately one hour, with a range of fifteen minutes to two and one-half hours in 1996.

Towns are authorized by statute to adopt rules or orders for the conduct of town meetings, and the vote on any item in the call of a town meeting may be by paper ballot at the meeting, provided no petition for a referendum on the item has been filed.[25] Furthermore, the assembled voters may adjourn a regular or a special town meeting to another day and time. As noted, assembled voters in eight towns act only on the proposed budget.

Role of the Board of Finance

Registered voters at any annual town meeting or special town meeting, warned and held for the purpose, may vote to establish a board of finance. If the voters approve the creation of the board, the selectpersons within ten days must appoint six electors (registered voters) who are taxpayers to the board to serve until their successors are elected and qualified in accordance with state election laws.[26] A town meeting is not allowed by statute to vote to abolish a board of finance during the first two years subsequent to its establishment.[27]

The Connecticut Supreme Court in 1940 explained that one of the reasons the General Assembly authorized the establishment of a board of finance was to provide a check against the incurring of school expenses by the town board of education that may not be reasonably necessary and that a town may not be able to finance.[28] In 1963, the court described the function of a town board of finance as the elimination of extravagant and wasteful expenditures by ensuring that town finances are viewed as a whole rather than from the viewpoint of individual departments.[29]

The Connecticut Superior Court in 1941 ruled that a town exceeded its powers in its attempt to establish a bipartisan board of finance since the statutes lacked a provision for minority party representation on such a board.[30] Not every registered voter is eligible to serve on the town board of finance. The Connecticut Supreme Court in 1936 held that membership on the town board of finance was incompatible with the position of deputy commissioner on a city board of finance when the two boards acted in concert in assessing, collecting, and appropriating taxes, and the city and town shared various governmental expenses.[31]

However, the Connecticut Superior Court in 1946 opined that membership on the town board of finance was not incompatible with the office of deputy judge of the Glastonbury Town Court so as to prohibit the deputy judge from being a member of the board.[32] Similarly, the Connecticut attorney general in 1952 advised that the election of a town board of finance member to the Connecticut General Assembly did not disqualify the member from continuing to serve on the board.[33]

As explained, the board of finance is required to hold a public hearing (pre–town meeting meeting) at least two weeks prior to the annual town meeting to present its itemized estimates of town expenditures for the forthcoming fiscal year. Subsequently, the board is required to hold a public meeting to consider the estimates and prepare a report for publication in a newspaper with a substantial circulation in the town containing detailed information on receipts from all revenue sources and expenditures during the previous year, information on a revenue surplus or deficit at the commencement of the fiscal year for which estimates are being prepared, and other related information.

The board of finance is directed to present its estimates with recommendations to the annual town meeting, which may reduce or delete recommended appropriations items but may not increase appropriations beyond the amounts recommended by the board or add items.[34] If the board's estimates and recommendations are submitted to a vote by voting machine, questions may be added as to whether the budget is too high or too low, but the votes on these questions are for advisory purposes only and are not binding on the board.[35]

Participants generally rely for advice on the board of finance, composed of fellow town citizens, which studies revenue sources and expenditures proposed by town officers and departments. Ten (18%) of fifty-seven reporting towns indicated that the town meeting always follows the recommendations of the board of finance, and forty-three (78%) towns checked that such recommendations are followed, most of the time. Four (7%) towns noted that the recommendations seldom are followed, and one respondent wrote that "we usually vote the budget down two or three times."

Role of Planning and/or Zoning Commission

Connecticut municipalities are not mandated by state law to have a planning commission and/or a zoning commission.[36] A town may create a five-member planning commission by ordinance, which must stipulate whether the members are to be appointed or elected and specify the term of office.[37] A town also may create a five-to-nine member zoning commission with minority party representation, and a town with a population under 5,000 by ordinance may designate the Board of Selectmen to act as the zoning commission.[38]

The Connecticut Supreme Court in 1991 ruled that the authority of a zoning commission is concerned with land use and that the authority of a planning commission focuses upon municipal development.[39] A town by ordinance may

Table 7.1
Connecticut Annual Town Meeting Attendance (Percent of Registered Voters, 1996)

Population Range	Number of Towns	Average Attendance	Attendance Range
499 and under	-	-	-
500-999	1	5.00	-
1,000-1,999	3	12.33	2 to 25
2,000-4,999	6	13.00	2 to 37
5,000-7,499	5	6.10	1 to 25
7,500-9,999	5	12.30	1 to 40
10,000-14,999	6	4.33	1 to 9
15,000-19,999	5	0.64	.1 to 2
20,000-24,999	5	1.09	.006 to 2
25,000 and over	1	0.90	-

designate its zoning commission or its planning commission as the planning and zoning commission.[40] A combined commission must have between five and ten members, excluding nonvoting members.

In common with similar bodies in the other New England states, Connecticut's town planning and zoning commissions exert great influence at town meetings. Seven (13%) of fifty-four responding towns reported that the town meeting always accepts the commission's recommendations, and the remaining forty-seven (87%) towns indicated that the commission's recommendations are accepted most of the time.

Town Meeting Attendance

Thirty-seven (57%) of sixty-five reporting towns with an open town meeting provided attendance data. The other respondents left the data attendance section of the questionnaire blank or reported they did not record attendance.

Table 7.1 contains data relative to town meeting attendance classified by the population of towns that differs from attendance data in the states to the north of Connecticut, where there generally is a positive correlation between the population size of a town and town meeting attendance, with the largest percentage turnout of registered voters in the small towns. The Connecticut data, however, may be skewed by the small number of reporting towns in each population class. The reporting towns had an unweighted average attendance of 8.8 percent of the registered voters and a weighted average attendance of 6.9 percent.

Relative to the open town meeting in Connecticut towns, it is important to understand whether the town meeting has full legislative authority or shares it with the Board of Selectmen or town council. In Coventry, for example, the town meeting acts on the adoption of the budget, appropriations other than the annual budget of $100,000 or more, and any item the town council deems appropriate for decision by the town meeting. Thirty-six (55%) of sixty-five reporting towns operate with a town meeting that has full legislative authority. However, it is not possible to draw conclusions relative to attendance at voter assemblies in towns with full legislative authority with assemblies in towns with shared authority because numerous towns failed to provide attendance data. One suspects that voters have less incentive to participate in the town meeting if most major decisions are made by the selectpersons or town council or referenda.

The number of town meeting attendees who speak on controversial issues ranged from none to 10 percent. In general, the highest percentage of attendees speaking on such issues was in the small towns. A longtime moderator in a small town wrote in 1996 that participation in discussions at town meetings had declined in conjunction with the decline in attendance. He noted that, in general, "only long-term residents now come to town meeting, and few of them participate in debate and discussion. At the same time, there seems to be a considerable increase in anger at 'government' in town, often directed at town meeting by those who do not attend, as well as at the Board of Selectmen, the School Board, and the Planning and Zoning Commission." He also explained that during the past five years voter petitions have resulted in the town budget's being decided by referenda, and participation in the referenda "has been somewhat higher, but not enormously, than attendance at town meeting."

Questionnaire recipients were requested to indicate whether a perception exists in their respective town that special interest groups pack the town meeting. Fifty-one (80%) of the sixty-four respondents answered in the affirmative, and thirteen (20%) replied in the negative. As in the other New England states, firemen, environmentalists, town employees and their families, schoolteachers and parents of schoolchildren, and taxpayer associations were identified as groups that tended to pack the town meeting.

A town clerk referred to the education and recreation groups and wrote that "they have the power to adopt or defeat a very important issue without being well-informed. They appear when prodded to attend a controversial warrant (sometimes people never seen at regular town meetings)." A second town clerk reported that each interest group will have a speaker at the town meeting "regardless of how many group members attend" and added that "personalities influence more than issues, it seems." A third town clerk wrote that budget town meetings "are generally 'packed' with parents of school age children with special interests; *i.e.*, gifted and talented program, computer education, sports."

Population mobility today is a common characteristic of numerous Connecticut towns, and many residents of a town are relatively recent arrivals. Hence, it is not surprising that only one of sixty-two respondents checked no as the answer to the question whether long-term residents held views on certain items in the call of the town meeting that differed from the views of newer residents. A second respondent qualified his response by indicating no with some exceptions. Two town officers who checked yes qualified their replies by adding "depending on the issues."

A town moderator wrote in 1996 that as the population of his town increased, the "newcomers generally went to the town meeting . . . and it was not long before they participated in the discussions as well as voting."

Quality of Debate and Decisions

Questionnaire recipients were requested to rate the quality of debate at the annual town meeting—in terms of explanations of budget items, exploring pros and cons of proposals, and neighbors influencing neighbors' opinions on town issues—as one of the following: excellent, good, fair, or poor.

Fifty-nine town officers rated the quality of debate. Eight (14%) rated the quality as excellent, thirty-four (58%) selected good, twelve (20%) checked fair, and five (8%) considered the debate quality to be poor. Comments on the quality varied considerably. A town clerk reported that debate was excellent because "more details are requested and received." On the other hand, another clerk explained that "budget items get very personal and education budgets are scrutinized and criticized as not effectively used." In response to a question inquiring whether the quality of debate had changed over the past decade, he wrote that "more personal, nastier, no one is listening." On the other hand, another town officer explained that "interspersed among perennial comments on the economy and taxes are questions which bring clarity to issues and consequences pertinent to the vote."

Questionnaire recipients were requested to make a similar rating of the overall quality of town meeting decisions. Twelve (19%) of sixty-three town respondents checked excellent, forty-two (67%) selected good, nine (14%) selected fair, and no respondent selected poor.

The ratings of debate quality and decisions quality in the same town were not always identical. Two respondents who judged debate quality to be fair rated town meeting decisions as excellent. Similarly, two respondents who rated debate quality as good were convinced decisions quality was excellent. One town officer rated debate as poor but evaluated decisions quality as excellent.

THE SPECIAL TOWN MEETING

A town that has adopted the uniform fiscal year must set at its annual town meeting a date for a special town meeting to act on the budget prepared by the board of finance.[41] A special town meeting may be convened at any time at the discretion of the Board of Selectmen, which also must issue a warning for such a meeting to be held within twenty-one days of receipt of a petition signed by twenty registered voters.[42] The Connecticut Superior Court, however, has ruled that the Board of Selectmen does not have to call a special town meeting upon receipt of such a petition unless the board is convinced that the object of the petition is lawful and not frivolous.[43]

Town charters can specify the subjects that may be considered at a special town meeting. The Portland town charter authorizes the Board of Selectmen to call special town meetings to act on the following subjects:

(a) The issuance of bonds, notes, and other obligations, and all other forms of financing, the terms of which are in excess of one (1) year, except as provided in section 1204 of this Charter;

(b) Any appropriation supplemental to those provided in the current General Fund operating budget which exceeds one-half of one percent (.5%) of the total of the current General Fund operating budget;

(c) Real estate purchases by the Town in excess of $10,000;

(d) Sale of any Town-owned real estate appraised for more than $10,000;

(e) The creation, consolidation, or abolition of any permanent Board or department not otherwise provided for in this charter;

(f) Leases and/or lease options to which the Town, including its Board of Education, is a party which involve a term or obligation of one (1) year;

(g) Any appropriation from the capital and non-recurring expense fund not included in the annual capital expenditures budget and any supplemental appropriation which exceeds $1,000;

(h) The application for or participation in any Federal, State, or private grant program that requires the Town to contribute cash or provide any in-kind participation which jointly together exceed $10,000;

(i) Such other matters or proposals as the Selectmen, in their discretion, shall deem to be of sufficient importance to be submitted to a special Town Meeting, including recommendations by the Selectmen for the adoption or repeal of any ordinance.[44]

Although the Portland selectpersons can refer items to a special town meeting, they never have done so.[45]

In contrast to open town meeting towns in New Hampshire and Vermont, where relatively few special town meetings are held, and many towns hold no special town meetings, such meetings are very common in Connecticut. Only three (5%) of sixty-five reporting towns do not hold special town meetings. A fourth town reported it typically did not hold a special town meeting, but on rare occasions one would be called. The number of special town meetings held on average in a town each year varied from one to twelve. One respondent did not provide a number but wrote ''too many.'' Most responding towns held four to six such meetings annually.

Routine items at special town meetings ranged from none to 99 percent. Nineteen (31%) of sixty-two towns indicated that 50 percent or more of such town meetings were devoted to routine items. Transfers of funds between accounts is a common item at special town meetings, and two towns reported that such transfers are handled by the board of finance and not by a special town meeting.

SUMMARY

The traditional annual open town meeting survives today in 106 Connecticut towns, and only a financial (budget) town meeting is held in eight additional towns. In fifty towns, the annual budget is approved by the town meeting in the form of a referendum. Power sharing is common in Connecticut towns and involves the town meeting where held, town council, Board of Selectmen, and board of finance. The Board of Selectmen in approximately thirteen towns, is in effect, a town council since the board possesses the ordinance-making power. In surrendering powers to the town council or Board of Selectmen, voters have retained power in the form of the initiative and protest referendum.

The board of finance in a Connecticut town possesses more authority than its equivalent—budget or finance committee—in towns in the states north of Connecticut, since the town meeting is limited to approving, reducing, or eliminating budget items recommended by the board. In common with towns in the other New England states, voters rely heavily upon the board of finance's recommendations when making decisions at a town meeting. Voters similarly express great faith in the planning and/or zoning commission as they always or most of the time accept its recommendations at town meeting.

With reporting towns having a weighted average attendance of only 6.9 percent of the registered voters at the annual town meeting, the question can be raised why the town meeting is retained. The answer to this question perhaps may be found in the survey data revealing that 86 percent of the responding town officials rated the quality of town meeting decisions as excellent or good. This finding also may be reinforced by the traditional belief in town meeting government as the purest form of democracy.

Chapter 8 examines the town meeting in another southern New England state—Rhode Island—where major changes have occurred.

NOTES

1. Benjamin Trumbull, *A Complete History of Connecticut: Civil and Ecclesiastical* (New London: H. D. Utley, 1898), pp. 9–10.

2. Bruce C. Daniels, "Contrasting Colony-Town Relations in the Founding of Connecticut and Rhode Island prior to the Charters of 1662 and 1663," *The Connecticut Historical Society* 3, April 1973, p. 60.

3. Trumbull, *A Complete History of Connecticut*, p. 71.

4. Bruce C. Daniels, *The Connecticut Town: Growth and Development, 1635–1790* (Middletown, Conn.: Wesleyan University Press, 1979).

5. For details, see Joseph F. Zimmerman, *The Recall: Tribunal of the People* (Westport, Conn.: Praeger Publishers, 1997).

6. *Simon v. Canty*, 195 Conn. 524 (1985).

7. *Constitution of Connecticut*, art. X, § 1; *Connecticut General Statutes Annotated*, chap. 99, §§ 7-187 to 7-201.

8. *Connecticut General Statutes Annotated*, chap. 99, § 7-188(a).

9. Paul Marks, "The Town Meeting: Alive, but Ailing," *Hartford Courant*, July 14, 1996, p. A5.

10. *Connecticut General Statutes Annotated*, chap. 90, § 7-1.

11. Ibid., § 7-388.

12. Ibid., § 7-3.

13. Ibid., § 7-1(b).

14. Ibid., chap. 171, § 10-242.

15. *Hayden v. Noyes*, 5 Conn. 391 (1824).

16. *Johnson v. Miller*, 13 Conn. Supp. 116 (1944).

17. *Wright v. North School District*, 53 Conn. 576 (1886).

18. *Welles v. Town of East Windsor*, 185 Conn. 556, 41 A.2d 174 (1981).

19. *Connecticut General Statutes Annotated*, chap. 90, § 7-7.

20. Ibid., § 7-6.

21. *Spahos v. Mayor & Councilmen of Savannah Beach*, 371 U.S. 106 (1962); *Spahos v. Mayor & Councilmen of Savannah Beach*, 207 F.Supp. 688 at 692 (S.D.Ga. 1962).

22. *Connecticut General Statutes Annotated*, chap. 90, § 7-406.

23. Ibid., chap. 106, § 7-344.

24. Ibid., chap. 90, § 7-7.

25. Ibid., § 7-7.

26. Ibid., chap. 106. § 7-340.

27. Ibid.

28. *Board of Education of Stamford v. Board of Finance of Stamford*, 127 Conn. 345, 16 A.2d 601 (1940).

29. *Board of Education of Ellington v. Town of Ellington*, 151 Conn. 1, 193 A.2d 466 (1963). See also *Board of Education of Trumbull v. Butler*, 32 Conn. Supp. 132, 343 A.2d 657 (1974).

30. *Koch v. Theis*, 10 Conn. Supp. 258 (1941). See also 24 *Opinions of the Connecticut Attorney General* 73 (June 6, 1945).

31. *State ex rel. Schenck v. Barrett*, 121 Conn. 237, 184 A. 379 (1936).

32. *State ex rel. Purtill v. Friel*, 14 Conn. Supp. 289 (1946).

33. 27 *Opinions of the Connecticut Attorney General* 381 (November 26, 1952).

34. *Connecticut General Statutes Annotated*, chap. 106, § 7-344.

35. Ibid.

36. *Levinsky v. Zoning Commission of the City of Bridgeport*, 144 Conn. 117, 127 A.2d 822 (1956).

37. *Connecticut General Statutes Annotated*, chap. 126, § 8-19.

38. Ibid., chap. 124, § 8-1.

39. *Cristofaro v. Town of Burlington*, 217 Conn. 103, 584 A.2d 1168 (1991).

40. *Connecticut General Statutes Annotated*, chap. 124, § 8-4a.

41. Ibid., chap. 90, § 7-388.

42. Ibid., § 7-1.

43. *State ex rel. Feigl v. Raacke*, 32 Conn. Supp. 237, 349 A.2d 150 (1975).

44. *Town of Portland (Connecticut) Charter*, §503.

45. Interview with Donald Goodrich, Portland finance director, Watertown, Conn., August 16, 1996.

Chapter 8

The Rhode Island
Financial Town Meeting

Rhode Island, in common with Connecticut, was settled by people who migrated from the Massachusetts Bay Colony in the 1630s and founded the towns of Newport, Portsmouth, Providence, and Warwick. The Rhode Island settlers differed from the Connecticut settlers in that the former were dissenters, and the latter were Puritan zealots.[1] This difference accounts for the centralization of political powers in the early Connecticut General Court in contrast to the retention of significant powers by the four towns that formed the colony of Rhode Island in 1643.

The first permanent European settler of Rhode Island was Episcopal preacher William Blackstone, who lived the life of a hermit and did not contribute to the settlement of a town.[2] The founder of Rhode Island was Roger Williams, a friend of Governor John Winthrop of the Massachusetts Bay Colony. A theologian, Williams declined the offer of a pastorage of the church in Boston on the grounds the Boston Church had not separated itself from the Church of England but accepted an offer from the church in Salem.[3] Soon thereafter he became the assistant to Pastor Ralph Smith of the church in Plymouth, which was Separatist.

Williams challenged the covenant theology of the Massachusetts Bay Colony and maintained, among other things, that the settlers did not rightly own their lands because they had not purchased them from the Indians. Williams held a different interpretation of the Bible than the one held by the Puritans with specific reference to Christ's incarnation and was convinced "that Christ had set forth new laws of worship which had stripped judges, kings, and civic magistrates of their right to enforce the first" four commandments.[4] In October 1635, the General Court issued a decree of banishment against Williams and ordered that he be returned to England.[5] Pleading that he was too ill to travel to England, Williams moved to the area of Rehoboth but was ordered by Governor Winslow of Plymouth Colony to move to the western bank of the Seekonk River outside the jurisdiction of the colony.

Settling at the head of Narragansett Bay in 1636 at a place named Providence, Williams and fellow settlers established a town government that involved a meeting every two weeks of the heads of families. Patrick T. Conley explained:

In the formative period of the Providence plantation, Williams's political posture was not as liberal as his religious views. His plan for the temporary submission of new inhabitants, his unfulfilled desire to reserve unto himself a veto over the admission of new settlers, and his establishment of a closed corporation of landed proprietors are examples of this political caution.[6]

Many settlers of Providence were unhappy with these restrictions and worked for a new plantation agreement that was adopted in 1640 and provided for a town meeting and the election for a three-month term of five "disposers" with responsibility for disbursing land to new inhabitants, managing the common stock, and settling disputes.[7]

Three other towns were founded shortly thereafter. William Coddington, leader of the Antinomians and other religious dissenters, founded Portsmouth in 1638, but he was removed as leader in 1639. He and his followers immediately moved to the south and founded Newport.[8] The fourth town, Warwick, was founded by Samuel Gorton in 1643 and accorded freedom of religion to all.[9]

Williams traveled to England in 1643 and obtained a patent from the earl of Warwick and his parliamentary Committee on Foreign Plantations providing for the uniting of Newport, Portsmouth, and Providence as the Providence Plantations in Narragansett Bay in New England.[10] Samuel Gorton was successful in having his town of Warwick protected by the patent. In 1647, the four towns met in Portsmouth and organized a government for the colony.[11]

Rhode Island is the second most densely populated state (approximately 900 persons per square mile) after New Jersey and has an area of 1,214 square miles that is smaller than the geographical reach of the city of Houston, Texas (1,234 square miles), which occupies 95 percent of Harris County. There are thirty-one towns in Rhode Island, ranging in population from 3,492 in West Greenwich and 4,316 in Foster to 29,268 in West Warwick and 31,083 in Coventry. In addition, there are eight cities, ranging in population from 17,637 in Central Falls to 160,728 in Providence.

Significant changes have occurred in town government over the decades, and town councils have replaced the Board of Selectmen in all towns. In 1950, North Providence abandoned the financial town meeting in favor of an elected, seven-member budget commission.[12] In 1963, for example, a financial town meeting (FTM) was held annually in thirty of thirty-one towns.[13] Today, eleven (35%) of the state's thirty-one towns have abandoned the town meeting completely and invested full legislative authority in a town council. Twenty towns (65%) legally have a provision for an annual FTM, but Warren did not hold one in fiscal years 1995, 1996, and 1997 because of the lack of a quorum, which is 125 registered voters for the annual town meeting or a special town meeting.

The town council, presided over by a president, shares legislative authority with the financial town meeting in twenty towns and also performs administrative duties unless there is a town manager or a town administrator.

To collect data, a questionnaire was mailed to each town with an open financial town meeting. Completed questionnaires were returned by sixteen towns (80%), but not every respondent answered each question. Telephone interviews also were conducted with a small number of knowledgeable individuals.

THE ANNUAL TOWN MEETING

State law requires that the financial town meeting be held annually or biennially on a date and at a time determined by the town.[14] In practice, the meetings are held in March, April, and May. The charter of the town of South Kingstown directs the qualified electors to assemble for the annual financial town meeting on the last Tuesday in April at 7:00 P.M., and the charter of the town of Warren sets the date of the annual financial town meeting as the third Monday in May at 5:00 P.M.[15]

The meeting is held in pursuance of a warrant issued by the town clerk notifying all registered voters of the place, date, and time of the meeting.[16] The town clerk is required to post a notice of the town meeting at least seven days prior to the meeting in a minimum of three public places in the town.[17] Notice of the meeting typically is published in a local newspaper.

Only items listed in the warrant issued by the town clerk and petitioned items may be acted upon by voters at the annual town meeting. Each petition article to be valid in Warren must be signed by a minimum of fifty qualified electors and filed with the town clerk by the fourth Monday in April.[18] A petition can be enacted or rejected only by a paper ballot vote at the Warren financial town meeting. Eleven (69%) of the sixteen reporting towns provided information on citizen-initiated petitions. Two (18%) responded that such petitions were frequent, seven (64%) checked seldom, and 2 (18%) selected never.

The Annual Report and Pre–Town Meeting Meeting

Each town with a financial town meeting publishes an annual report prior to the town meeting, containing information on the organization of the town government; reports of officers, committees, and departments; minutes of the preceding annual financial town meeting; the independent auditor's report on town finances; and often the warrant for the forthcoming financial town meeting.

Twelve (75%) of the responding sixteen towns held a pre–town meeting meeting in 1996, where warrant articles were explained, and questions were raised by citizens and answered by town officers. The purpose of this meeting was to help voters make intelligent decisions when voting at the financial town meeting.

In common with the other New England towns of the same population classes with an open town meeting, attendance at these meetings is very small and averages less than 1 percent of the registered voters. One town clerk reported attendance was minimal, and the highest reported attendance was 4 percent of the eligible voters.

Conduct of Business

The moderator, the presiding officer of the financial town meeting or special town meeting, is elected at the annual or biennial town meeting and serves until his or her successor is elected and qualified.[19] The charter of the town of Little Compton, for example, provides for the election of a moderator for a two-year term at the general election in the town and authorizes the town council to appoint an assistant moderator with the approval of the moderator.[20]

Voters view the moderator as an impartial person who is granted considerable discretion relative to the conduct of a meeting. The general laws stipulate:

If any person shall conduct himself in a disorderly manner in any town, representative district, or voting district meeting, the moderator may order that person to withdraw from the meeting; and, on the person's refusal, may order the town sergeant, or any constable present, or any other persons, to take him or her from the meeting and to confine him or her in some convenient place until the meeting shall be adjourned; and the person so refusing to withdraw shall, for each offense, be fined not exceeding twenty dollars.[21]

The moderator may distribute a set of ground rules for the conduct of business prior to action on warrant articles and/or verbally explain the rules for conducting the meeting. In general, a voter may not speak more than once on an article until every other person so desiring has spoken on the article. Voting may be *viva voce* or by ballot. Town meeting rules can be incorporated into town charters. The South Kingstown town charter authorizes a vote by ballot when requested by 20 percent of the assembled voters on any question involving expenditures or incurrence of a liability.[22]

The skill of the moderator determines, in part, the length of the annual financial town meeting, which averaged three hours in 1996. The length also is influenced by the number of controversial articles in the warrant. The longest town meeting in recent years occurred in New Shoreham (Block Island) in 1991 and continued for four and one-half days.

The general laws established a minimum of seven voters as a quorum in towns with a population under 3,000 and a minimum of fifteen voters in larger towns.[23] Each town is free to establish a quorum requirement higher than the statutory minimum one for the conduct of business at the annual town meeting and/or special town meeting. Of the sixteen reporting towns, only New Shoreham lacked a town established quorum. In the other towns, the number required for a quorum varies from fifteen voters at each type of meeting in Barrington

(15,849), Foster (4,316), Hopkington (6,873), Scituate (9,796), and West War-wick (29,268) to 200 in Tiverton (14,312). Gloucester (9,227) established a quorum of twenty-five at the annual meeting and 10 percent of the registered voters (5,450) or fifty-five at a special town meeting. Little Compton (3,339) established the quorum as 5 percent of the registered voters (2,640) or thirteen at both types of meetings.

Role of the Budget Committee

The financial town meeting may establish a finance committee to provide guidance to the assembled voters on the appropriation of town funds. Twelve (75%) of the reporting sixteen towns have established such a committee. The town council acts as the finance committee and provides advice to the town meeting in one town. In another town lacking a committee, the town council and the town manager advise the town meeting. Two towns reported that they lacked such a committee.

In eight of the towns with committees, recommendations are made by the committees on all warrant articles. In the remaining towns, the committee provides advice on only certain warrant articles.

Town meeting participants in Rhode Island, as in the other New England states with open town meetings except Vermont, rely heavily on the finance committee for advice. Of the twelve reporting towns with committees, two towns (17%) reported that the town meeting accepted all of the recommendations of the committee, and ten towns (83%) reported that meeting participants followed the committee's recommendations most of the time. No town reported that the committee's recommendations seldom or never were followed by the assembled voters.

Town Meeting Attendance

Thirteen (81%) of the sixteen reporting towns provided data on attendance at the annual financial town meeting in 1996. As noted, Warren did not hold a financial town meeting in 1996 because of the lack of a quorum. Table 8.1 reveals that attendance varied from 1 percent to 20 percent, with the smaller towns in general having a slightly higher turnout on a percentage basis of registered voters than the larger towns. The unweighted average attendance was 6.54 percent, and the weighted average attendance was 5.33 percent.

Not surprisingly, town meeting attendance varied over the past three decades. Tiverton, for example, reported the following data on attendance as a percentage of the registered voters: 14.2 percent in 1966, 10.5 percent in 1976, 8.6 percent in 1986, and 5.1 percent in 1996. Foster reported attendance of 14.0 percent in 1966, 16.0 percent in 1976, 6.0 percent in 1986, and 10.0 percent in 1996. The downward trend revealed by these data mirrors in general the decline in attendance at town meetings in the other New England states. South Kingstown

Table 8.1
Rhode Island Annual Financial Town Meeting Attendance (Percent of Registered Voters, 1996)

Population Range	Number of Towns	Average Attendance	Attendance Range
499 and under	-	-	-
500-999	-	-	-
1,000-1,999	-	-	-
2,000-4,499	1	10.00	-
5,000-7,499	4	6.75	1.1-20.1
7,500-9,999	1	7.00	-
10,000-14,999	3	2.70	1.0-5.1
15,000-19,999	2	4.60	2.0-7.2
20,000-24,999	1	2.00	-
25,000 and over	1	6.00	-

reported attendance data for the 1976 annual financial town meeting, which extended over three nights. Attendance was 15.0 percent the first night but declined to 10.0 percent on the second night and to 7.0 percent on the third night.

Respondents indicated that the percentage of the financial town meeting participants who speak on a controversial issue varies from less than 1 percent to 10 percent. The average percent of participants who speak is approximately 2 percent.

Questionnaire recipients were requested to indicate whether a perception exists in their respective town that special interest groups pack the town meeting. Thirteen (87%) of the fifteen town officers who answered the question checked yes, and two (13%) selected no. Written comments indicated that school supporters, including teachers and parents of children, policemen, and library supporters have excellent attendance records at the annual financial town meeting. One town officer reported that the school and public safety supporters exerted "enough influence to control the outcome," and school supporters were at every town meeting, whereas the public safety supporters tended to be present only when the warrant affected them. A second town correspondent wrote that town employees and their families regularly attend the town meeting but "never pack the meeting." A third town officer identified four different groups but noted that the "police almost always are successful and the others usually fail."

Rhode Island towns have a relatively mobile population, and not surprisingly, the views of newer residents on key issues may differ from the views of long-term residents. Only one of the fifteen responding towns indicated that newer residents held the same view on issues as long-term residents. The other fourteen towns (93%) indicated there were differences in views depending on the issue in question.

Quality of Debate and Decisions

Each recipient of a questionnaire was asked to assess the quality of debate at the annual financial town meeting—in terms of explanations of budget items, exploring pros and cons of proposals, and neighbors influencing neighbors' opinions on town issues—as excellent, good, fair, or poor.

Twelve (75%) of the sixteen questionnaire respondents rated the quality of the debate. Two (17%) rated the debate quality as excellent, five (41%) as good, three (25%) as fair, and two (17%) as poor. A town officer who judged debate quality to be fair wrote that the quality has "gone down till mostly anger." A second town officer wrote "worsened" relative to the change in debate quality over the years. A third town officer noted that the amount of debate has increased since the formation of a citizen group but added that the quality had not necessarily improved. An insightful town correspondent explained:

For those with genuine concern, the debate is excellent, with excellent results. For the politicos or those with axes to grind, the debate is long-tiring-inflammatory and causes the meeting to go on too long which causes many to leave.

Questionnaire recipients also were requested to make a similar rating of the overall quality of town meeting decisions. Fifteen town officers responded. Three (20%) rated the quality of decisions as excellent, seven (47%) selected good, four (27%) checked fair, and one (6%) checked poor. A respondent who rated debate quality as poor judged the quality of decisions to be good. Two town officers who judged debate quality to be fair evaluated town meeting decisions as good.

THE SPECIAL TOWN MEETING

The general laws authorize a town council at any time to direct the town clerk to call a special town meeting.[24] In addition, the clerk must call such a meeting when petitioned by 10 percent of the registered voters unless the subject(s) proposed to be considered at the special town meeting is one that has been acted on by the town at any time within the previous six months.[25] If the subject of a petition has been acted upon by the town meeting during the previous six months, the clerk may call such a meeting only with permission of the town council.[26]

In adopting a "home rule" charter, a town may change the procedures for calling a special town meeting. The South Kingstown town charter has made a slight change in the procedures by specifying:

Special financial town meetings shall be called by the town clerk upon the resolution of the town council or whenever ten (10) per centum of the qualified electors of the town shall make a request in writing and direct the same to the town clerk.[27]

The charter of the town of Warren has made a more major change in the procedures by specifying that the town clerk must call a special financial town meeting upon the adoption of a resolution by two-thirds of the members of the town council directing that such a meeting be called or the receipt of a petition signed by 5 percent of the town's registered voters.[28]

Special town meetings are uncommon in Rhode Island towns with a financial town meeting. Of fifteen responding towns, eight (53%) reported that no special town meetings were held. One town officer reported that such meetings are held "rarely." Three special town meetings were held in one reporting town in 1996, two special meetings were held in another town, and one special meeting was held in each of four towns.

SUMMARY

The state of health of town meeting government in Rhode Island is poor. None of the state's thirty-one towns hold an open town meeting today, and only twenty towns have a legal provision for a financial town meeting. One of these towns—Warren—did not hold a financial town meeting in fiscal years 1995, 1996, and 1997 because of the lack of quorum, which is only 125 voters in a town with a 1990 population of 11,385.

Attendance data for the 1996 financial town meetings do not bode well for the future of this type of town meeting. The weighted average attendance at the 1996 meetings was only 5 1/3 percent of the electors, and only a small minority of electors participating in the meetings spoke on controversial issues.

Available evidence suggests that individual Rhode Island towns gradually will replace the financial town meeting by confiding authority for financial decisions in the town council. This approach contrasts sharply with the approach in Massachusetts, where the open town meeting was replaced between 1915 and 1972 in a significant number of the larger towns by the representative town meeting (RTM). Chapter 9 examines the RTM in forty-two Massachusetts towns, seven Connecticut towns, one Maine town, and one Vermont town.

NOTES

1. Bruce C. Daniels, "Contrasting Colony-Town Relations in the Founding of Connecticut and Rhode Island," *The Connecticut Historical Society* 3, April 1973, p. 60.

2. Bertram Lippincott, *Indians, Privateers, and High Society* (Philadelphia: J. B. Lippincott Company, 1961), pp. 27–29.

3. Ibid., pp. 31–32.

4. Patrick T. Conley, *Democracy in Decline: Rhode Island's Constitutional Development 1776–1841* (Providence: Rhode Island Historical Society, 1977), p. 11.

5. Ibid., p. 8.

6. Ibid., p. 15.

7. Ibid., pp. 15–16.

8. Ibid., p. 16.

9. Ibid., p. 18.

10. Ibid., pp. 17–18.

11. Ibid., pp. 18–19.

12. *Rhode Island Acts and Resolves of 1950*, chap. 2530.

13. Edwin W. Webber, *Rhode Island Local Government and Administration* (Kingston: Bureau of Government Research, University of Rhode Island, 1963), p. 28.

14. *General Laws of Rhode Island Annotated*, § 45-3-1.

15. *Charter of the Town of South Kingstown, Rhode Island*, § 2310; *Charter of the Town of Warren, Rhode Island*, § 16.01.

16. *General Laws of Rhode Island Annotated*, § 45-3-5.

17. Ibid., § 45-3-8.

18. *Charter of the Town of Warren, Rhode Island*, § 16.06.

19. *General Laws of Rhode Island Annotated*, §§ 45-3-15, 45-3-16.

20. *Home Rule Charter, Town of Little Compton, Rhode Island*, art. III, § 303.

21. *General Laws of Rhode Island Annotated*, § 45-3-19.

22. *Charter of the Town of South Kingstown, Rhode Island*, § 2343.

23. *General Laws of Rhode Island Annotated*, § 45-3-14.

24. Ibid., § 45-3-6.

25. Ibid., § 45-3-7.

26. Ibid.

27. *Charter of the Town of South Kingstown, Rhode Island*, § 2313.

28. *Charter of the Town of Warren, Rhode Island*, § 16.04.

Chapter 9

The Representative Town Meeting

Townspeople have cherished their right to participate directly in the process of determining town policies since 1630 and only reluctantly have agreed to the substitution of a representative policy-determining mechanism for the open town meeting. Sentiment and tradition work against any major change in the open town meeting.

The limited or representative town meeting (RTM) is a hybrid political institution that seeks to combine certain features of the open town meeting with a representative body; the voters delegate legislative powers to a relatively large number of elected representatives yet reserve the right to attend and speak at town meetings and by means of referenda reverse most actions of their elected representatives. Forty-two Massachusetts towns, seven Connecticut towns, one Maine town, and one Vermont town have abandoned the open town meeting in favor of an RTM.

ORIGIN

The date of the origin of the concept of a representative town meeting as a substitute for the open town meeting cannot be determined with precision. Dissatisfaction with the traditional form of town government manifested itself in Boston as early as 1708, when the selectmen reported that by-laws were not being executed properly for "the want of a proper head or Town officer or officers impowered for that purpose" and urged the appointment of a committee to draft a charter of incorporation for the town.[1] The town meeting held on December 27, 1708, voted that such a committee be chosen, but the March 14, 1709, town meeting rejected the report of the committee.[2]

Town records indicate that the open town meeting functioned adequately, albeit tumultuously on occasion, for at least its first century and one-half in all towns. Not until the 1780s did rumblings of discontent with the plenary meeting as the local legislative body begin to develop in Boston as its population increased.

Acting upon the petition of a large number of citizens that the sense of the town be taken on the question of the expediency of transforming the town of Boston into an incorporated city, a town meeting held in Fanuiel Hall on May 11, 1784, voted the appointment of a thirteen-member committee headed by Samuel Adams to consider whether the form of government should be altered.[3]

On June 4, 1784, the committee reported two plans for a municipal corporation. The first plan provided for "incorporating the Town of Boston into a Body Politic by the Name, Style and Title of the Mayor, Aldermen and Common-Council of the City of Boston," and the second plan provided "for incorporating the Town of Boston into a Body Politic, by the Name, Style and Title of the President and Selectmen of the City of Boston." A town meeting held on June 17, 1784, rejected the plans by a great majority.[4]

An article representing the views of a considerable number of citizens was inserted in the warrant for a town meeting held on December 30, 1791, and called for the appointment of a twenty-one-member committee to consider "the Present State of the Town"; the meeting approved the appointment of the committee.[5] It reported on January 13, 1792, a plan authorizing the selectmen to divide the town into nine wards of equal population and each ward annually to elect by ballot two voters residing in the ward who together with the selectmen would constitute a "Town Council" possessing the power to make "all such By Laws as the Town have now in their corporate capacity A right to make and establish the same ... and to alter and repeal them."[6] The town council would have been authorized to appoint all executive officers except the selectmen, town clerk, overseers of the poor, assessors, town treasurer, school committee, auditors of account, "fire wards," collector of taxes, and constables.[7] This plan was defeated on January 26, 1792, by a vote of 701 to 517.[8]

On May 12, 1803, the Boston town meeting voted that a committee be organized to inquire into the affairs of Suffolk County. The committee reported on December 21, 1803, and on January 2, 1804, a committee of twenty-four, two from each ward, was elected "to procure any alteration in the County and Town Government."[9] The report of the committee, dated February 29, 1804, was received by a town meeting held on March 12, 1804, which adjourned until April 9, 1804, at which time the report was read, and the meeting after considerable debate voted to dissolve itself.[10]

The committee recommended that a town council composed of the selectmen and two delegates elected in each ward be created with the power "to make all such Bye-Laws, Ordinances, Rules and Regulations, for the orderly government of the Town, and for the management of its concerns, as they may judge necessary."[11]

On October 16, 1815, a committee that considered the question of altering the town government reported to the town meeting that it rejected the concept of a city government but urged the establishment of a chief executive termed "the Intendant" and a change in name to "the Intendant and Municipality of the Town and City of Boston."[12]

The committee advanced succinct arguments against the open town meeting in large towns, arguments that have a familiar ring today:

It is impossible that all the individuals of which they are composed should be well acquainted with the principles on which depend the prosperous conduct of the monied concerns of a corporation, and with those other subjects of internal regulation, by which the prosperity of a city is increased, and by which it is best enabled to encourage & protect the industry of its own citizens. If all the inhabitants of such towns assemble, it is obvious that business cannot be well transacted by so numerous a body, liable as it always must be, to be swayed by local views, party feelings, or the interests of designing men: If the meetings be, as it most frequently will be, but thinly attended, those present must act as the representatives of the whole; and it is very seldom, that men of the best intelligence and most capable of conducting publick business will leave their important private concerns to attend to affairs in which they have only a general interest; it therefore unavoidably happens that the affairs of a large town are conducted by a very small number of persons, who represent and act for the whole, but who are not chosen by them, who do not possess their confidence and act under no, or a very slight responsibility.[13]

The committee added that "all great bodies of men," including state governments, banking institutions, and corporations, are managed by representatives or directors who "act for the joint interest under general laws."[14] A bill drafted by the committee provided that the selectmen, twenty-four delegates, of whom two would be elected in each ward, and the "Intendant" would be "a body corporate & Politic" with power to adopt by-laws and ordinances. The "Intendant" was to be elected annually by the joint ballot of the selectmen, delegates, overseers of the poor, and the board of health and, with the concurrence of the selectmen, was to be responsible for the faithful execution of laws.[15]

By a vote of 950 to 920 the meeting refused to accept the report of the committee.[16] The chief reason for the rejection of the plan apparently was the lack of a constitutional provision authorizing the General Court (state legislature) to incorporate city governments. No variation in the traditional form of town meeting government was allowed under the 1780 constitution of the commonwealth. The Second Amendment to the constitution, adopted in 1821, empowered the General Court to establish limited town meetings in towns with a population in excess of 12,000 upon the application of, and with the consent of, a majority of the electorate at a town meeting called for the purpose. The 12,000 population figure appears to have been selected as a compromise, as figures as high as 30,000 and as low as 5,000 had been considered.

A committee appointed on October 22, 1821, to consider "[a] complete system relating to the administration of Town and County" reported on December

10, 1821. The town meeting voted to recommit the report to the committee, which was enlarged by the addition of one person from each ward and instructed "to report a system of Municipal Government for this town."[17]

The committee reported on January 2, 1822, and urged a city government but proposed:

> That general meetings of the citizens, qualified to vote in City affairs, may from time to time be held, to consult upon the common good, to give instructions to their Representatives, and to take all lawful measures to obtain a redress of any grievances, according to the right secured to the people, by the Constitution of this Commonwealth. That such meetings shall be duly warned by the Mayor and Aldermen, upon the requisite of fifty qualified voters of said city.[18]

In 1822, Boston, with a population in excess of 43,000, abandoned the town form of government in favor of a city charter because of attendance problems. Fanuiel Hall was overcrowded when a controversial article was on the warrant, and only voters near the moderator could hear the deliberations. When routine articles constituted the warrant, only the selectmen and thirty or forty other voters were present and acted upon the articles and reports that the majority had not considered carefully.

Role of Alfred D. Chandler

The institutional history of the representative town meetings in Massachusetts is traceable to Brookline in 1915. Newport, Rhode Island, however, in 1915 became the first local government to adopt the equivalent of a RTM when its city charter was amended to provide for a council of 195 members.

Brookline was experiencing difficulties with its open town meeting late in the nineteenth century, at which time Alfred D. Chandler advanced the concept of a representative town meeting as an alternative to the city form of government. To secure adoption of an RTM, Chandler had to overcome the firmly established beliefs that every town voter had the right to participate fully in town meetings and that the RTM would weaken or destroy grassroots democracy. Fear also was expressed that citizen apathy would be multiplied by the adoption of an RTM, as citizens would become convinced there is no logical reason to attend town meetings, as they would have no effective voice in the decision-making process unless they were elected town meeting members. In fact, relatively few non-town meeting members attend representative town meetings.

In response to a petition filed by a citizen group organized by Chandler, the 1915 General Court enacted a law authorizing the question of the adoption of an RTM to appear on the Brookline ballot.[19] Brookline voters adopted the plan by a vote of 3,191 to 1,180.[20] Watertown adopted a representative town meeting acceptance statute on November 4, 1919.

The Massachusetts RTM

The granting of woman suffrage in 1920 doubled the pressure for the abandonment of the open town meeting. Twelve towns accepted, and Wakefield rejected, representative town meeting acceptance statutes during the 1920s; thirteen towns accepted, and three towns rejected, acts during the 1930s; three towns accepted, and Palmer rejected, acts during the 1940s; and eleven towns accepted, and Wakefield rejected, acts during the 1950s. During the 1960s, Southbridge rejected an RTM act, and Lee and Montague accepted one. Burlington, Chelmsford, Holbrook, North Attleborough, and Walpole adopted RTMs during the 1980s, and West Springfield followed suit in 1992.

Interest in the representative town meeting among several towns with a population under 12,000 led to the adoption in 1926 of the Seventieth Amendment, which amended the Second Amendment by empowering the General Court to establish representative town meetings in towns with a population in excess of 6,000. Only three RTM towns currently have a population under 12,000: Athol (11,678), Lee (5,798), and Montague (8,444). In 1967, sixteen open town meeting towns had larger populations than Montague, which was the smallest RTM town. Today, 121 open meeting towns, ranging in population from Merrimac (5,803) to Andover (31,317), are larger than Lee. Twelve of these towns have a population exceeding 20,000.

The desirability of restricting representative town meetings to towns with a population in excess of 6,000 is questionable. Logically, a requirement of a prescribed minimum population to be eligible to have a representative town meeting has no validity. If the voters prefer a representative town meeting, they should be free to adopt it. Furthermore, the number of registered voters is of greater significance than the population of a town, and the restriction of representative town meetings to towns with a population in excess of 6,000 has led to the paradoxical situation in which eight surveyed towns with populations under 6,000 in 1996 had more registered voters than Ayer (6,300), which is eligible under the state constitution and statutes to adopt an RTM. Manchester-by-the-Sea (5,512), for example, had 3,517 registered voters in 1996 compared to 2,893 such voters in Ayer.

Reasons for Adoption

Four major reasons have been advanced in support of the adoption of an RTM. First, a large town lacks the facilities to accommodate all voters. The number of registered voters exceeds by several times the capacity of the largest hall in the town, and the use of two or more halls connected to the same public address system is cumbersome and less than satisfactory. Even a large attendance in one hall restricts the amount of genuine deliberation.

Surprisingly, this reason appears to have little validity; most towns that adopted the representative town meeting did so because they had experienced quorum problems with the open town meeting except when the warrant contained an exceptionally controversial article. Auburn, for example, had difficulty in attracting a quorum of fifty voters prior to the adoption of the representative town meeting. Athol in 1956 sounded the fire alarm at the town hall in an attempt to attract a quorum; the alarm was an attraction, but citizens did not go into the meeting in sufficient numbers to establish a quorum.

Second, the conduct of an open town meeting with several thousand voters in attendance is difficult, if not next to impossible. Only the failure of large numbers of voters to attend in the larger towns has prevented meetings from becoming unwieldy.

Third, the alleged unrepresentativeness of the open town meeting in larger towns, in the view of critics, is a serious problem. The RTM substitutes legal representation for chance or accidental representation. The small attendance of registered voters at the typical open town meeting may permit a minority group to pack the meeting and control town policies; a neighborhood sporadically could turn out in large numbers and vote appropriations for expensive capital improvements for the neighborhood. RTM proponents are convinced that a *de jure* RTM provides better representation for all voters than a *de facto* RTM (see Chapter 10).

Fourth, it is argued that town meeting members become well educated with respect to town problems and, consequently, are better prepared than the average citizen to vote intelligently on the articles in the warrant. Furthermore, RTM supporters maintain that conclusions can be reached with less difficulty.

LEGAL PROCEDURES FOR ADOPTION

Neither the constitution of the commonwealth of Massachusetts nor the General Court authorized towns by their own action to adopt a representative town meeting until 1966, when the home rule constitutional amendment was ratified by voters.[21]

Prior to 1966, a town wishing to adopt a representative town meeting voted at a town meeting to authorize the drafting and filing of a petition in the General Court requesting the enactment of a special act providing for an RTM and making the act effective upon its acceptance by the town.

A special state commission reviewed the RTMs in 1931 and drafted a standard RTM bill, which was enacted by the General Court the same year.[22] Only a town that accepted a special act providing for an RTM may adopt the standard representative town meeting act. To date, only Arlington and Brookline have adopted the standard act.[23]

The standard and special RTM acts are fundamentally the same; the details such as the number of members and *ex officio* members vary considerably from town to town. Most special acts were copied from earlier special acts. All acts contain ephemeral provisions that should be left to by-law determination.

The home rule constitutional amendment authorizes towns to create a charter commission that may draft a new charter or amendment for submission to the voters for their action. Hopefully, a charter commission will not copy *verbatim* the provisions of a special representative town meeting statute that has been accepted by another town.

To collect information and data on RTMs, a questionnaire was mailed to each of the forty-two towns with an RTM. Responses were received from thirty-eight (90%) towns. With a few exceptions, respondents answered each question.

NOMINATION AND ELECTION OF MEMBERS

The standard RTM act provides for the division of the town into precincts by the selectpersons, and the special acts and town charters provide for the division of the town into precincts by the selectpersons or others specified in the acts. Town meeting members, except in Montague, are elected by nonpartisan ballots from among the registered voters of each precinct.

Twenty-three special acts specify a minimum and maximum number of precincts, seven acts specify a minimum number of precincts, Framingham and Ludlow acts specify the number of precincts, and the remaining acts leave the number of precincts to by-law determination. Twenty-six acts establish a minimum number of voters in each precinct. Thirteen acts stipulate that each precinct shall have an approximately equal number of voters. The standard act does not stipulate the number of precincts but does stipulate that each precinct must contain at least 400 voters.

Experience clearly indicates it is preferable for town by-laws to specify the number of precincts and the number of voters in each precinct. If a limitation is incorporated in the act or town charter relative to the RTM's size, it would be preferable to limit the number of town meeting members rather than the number of voters per precinct.

Candidates for town meeting members are nominated by petitions that bear no political party designations except in Montague; the required number of signatures of precinct voters on nomination petitions varies from ten in most towns to thirty in Milford. Ten signatures should be sufficient on a nomination petition, as barriers preventing voters from becoming candidates should be kept to a minimum.

An incumbent in most towns automatically is renominated if he or she submits his or her written intention to seek re-election to the town clerk at least thirty days prior to the election. Fourteen special acts specify that the words "candidate for re-election" must be printed on the ballot under the names of incumbents seeking re-election. Re-election of incumbents is nearly automatic in every town. The designation "candidate for re-election" is undesirable, as it grants an unfair advantage to incumbents and eliminates potential candidates who know it is difficult to defeat an incumbent who is so labeled on the ballot.

Forty-one towns elect town meeting members in March; Saugus elects its town meeting members on the first Tuesday after the first Monday in November of odd-numbered years. All RTM acts provide that town meeting members, are the judges of the election and qualifications of their members, who receive no compensation for their service.

Number and Term of Elected Members

The number of elected town meeting members ranges from 50 in Saugus to 429 in Fairhaven. The most common number is 240, which was selected in emulation of the 240 members of the House of Representatives of the General Court until the number of members was reduced to 160 by voter employment of the initiative and referendum in 1968.

With the exceptions of Framingham and Saugus, an RTM is a continuing body; one-third of the town meeting members are elected each year for a three-year term. Framingham and Saugus elect all town meeting members simultaneously for a two-year term.

The acceptance statute either stipulates the total number of elected town meeting members or specifies the formula to be used in determining the number of elected members. The Adams acceptance statute, for example, provides that the number of town meeting members in each precinct shall "consist of the largest number divisible by three which will admit of a representation of all precincts by an equal number of members and which will not cause the total elected town meeting membership to exceed one hundred and fifty."[24] The Amherst act stipulates that one town meeting member shall be elected for every twenty registered voters in each precinct, and the Winthrop act restricts the number of elected town meeting members in each precinct, to the largest number divisible by three that is less than 3 percent of the registered voters in the precinct.

The standard representative town meeting act mandates that the "membership shall in each precinct consist of the largest number divisible by three which will admit of a representation thereof in the approximate proportion which the number of registered voters therein bears to the total number of registered voters in the town, and which will cause the total membership to be as nearly 240 as may be."[25]

The number of women town meeting members has increased greatly since 1967, when they constituted from 3 percent to 10 percent of the total RTM membership in various towns.[26] In 1977, 40 percent of the town meeting members were women.

Vacancies

A town meeting member may resign by filing a written notification of resignation with the town clerk, which is effective upon filing. A member automatically vacates his or her office by moving from the town. If a member moves to another precinct, he or she continues to hold office until the next annual town election.

Most acts provide that a vacancy may be filled until the next annual election by the remaining members of the precinct from among the voters thereof. However, Auburn, Billerica, Chelmsford, Falmouth, Natick, Saugus, Shrewsbury, Wellesley, and West Springfield fill a vacancy with the unsuccessful candidate who received the most votes provided he or she consents to serve.

The number of vacancies caused by resignations is apparent upon examination of the ballot in a typical town; in each precinct the voters are instructed to vote for one or more candidates for a one- or two-year term to fill vacancies.

EX OFFICIO MEMBERS

Representative town meeting statutes—except in Framingham, Montague, Saugus, and Swampscott—designate or authorize the town to designate by by-law specified town officers as members *ex officio* to participate in the meeting as members at large. Although Athol is authorized to designate *ex officio* members by by-law, it has not done so.

The standard representative town meeting act authorizes the town by by-law to designate *ex officio* members, which is preferable to statutory designation, as it introduces flexibility instead of rigidity in the procedure for designating such members. The Amherst statute specifies a number of officials as *ex officio* members and authorizes the designation of other town meeting members at large by by-law.

The number of such members varies from none in sixteen towns to twenty-four in Ludlow and South Hadley. As a courtesy, most RTM statutes extend *ex officio* membership to any member of the General Court residing in the town. The number of *ex officio* members in a town varies annually with changes in membership in the General Court and the number of town offices held by an individual entitling him or her to *ex officio* membership.

The theory behind *ex officio* membership for key town officials is to ensure their presence at town meetings. The importance of having major town officials present at RTMs is apparent, yet the desirability of designating them *ex officio* members is questionable, as they undoubtedly would attend meetings as non-members and have the same right as other non-town meeting members to speak. Furthermore, they are eligible to serve as elected town meeting members.

No serious arguments have been advanced against the practice of having members at large, provided the number of such members is small. Opponents of a large number of *ex officio* members approve the designation of the moderator, town clerk, selectpersons, and chairpersons of the finance committee as *ex officio* members but oppose extending the list for fear that an administrative bloc with its better sources of information would control the meeting.

The Athol representative town meeting act resolves the problem of attendance of key town officials by stipulating that "it shall be the duty of the chairman of each board or committee of the town, elected or appointed, and the head of each department to attend throughout that part of each town meeting at which matters other than those to be acted upon and determined by ballot are to be considered."[27]

The designation by statute or by-law of specified town officials as *ex officio* members of the representative town meeting apparently is of no great consequence, as it is not unusual for such members to be elected town meeting members by the voters of their precincts. The town clerk in Belmont in 1966, for example, was both an *ex officio* and an elected RTM member. It is common practice in towns where few or no town officers are designated as *ex officio* members for the officers to be elected in their precincts as town meeting members.

TOWN EMPLOYEES AS TOWN MEETING MEMBERS

A subject of controversy is whether paid town employees should be allowed to serve as elected town meeting members. Critics occasionally maintain that town employees dominate town meetings and vote themselves higher wages and shorter working hours.

Robert J. Tilden wrote in 1957 that "it is not expected that voting trends in meetings will divide strictly along employment lines. The significant point is that many issues are carried or lost by a few votes. Every decision reached by a margin which is less than the size of the 'employee bloc' is immediately suspect. If the issue involves employee wages or benefits the vote is *prima facie* a result of self-interest. What the outcome would be if such a vote were tested in the courts is an interesting question."[28]

Should the representative town meeting not respect the wishes of the town on matters of wages and working hours, the disgruntled citizens may initiate corrective action by a petition for a referendum and at future annual town meetings elect new town meeting members to replace incumbents who do not represent the majority views of the town. Only citizen apathy can allow paid town employees to dominate a town meeting, and citizen action is the proper corrective.

A Framingham study committee investigated the charge that town employees serving as town meeting members would vote as a bloc and control the meeting. The committee concluded in 1965 that "there was no merit to the belief that town employees were exerting any great influence on the meeting."[29]

A 1967 survey of RTM towns and an examination of their records fail to reveal town meetings dominated by town employees.[30] Officers in only six RTM towns in 1996 reported that town employees exerted major influence on decisions as town meeting members. Officers in the other towns indicated that town employees did not exert undue influence.

The proposal has been made on numerous occasions that paid town employees should be made legally ineligible to serve as town meeting members. Whether the General Court possesses the constitutional power to disbar town employees from service as elected town meeting members is debatable and has not been resolved by the courts. It has been pointed out that the General Court has forbidden city employees to serve on a city council. Agreement has been reached on one point: the General Court may forbid a town employee serving as an elected town meeting member to vote on articles that personally affect him or her.

PRECINCT AND PRE–TOWN MEETING MEETINGS

Meetings were held prior to the 1996 annual town meeting in some or all voting precincts in thirteen (34%) of thirty-eight reporting RTM towns, attended by town meeting members and voters, to discuss the articles in the warrant for a forthcoming town meeting. Members of the finance committee usually attend the precinct meetings to explain the committee's recommendations.

Such meetings were sponsored by the moderator in Plymouth and Shrewsbury, by the town manager in Chelmsford, and by the finance or advisory committee, League of Women Voters, selectpersons, or taxpayers' association in the remaining towns. Attendance by registered voters other than town meeting members is very poor. However, the meeting is televised in Plymouth, and a significant number of voters may watch all or part of the meeting.

Auburn has a by-law that provides that one town meeting member in each precinct is charged with the duties of keeping town meeting members informed and calling them for meetings. The Auburn Representative Town Meeting Review Committee in 1963 recommended establishing a "cadre" of town meeting members from each precinct to promote attendance at town meetings and help educate members. The committee suggested that a copy of the finance committee's report be mailed with the warrant to each town meeting member. Furthermore, sponsors of articles and others possessing special knowledge of articles should prepare and transmit reports to the members.[31]

RTM POWERS AND PROCEDURES

The representative town meeting possesses all powers of an open meeting *ad referendum*. The acceptance statutes empower an RTM to act for, and bind, the town by stipulating that "all powers vested in the municipal corporation so far as conforms with the provisions of law now or hereafter applicable to the transaction of town affairs and town meetings shall, when taken by any representative town meeting in accordance with the provisions of this act, have the same force and effect as if such action had been taken in a town meeting by the voters of the town."

Procedures

An RTM is called and conducted in the same manner as an open town meeting, with one exception: only town meeting members may vote. The selectpersons call the meetings by the issuance of a warrant at least seven days prior to each meeting. The Supreme Judicial Court rendered an advisory opinion that "it is within the competency of the General Court to enact a law which would provide for the conducting of a representative town meeting . . . because the Selectpersons unreasonably refuse to call a town meeting.''[32] In the event the selectmen unreasonably refuse to call a town meeting, a justice of the peace upon the written petition of 100 registered voters or 10 percent of the registered voters may call a meeting by issuing a warrant, and notice must be given to town meeting members as provided by law.[33]

The issues that come before an RTM generally are similar in nature to the issues resolved by the open town meeting but differ to an extent because of the greater average population of the RTM towns. The length of the 1996 RTM annual meetings ranged from one and one-half to thirty hours. Ten RTMs held their annual meeting over a period of several days, including Arlington, which had eleven adjourned sessions in 1996.

Framingham holds ten to fifteen special town meetings per year. The other RTM towns hold one to four special meetings, with the exception of Lexington, which held no special town meeting in 1996. Chelmsford held a special town meeting within the 1996 annual town meeting. The length of the 1996 special town meetings varied from one hour to twelve hours in Amherst.

The town clerk is charged with the responsibility of notifying the members of a town meeting and is required to give them at least seven days' notice, with the exception of four towns; five days' notice is required in Falmouth and Wellesley, and three days' notice is required in Milton and South Hadley.

With the exception of Saugus, the moderator is popularly elected at the annual town meeting for a term of one or three years and serves until his or her successor is elected and qualified. The Saugus moderator is elected by the representative town meeting from its membership. The Supreme Judicial Court ruled in 1940 that the powers granted by statute to the moderator to preside and preserve order at town meetings are unaffected by the adoption of the limited or representative town meeting.[34] In the absence of the moderator, town meeting members are authorized to elect a moderator *pro tempore*. Commonly, all motions are required to be in writing. The Needham moderator expedites action at town meetings by mailing to each town meeting member prior to a meeting a letter stating that he or she as moderator considers certain specified articles routine and urges each member to review the warrant prior to the town meeting "to determine those articles which should be adopted unanimously without debate.''

In spite of an Arlington by-law providing for the use of *Robert's Rules of Order*, the Supreme Judicial Court held that a town that had accepted the standard RTM act could amend its by-laws by a majority vote of the members present regardless of the provision in *Robert's Rules* that a majority vote of the entire membership would be necessary.[35] Several acceptance statutes forbid the meeting to delay indefinitely action upon an article.

The Framingham annual town meeting on March 11, 1964, adopted a code of ethics for debate patterned after the Massachusetts conflict of interest law:

ARTICLE FIRST: Any person who is employed as an attorney, engineer, architect, land surveyor, broker, employee or in any other capacity by another interested in the Article under discussion shall disclose his or her employment before speaking thereon.

ARTICLE SECOND: Any person who has a financial interest in the Article under discussion shall disclose his or her financial interest before speaking thereon.

ARTICLE THIRD: Any person who is the spouse, parent, child, brother or sister of a person who has a financial interest in the Article under discussion shall disclose such relationship before speaking thereon.

ARTICLE FOURTH: A Town Meeting Member shall have the right to raise a "point of order" and request that the moderator inquire of the speaker whether he or she has an interest in the Article required to be disclosed by the rules of Town Meeting and if the speaker has such an interest, why it was not disclosed before speaking on the merits of the Article.

The Framingham meeting rejected a section of the proposed code that would have required any person speaking on an appropriation article to disclose "his or her vocation or principal type of employment."

Quorum. The 1915 Brookline act established a majority of the town meeting members as the quorum, and a similar quorum requirement has been established by the standard RTM act. Arlington, Belmont, Burlington, Fairhaven, and Framingham have established less than a majority as the quorum. Only four RTM towns reported an occasional quorum problem, and one town lacked a quorum at one meeting. A number of town meeting members less than a quorum is authorized to organize temporarily and adjourn from time to time.

Secret Ballots. Towns are authorized by general law to enact by-laws regulating proceedings at town meetings, and an RTM by a two-thirds vote may use secret ballots.[36] The Stoughton RTM act, however, was amended in 1960 by stipulating that all votes must be taken by standing vote or voice.[37]

Whether secret ballots should be used in a representative town meeting is a subject of considerable controversy. The Associated Fire Fighters of Massachusetts, American Federation of Labor–Congress of Industrial Organizations (AFL-CIO) in 1961 introduced a bill in the General Court forbidding the use of secret ballots at RTMs, which was amended to allow their use if two-thirds of the town meeting members vote to authorize their use; the bill was vetoed by the governor.[38] In a veto message, dated February 27, 1961, returning a similar bill, Governor John A. Volpe wrote:

The question as to whether a town should require a two-thirds vote or any other percentage to have a secret ballot is not the issue. The important and traditional right of home rule and self government in the Towns of the Commonwealth should not be interfered with and it is my sincere belief and opinion that the people of each Town should have the right as they presently do under existing statutes, to adopt such by-laws and parliamentary procedure as best meets the needs of their respective Towns. This bill, if signed by me, would violate the time honored custom of home rule.[39]

An amendment to the general laws enacted in 1963 provides that secret ballots may not be utilized unless their use is authorized by a two-thirds vote of the town meeting members present.[40]

The Massachusetts Selectmen's Association, Incorporated, introduced in 1965 a bill requiring all votes on all bond issues be by roll call vote, but the General Court referred the bill to the next annual session, a technique utilized to kill a bill without directly voting to do so.[41]

Advocates of the use of secret ballots on highly controversial articles maintain that a secret ballot is a mechanism that protects town meeting members from possible reprisals by town employees, neighbors, and others. According to a study committee, the non-use of secret ballots in Framingham resulted in the reluctance of a significant number of town meeting members to vote on important articles.[42] It also is maintained that the absence of a secret ballot provision decreases the number of candidates for town meeting members, as businessmen hesitate to seek office for fear of losing customers, and other citizens may fear incurring the wrath of their employers. Although the arguments in favor of the use of secret ballots have a degree of validity, elected representatives can be held responsible and their performance evaluated only if they vote publicly.

A survey of twenty-five representative town meeting towns in 1940 revealed there was no by-law providing for secret ballots in sixteen towns; in six towns secret ballots were used when a majority of the town meeting members voted to use them; in Ludlow secret ballots were used if the vote was questioned by seven voters or the moderator was in doubt after a second show of hands; in Fairhaven secret ballots were used if a motion to use them was supported by twenty-five town meeting members and was made prior to the vote; and in Dartmouth secret ballots were used on the demand of forty town meeting members.[43]

A survey of the forty-two representative town meeting towns in 1964 and 1965 disclosed that secret ballots seldom were used; twenty-six towns reported that secret ballots were not used, and the remaining towns indicated that secret ballots had been used on rare occasions in the past.[44] Respondents to a 1996 survey indicated that secret ballots were used infrequently in one town, on rare occasions in seven towns, and never in remaining towns.

REFERENDUM

The voters in accepting an RTM act or adopting an RTM charter did not forsake all policy-determining powers; every RTM act or charter grants voters power, with a few exceptions, to veto actions taken at a representative town meeting by means of a protest referendum. Direct democracy can override representative democracy.

The provisions for referenda vary. A referendum in many towns may be held on any action of the representative town meeting, but in other towns the use of the referendum is restricted to actions appropriating funds in excess of a specified amount. The standard RTM act allows a referendum to be held on any vote appropriating in excess of $20,000, establishing a new board or town office, merging two or more boards or offices, fixing the term of office of town officials if the term is optional, increasing or decreasing the number of members of a board, and adopting or amending a by-law.[45] To cite only one other example, Amherst voters are precluded from utilizing the referendum to reverse actions of the representative town meeting appropriating less than $5,000 or money to pay maturing bonds or notes, authorizing borrowing in anticipation of taxes, or a vote passed by two-thirds of the members as an emergency measure to preserve the peace, health, safety, or convenience of the town.[46] If voters are to control policies, a referendum should be permitted to reverse all actions of the town meeting except actions necessitated by *bona fide* emergencies.

Procedure

With the exceptions of specified actions in the acceptance statute, standard act, or town charter, no vote taken at a representative town meeting becomes effective until a specified number of days, five to ten excluding Sundays and holidays, have elapsed in order to permit circulation of petitions calling for a protest referendum. The specified period for filing a referendum petition commences with the dissolution of the town meeting regardless of the number of adjourned sessions held subsequent to the vote in question. Opponents of an action taken by a representative town meeting may collect signatures prior to the dissolution of the meeting.[47]

The procedure for holding a referendum is initiated by the filing of a petition signed by a specified number or percentage of registered voters. The percentage requirement varies from 3 percent in several towns to 25 percent in Montague. The required percentage or number of signatures in eight towns must be obtained in each voting precinct.

The standard representative town meeting act permits a referendum if 3 percent of the registered voters sign petitions within seven days of the dissolution of the meeting; a majority vote in the referendum reverses the action of the RTM, provided the majority is composed of at least 20 percent of the registered voters.[48] The Watertown and Winchester acts also specify that the RTM vote is not reversed unless the majority voting to reverse is composed of at least 20 percent of the registered voters. The stipulation of a majority composed of at least 20 percent of the registered voters is desirable, as it ensures that there is substantial town support for the reversal of the RTM action and prevents a small minority that lost at the meeting from winning its point in a referendum in which participation may be slight.

Recision of an RTM action by the voters in a referendum does not preclude the RTM from adopting a similar or identical article in a warrant for a subsequent meeting.

In drafting a representative town meeting charter provision, it clearly is preferable to express the number of signatures required to initiate a referendum in terms of a fixed percentage of the registered voters. The required percentage should not be so low that it encourages referenda on most actions of the town meeting but not be so high that it effectively prevents dissatisfied citizens from collecting the required number of signatures. Three to 5 percent of the registered voters would appear to be a reasonable requirement.

Considering the number of controversial issues resolved by representative town meetings, it is surprising there have been so few referenda. Sixteen (38%) of the forty-two RTM towns in 1965 reported they had never had a referendum.[49] In most of the remaining RTM towns referenda were uncommon, and the action of the representative town meeting usually was upheld by voters in the referenda.

A 1996 survey of thirty-eight RTM towns revealed that a referendum had never been held in twenty-three (61%) towns and was held on rare occasions in the other RTM towns. Burlington, for example, held four referenda during the previous twenty-five years. In general, the voters tend to be more economically minded than the town meeting members and reverse the vote if the RTM authorized large expenditures.

Committees

Elected town meeting members, in common with open town meeting participants, rely heavily upon the recommendations of the finance committee and the planning board in deciding how to vote on the various warrant articles. In response to a 1996 survey, town officers reported the finance committee made recommendations on all warrant articles in nineteen towns and on financial articles only in the other towns. Reading reported that elected town meeting members always accepted the committee's recommendations, and all other towns checked most of the time.

The 1996 survey revealed an identical response relative to whether the town meeting accepted the advice and recommendations of the planning board. Reading reported that its planning board's recommendations are always followed by the meeting, and the other towns indicated that such recommendations are followed most of the time.

Although a representative legislative body, an RTM traditionally lacked a system of standing committees. In 1965, a Shrewsbury town government study committee recommended the creation of standing committees of town meeting members that would allow members to become thoroughly familiar throughout the year with the town functions assigned to the jurisdiction of their respective committees. The study committee suggested the following committees be organized and composed of town meeting members: finance, streets and sidewalks, sewers, water, police department, fire department, public buildings, education, legislative matters, recreation, planning and zoning, electric power and light, personnel, public health, claims, and by-laws.[50]

The study committee also recommended that committee members be appointed by the moderator and that each town meeting member should serve on at least one committee; each precinct would have equal representation on each committee. To provide continuity, the study committee suggested that two members of each of the six precincts should serve on each committee. "A system of representation among the various committees with promotion from the less important to those of major importance might well serve to broaden the town meeting members' knowledge and sustain interest in town meeting government."[51]

One Shrewsbury department head in 1965 opposed committees of town meeting members on the grounds that they would encroach upon the prerogatives to the town manager to the point that the department heads no longer would have one superior as they currently had under the town manager system because the standing committees would be interposed between the manager and the department heads. Other Shrewsbury officials at the time were convinced that the existing boards and commissions—such as the sewer commission, lighting commission, and planning board—could function better than standing committees of town meeting members, who would promote improvements in their respective precincts rather than the overall good of the town. Surveyed officers in other RTM towns in 1965 generally believed that RTM standing committees would duplicate the work of the finance committee or usurp its functions.

Currently, the Shrewsbury by-laws direct the moderator to appoint annually three members of the finance committee to serve terms of three years, thereby ensuring that the committee is a continuing one with overlapping terms of office.[52]

Stoughton voters in a 1971 referendum approved a proposed RTM charter, effective in 1972, that continued the town manager system and created five standing committees—finance and taxation, municipal regulations, municipal operations, intergovernmental relations, and rules.[53] The finance and taxation committee is the only one to include non-town meeting members. The moderator and precinct chair each appoints one member from each precinct to serve on each committee. Stoughton's lead has been followed by Billerica and Reading.

The Stoughton charter directs that all warrant articles shall be referred automatically to the rules committee, which is composed of the moderator as chairman, deputy moderator *ex officio*, and each precinct chairman. The committee refers each article to the appropriate standing committee(s), which must hold a public hearing, study the article, and make a recommendation to the RTM. The charter specifically provides that "no floor action may be taken at town meetings without a public hearing and a standing committee report on the article."[54]

The Stoughton charter does not detail the functions of the standing committees, but their titles suggest the nature of their respective functions. To ensure that committee members meet their charter obligations, town moderator Howard Hansen in 1992 prepared *A Town Meeting Committee Guide*, which answers the most commonly asked questions about the organization and functions of the committees. The guide explains the appointment of members of the standing committees, the role of the rules committee, establishing a committee agenda and voting in committee, conduct of a public hearing, reports, pre–town meeting and precinct meetings, and duties of each committee.

Moderator Hansen is convinced that a standing committee system can be effective only if the moderator offers guidance to the committees and ensures they hold meetings and public hearings and issue reports.[55] He explained that there has been a problem relative to "the logistics of scheduling hearings so that petitioners have equal access when they are involved with more than one committee."[56]

Debate and Decision Quality

Each recipient of a 1996 questionnaire was requested to judge the quality of town meeting debate—in terms of getting explanations of budget items, exploring pros and cons of proposals, and members influencing other members' opinions on town issues—as excellent, good, fair, or poor. Officials in thirty-five towns provided ratings. Eleven (31%) respondents rated the debate as excellent, twenty-two (63%) selected good, and two (6%) selected fair.

Town officers were slightly more positive relative to the quality of RTM decisions. Officials in thirty-six towns provided ratings. Twelve (33%) graded such decisions as excellent, and twenty-four (67%) selected good. No officer rated the quality as fair or poor. The two officers who rated the quality of debate as fair judged the quality of decisions to be good. Another two officers who rated debate quality as good were convinced the quality of decisions was excellent.

Several survey respondents explained their decision quality ratings by referring to the detailed reports prepared by the finance committee and transmitted to elected town meeting members well in advance of the annual town meeting. The Adams finance committee report, for example, contains an overview of town finances, a table of the effect of budget increases on the property tax rate, town budget recommended decreases, a section on town issues, reserve fund transfers, recommendations on all financial articles, estimated tax levy, sources and uses of funds, summary of revenues and expenditures for fiscal years 1988 and 1997, excerpts from a *Guide for Representative Town Meeting Members*, prepared by Stuart DeBard of the Association of Town Finance Committees, and telephone numbers of major town offices.

RTMs IN OTHER STATES

As the population of numerous Connecticut towns became large, pressures grew for abandonment of the open town meeting in favor of a town council and a financial town meeting (see Chapter 7), a town council with plenary power, or a representative town meeting. Currently, seven Connecticut towns, Sanford (Maine), and Brattleboro (Vermont) have adopted an RTM.

With one exception, the size of Connecticut RTMs is relatively small—30 in Branford, 100 in Darien, 50 in Fairfield, 230 in Greenwich, 45 in Groton, 21 in Waterford, and 36 in Westport, which has no *ex officio* members.[57] The number of *ex officio* members is two in Branford, thirteen in Fairfield, eighteen in Greenwich, thirteen in Groton, and six in Waterford. Women constitute a significant percentage of elected town meeting members—Branford (20%), Fairfield (50%), Greenwich (30%), Groton (55%), Waterford (24%), and Westport (36%). The number of town employees who serve as elected town meeting members varies from none in Branford to four in Greenwich.

Five towns—Branford (16), Fairfield (26), Groton (21), Waterford (11), and Westport (18)—have established a quorum for the RTM to act on warning articles. No RTM town has experienced a quorum problem, and no RTM town uses secret ballots. Special town meetings are relatively uncommon, and Groton does not hold such meetings, since monthly representative town meetings are held. Questionnaire recipients reported their respective RTM followed the recommendations of the finance committee (town council in Groton) most of the time, with the exception of Waterford, where the recommendations always are adopted. The annual meeting lasts from two and one-half to twelve hours, and special meetings last one to four hours.

Voters in each Connecticut RTM town may utilize the protest referendum by filing signatures equal to 3 percent to 10 percent of the registered voters, in an attempt to reverse certain RTM decisions. A majority vote reverses an RTM decision provided it is equal to 5 percent of the registered voters in Branford, 15 percent in Groton and Waterford, 20 percent in Westport, and 25 percent in Fairfield. RTM town officers reported that no referendum had been held, with the exception of one in Fairfield, during the previous five years.

The quality of debate at Connecticut representative town meetings was rated by questionnaire respondents as excellent in Branford and Westport; good in Greenwich, Groton, and Waterford; and fair in Fairfield. The ratings of the quality of RTM decisions mirror the ratings of the quality of debate, with the exception of a good rating in Branford. According to respondents, there is general satisfaction with RTMs, and the only attempts to change the form of town government were a rejected referendum proposition in Greenwich to reduce the number of elected town meeting members and a rejected proposal in Fairfield to adopt a city charter.

Sanford (Maine) adopted a special act charter creating a representative town meeting in 1935, when its population was approximately 13,000, and the number of registered voters was approximately 8,000.[58] Sanford had a 1996 population of 20,570 and 13,103 registered voters. In 1980, the town adopted a charter providing for a continuation of the representative town meeting. Forty-three (29%) of the 147 elected members are women, and 14 (10%) are town employees. The latter play a minor role in the proceedings and decision-making by the representative town meeting. Attendance by town meeting members is approximately 90 percent at the annual town meeting and 80 percent to 90 percent at special town meetings. Secret ballots never are utilized.

The finance committee makes recommendations on all warrant articles, and the recommendations are followed most of the time by the representative town meeting. The average length of the annual town meeting is seven hours, and no special town meetings are held. Town officers rate the quality of debate as good and assign a similar rating to the quality of decisions. Although the charter authorizes voters to file petitions, signed by 5 percent of the registered voters, to initiate a referendum on the question of reversing an RTM decision, no referendum has been held. Voter satisfaction with the RTM is reflected in their decision to reject the adoption of a town council as a replacement for the representative town meeting.

Brattleboro (Vermont) voters, by a 1,293 to 749 margin, adopted a special act charter in 1960 because of the lack of an auditorium capable of accommodating all voters desiring to participate in the open town meeting and the fear that special interest groups would pack the town meeting.[59] The town in 1996 had a population of 12,141 and 7,430 registered voters. Fifty-six (43%) of the 129 elected members are women, and three (2%) are town employees who play a minor role in RTM proceedings and decision-making. Attendance by town meeting members is approximately 90 percent at the annual meeting and one special meeting held each year. All voting at the town meeting, as required by the charter, is *viva voce*, with the exception of proposed bond issues, which are decided by secret ballot.

The finance committee makes recommendations on financial articles only, and its recommendations seldom are accepted by the representative town meeting. Land use recommendations of the planning board, however, are accepted by the town meeting members most of the time. Town officers rate the quality of town meeting debate as excellent and the quality of town meeting decisions as good. The charter authorizes the filing of petitions, signed by 250 registered voters, providing for a referendum on an action taken by the RTM, but no referendum has been held. Attendance by voters other than elected town meeting members is very small at representative town meetings. Nevertheless, voters generally are satisfied with the system, as no attempt has been made since 1968 to abandon it. In 1964, voters approved a proposal for the continuance of the representative town meeting by a 1,380 to 859 margin.[60] In 1968, voters approved a proposal, 777 to 766, to return to the open town meeting but one month later reversed themselves by a vote of 954 to 701.[61]

SUMMARY AND CONCLUSIONS

Dating to 1915, the representative town meeting allows a town with a large population to retain traditional governance procedures by restricting voting at town meetings to elected town meeting members. A total of fifty-one New England towns currently have an RTM, and the number of such towns has remained relatively steady, as Massachusetts towns that abandoned it for a charter providing for a town council have been replaced by open meeting towns that adopted an RTM. Massachusetts in 1967, for example, had forty-two RTM towns and today has the same number, but the lists of such towns are not identical.

The RTM as a legislative body has failed to develop roots in Rhode Island and New Hampshire and has been adopted by only one Maine town and one Vermont town. Furthermore, its roots are not deep in Connecticut. Currently, voters in Massachusetts RTM towns are satisfied with their respective RTM, although nine towns, commencing with Agawam in 1971, abandoned town meeting governance in favor of a town council. Five of these nine towns have a town manager as the chief executive, and four have a mayor as chief executive.

Chapter 10 assesses the strengths and weaknesses of the open town meeting, the official ballot referendum type of town meeting, and the representative town meeting and draws conclusions relative to their effectiveness in terms of representing adequately their respective citizens.

NOTES

1. *A Report of the Record Commissioners of the City of Boston, Containing the Boston Records from 1700 to 1728* (Boston: Rockwell and Churchill, 1883), p. 55.
2. Ibid., pp. 56–59.
3. *A Volume of Records Relating to the Early History of Boston Containing Boston Town Records, 1784 to 1796* (Boston: Municipal Printing Office, 1903), p. 25.
4. Ibid., p. 42.
5. Ibid., p. 272.
6. Ibid., p. 274.
7. Ibid.
8. Ibid., p. 275.
9. *A Volume of Records Relating to the Early History of Boston Containing Boston Town Records, 1796 to 1813* (Boston: Municipal Printing Office, 1905), pp. 153–54.
10. Ibid., pp. 159–60.
11. *Report of the Town Convention*, February 29, 1804, pp. 1–2.
12. *A Volume of Records Relating to the Early History of Boston Containing Boston Town Records, 1814 to 1822* (Boston: Municipal Printing Office, 1906), pp. 38–42.
13. Ibid., p. 43.
14. Ibid.
15. Ibid., pp. 45–46.
16. Ibid., p. 48.

17. Ibid., p. 254.

18. Ibid., pp. 256–59.

19. *Massachusetts Special Acts of 1915*, chap. 250.

20. *Town Reports* (Brookline, Mass.: 1915), p. 74.

21. *Constitution of the Commonwealth of Massachusetts*, art. LXXXIX of the articles of amendment.

22. *Massachusetts General Laws*, chap. 43A.

23. Arlington and Brookline adopted the standard act on March 4, 1935, and March 10, 1942, respectively. See *Fitzgerald v. Selectmen of Braintree*, 296 Mass. 362, 5 N.E.2d 838 (1937).

24. *Massachusetts Acts of 1935*, chap. 235, § 2.

25. *Massachusetts General Laws*, chap. 43A.

26. Joseph F. Zimmerman, *The Massachusetts Town Meeting: A Tenacious Institution* (Albany: Graduate School of Public Affairs, State University of New York at Albany, 1967), p. 60.

27. *Massachusetts Acts of 1954*, chap. 382, § 6.

28. Robert J. Tilden, "Separation of Powers and the Representative Town Meeting," *Massachusetts Law Quarterly* 42, March 1957, p. 28.

29. *Report of the Committee Studying Changes in the Town Government* (Framingham, Mass.: March 1965), pp. 14–15.

30. Zimmerman, *The Massachusetts Town Meeting*, p. 63.

31. *Report of the Representative Town Meeting Review Committee* (Auburn, Mass.: January 14, 1963).

32. *Opinion of the Justices to the House of Representatives*, 347 Mass. 792 (1964).

33. *Massachusetts General Laws*, chap. 39, § 12.

34. *Doggett v. Hooper*, 306 Mass. 129 (1940).

35. *Blomquist v. Town of Arlington*, 338 Mass. 594 (1959).

36. *Massachusetts General Laws*, chap. 39, § 15.

37. *Massachusetts Acts of 1960*, chap. 394.

38. *Massachusetts House No. 2345*, 1961.

39. *Massachusetts House No. 2790*, 1961.

40. *Massachusetts Acts of 1963*, chap. 320.

41. *Massachusetts House No. 2240*, 1965.

42. *Report of the Committee Studying Changes in the Town Government*, p. 14.

43. "Representative Town Meetings in Massachusetts," p. 21.

44. Zimmerman, *The Massachusetts Town Meeting*, p. 69.

45. *Massachusetts General Laws*, chap. 43A, § 10.

46. *Massachusetts Acts of 1936*, chap. 10, § 8.

47. *Hinch v. Lindsey*, Essex Superior Court Docket No. 103390 (1955).

48. *Massachusetts General Laws*, chap. 43A, § 10.

49. Zimmerman, *The Massachusetts Town Meeting*, p. 72.

50. *Report of Town Government Study Committee* (Shrewsbury, Mass.: 1965), p. 8.

51. Ibid.

52. *General By-Laws of the Town of Shrewsbury* (Shrewsbury, Mass.: n.d.).

53. *Town of Stoughton, Commonwealth of Massachusetts, Town Charter*, §§ 7–14.

54. Ibid.

55. Letter to author from Stoughton, Mass., town meeting moderator Howard Hansen dated November 28, 1996.

56. Ibid.

57. Groton is unique in that it has a town manager, a nine-member town council, and a representative town meeting.

58. *Maine Special Laws of 1935*, chap. 72.

59. *Vermont Acts of 1959*, no. 302. See also Fred Stetson, "The Brattleboro Way: Is This the Future of Town Meetings?" *Vermont Life*, Spring 1989, pp. 17–18.

60. Ibid., p. 19.

61. Ibid.

Chapter 10

Democratic Law-Making

Law-making by assembled voters continues to be the distinguishing feature of most New England towns in spite of the very low voter participation, except in small towns, which contradicts the romantic stereotypical image of town meeting government. To many, it is amazing that a deliberative governance institution devised in small rural Massachusetts towns in 1630 continues to be the paramount town governance instrumentality.

The system of New England town governance was modified commencing in the late nineteenth century in a number of towns with the establishment of a finance committee to advise the town meeting. More recently, the open town meeting in fifty-one towns has been converted from a *de facto* representative body into a *de jure* one by adoption of a charter providing for a representative town meeting (RTM) in which voting on warrant articles is restricted to elected town meeting members. An additional thirty-four towns retain the town meeting only to appropriate funds. Nine Massachusetts towns, ten Rhode Island towns, six Maine towns, and two New Hampshire towns have replaced town meeting government completely with a town council possessing full legislative authority. Thirty-five New Hampshire towns and eight Vermont towns hold only a deliberative town meeting, with voters subsequently going to the polls to vote on warrant articles by the Australian or official ballot (OB). Most surprisingly, Seekonk and Webster, Massachusetts, abandoned the RTM for the open town meeting, and Hudson, New Hampshire, reverted from a town council to the primary assembly of voters.

This chapter draws upon the evidence presented in Chapters 3–8 to assess Jefferson's town meeting encomium today and the thesis that the New England open town meeting is a *de facto* representative legislative body, with a changing membership, that considers all viewpoints on warrant articles and makes decisions that generally are in the best interests of the town. Special attention is paid to the views of critics, and recommendations are advanced to make the open town meeting more participant-friendly and effective. Also evaluated are the official ballot referendum type of town meeting, the representative town meeting, and the town council as alternatives to the primary assembly. Conclusions are drawn with respect to the future of town meeting government.

CRITICISMS ASSESSED

Citizen apathy is a common charge against town meeting government and cannot be denied if attendance is an accurate barometer of such apathy. The gravitational pull of the town meeting has been diminishing over the decades, and for sundry reasons an exceptionally large percentage of the registered voters in New England open meeting towns voluntarily abdicate power that is rightfully theirs.

A related criticism is the modicum of debate on warrant articles, except highly controversial ones, as most participants sit in the meeting hall *sub silentio*. Debate, it should be noted, was not widespread in fifth-century B.C. Athens. According to M. I. Finley, "few actually exercised the right to speak in the Assembly, which did not suffer fools; it acknowledged, in its behavior, the existence of political as well as technical expertise, and it looked to a few men in any given period to lay down alternative policy lines from which to choose."[1]

The failure of the vast majority of voters, except in small towns, to attend town meetings allegedly makes it possible for special interest groups, particularly town and school district employees, to conspire to control the meetings and approve warrant articles benefiting members of these groups. This criticism finds a degree of support in our surveys of town officers in each New England state who reported that a sizable percentage of voters perceive the town meeting to be controlled by special interest groups. Although low attendance would appear to facilitate interest group control of meetings, a careful study of town meetings leads to a different conclusion relative to whether decisions are *pro bono publico* ones.

Declining Attendance

Lord James Brace wrote that meeting attendance generally was good during the latter half of the nineteenth century.[2] No regular observer of town meetings today would write such a statement in view of the lamentable decline in participation.

Table 10.1 reveals that the average weighted and unweighted percentages of registered voters participating in the 1996 annual town meetings exceeded 20.0 percent only in New Hampshire and Vermont, although the weighted average participation rate was 28.17 in Maine. A higher percentage of small towns is

Table 10.1

New England Annual Town Meeting Average Business Attendance (Percent of Registered Voters by State, 1996)

Population Range	37 Connecticut Towns	121 Maine Towns	138 Massachusetts Towns	60 New Hampshire Towns	13 Rhode Island Towns	81 Vermont Towns
499 and under	-	36.20	44.50	38.00	-	36.21
500-999	5.00	20.30	20.67	33.36	-	25.51
1,000-1,999	12.33	12.52	16.58	18.15	-	22.26
2,000-4,999	13.00	6.60	12.57	18.40	10.00	25.25
5,000-7,499	6.10	9.30	7.31	17.60	6.50	14.33
7,500-9,999	12.30	-	9.60	12.50	7.00	-
10,000-14,999	4.33	-	6.54	8.00	2.70	-
15,000-19,999	0.64	13.00	9.60	-	4.60	-
20,000-24,999	1.09	-	6.80	-	2.00	-
25,000 and over	0.90	-	3.00	14.00	6.00	-
Unweighted Average	8.80	16.32	13.72	20.00	6.54	24.50
Weighted Average	6.90	28.17	11.89	22.60	5.33	26.03

found in these northern New England states, which have made the fewest changes in the traditional town meeting form of government.

The data also indicate there is a positive correlation between the average participation rate and the two states where the powers of the town meetings have been curbed the most. In twenty-one Rhode Island towns, the annual town meeting may act only on the proposed town budget, and all other legislative matters are the province of the town council. A Rhode Island special town meeting may act only on proposed appropriations. Similarly, eight Connecticut towns have only a financial town meeting, and in many other towns the primary assembly shares power with the Board of Selectmen and the board of finance. This direct correlation is not surprising, as numerous voters apparently have concluded that the town meeting no longer addresses major issues that would attract their participation.

The unweighted average percentage of registered voters who participated in open town meetings in the six states in 1996 was 19.17, and the weighted average percentage was 16.82. As noted in the individual chapters on each state, there is isomorphic direct correlation between the population of a town and the attendance rate, with the latter declining as the population of towns increases.

The percentages of voters attending meetings are depressed by the National Voter Registration Act of 1993, which does not allow the purging of the checklist (enrolled voters) used to elect federal officers until two federal elections have been held unless there is written confirmation that registrants have changed their residence to another local government.[3] Although the act applies only to federal elections, towns are reluctant to maintain two checklists—one for elections of national officers and one for election of state and local government officers. Currently, residents who move to, and register in, another city or town will remain on the checklist in the previous place of residence for a period of time that may extend to four years unless they notify the registrar of the checklist in the previous town of residence that they have moved. Population mobility is increasing, and it is estimated that at least 10 percent to 12 percent of the voters on the checklist in the typical town are ''deadwood.'' Nevertheless, only a small minority of those eligible and residing in most towns participate in the annual primary assembly.

The growth of political apathy has been a salient characteristic of life in the twentieth century and is a reflection of a changing society that is becoming less communal in nature, as witnessed by the small number of citizens who seek election to town offices and the steep decline in participation in social clubs and voluntary activities, including the sharp decrease in the number of volunteer firemen.

Philosopher John Dewey in the 1920s commented on the principal reason for the loss of community:

The increase in the number, variety, and cheapness of amusements represents a powerful diversion from political concern. The members of an inchoate public have too many ways of enjoyment, as well as of work, to give much thought to organization into an effective public. . . . What is significant is that access to means of amusement has been rendered easy and cheap beyond anything known in the past.[4]

Lester W. Milbrath concluded in 1965 that approximately one-third of voters were apathetic and generally ''are unaware, literally, of the political part of the world around them.''[5] He added that spectator roles were played by 60 percent who did little more than observe and vote.[6]

Charles Johnson of the U.S. Bureau of the Census reported that presidential elections traditionally had low voter participation and that 50 percent of the voting-age population did not vote until 1928.[7] Only 49 percent of the registered voters cast ballots in the 1996 presidential election. Director Curtis B. Gans of the Committee for the Study of the American Electorate explained in 1997 that ''most people who are over age 45 and don't vote tend to be angry and alienated, and people under that age tend to be indifferent . . . our values have changed.''[8] It is apparent that the removal of legal barriers to voting in the United States has not removed the motivational barriers, which, on the contrary, have grown in strength.

A Connecticut moderator with thirty years' experience explained in a 1996 letter that he was uncertain what caused voter alienation in his small town, where the sense of community had been strong. He noted that ''people seem to prefer . . . the isolation of the voting booth, and the secret retention of their political acts, to the public discussion of issues and public debate over actions that directly control what their own town government does.''

An interviewed, long-serving New Hampshire town moderator was convinced in 1996 that "most people don't give a damn. They pay taxes and bitch" but do not come to town meetings. He added that it is usually the same people who attend town meeting. Similarly, an experienced Massachusetts town clerk compared current citizen dedication to the town with the dedication of twenty-five to thirty years ago: "Today there seems to be less interest in all town affairs, including town elections, committee appointments, of anything that requires personal commitment. Where once it was considered an honor to be asked to serve, today the response is 'I'm too busy' or 'what's in it for me?' Is this a general trend?"

The secular decline in town meeting attendance suggests that the primary assembly emits anti-magnetic as well as magnetic forces that assume several forms. The numerous problems encountered by rapidly growing towns and increased federal government and state government regulation of towns have lengthened significantly the typical warrant and the meeting, thereby producing participant fatigue and encouraging a significant number of voters to avoid the meeting. As the primary assembly drags on, voters gradually leave the hall as action is completed on articles of the greatest interest to them, and the number of voters making decisions on the last few articles in a long warrant often is minuscule. Numerous citizens do not wish to devote the required time to town affairs, especially when the annual meeting requires multiple sessions over a period of one week or more to consider and act on all articles.

A school superintendent in a Massachusetts suburban town who attended all town meetings for more than thirty years noted in a 1996 letter that "younger voters, when they do attend (often out-of-curiosity) get easily turned off by debate that drags, is repetitive, and seems to take forever to get to a vote. They do not come back to subsequent sessions." This comment suggests that a number of town meetings may not be participant-friendly.

The annual assembly has ceased to be a holiday and a pageant in all but the small towns and no longer performs its earlier social functions because the increased warrant length leaves no time for a town meeting supper and other social gatherings. It is not unreasonable to assume that a number of voters in the past were as interested in the social functions as the issues to be resolved at the town meeting.

The entertainment attraction of the town meeting also has declined. Long warrants undoubtedly have decreased attendance by necessitating tighter parliamentary control; towns no longer can afford the luxury of allowing the meeting to be conducted as a vaudeville show for attendees, as was the case in certain towns. Today, the meeting generally is orderly and not obstreperous and tumultuous as in the past in a number of towns.

Night meetings discourage participation by many senior citizens who, for a variety of reasons, tend not to venture outside their homes in the darkness of night in an era when the senior citizen population is growing in most towns.

"Commuteritis" is a problem in suburban towns; voters may be tired by the time they return home from work in another town or city. A related development contributing to low voter turnout at meetings is the greater mobility of citizens. New voters may have no strong attachment to the town and/or believe they are not well enough acquainted with the candidates and issues to vote intelligently.

Television is responsible for a significant decline in town meeting participation. When a choice has to be made between the meeting and one or more favorite television programs, the former is apt to be the loser as far as a significant number of voters are concerned, especially if the warrant contains primarily non-controversial articles.

The small percentage of voters participating in the primary assembly in the larger towns may be explained, in part, by residents who rationalize that their individual vote does not carry as much weight as it would in a small town, and hence their attendance at the meeting would have no effect on the ultimate decisions made. Furthermore, it is difficult to establish a sense of community in a large town where many residents do not know other residents personally as they would in a small town.

The modification of the traditional open town meeting by the creation of committees, the finance committee in particular, has contributed to the decline in town meeting attendance. Public understanding of town affairs is facilitated by the finance committee, the Argus of the primary assembly, which translates financial and other complexities into understandable terms and relieves the average townsperson of the inordinate burden of making a detailed investigation of each warrant article. In addition, the committee speeds up the decision-making process, thereby enabling the meeting to complete action on an ever-lengthening warrant in growing towns without producing voter fatigue. In other words, the committee makes the meeting more participant-friendly, which should encourage voter attendance.

Ironically, these benefits of the finance committee may, however, be offset, in part, by a decline in meeting attendance if numerous voters become convinced that their presence is not needed at the meeting because attendees will follow the published recommendations of the committee. Our 1996 survey of New England towns with open meetings reveals that the committee's recommendations are approved, with rare exceptions, all or most of the time. Our survey also reveals that townspeople generally place a similar faith in the planning board as the protector of the public's interest with respect to land use matters.

The published reports of the finance committee, planning boards, other boards and committees, and town officers generate discussion of the town meeting warrant and, combined with a "pre–town meeting meeting" in a number of towns, often lead to a tacit consensus among voters on warrant articles in advance of the annual town meeting. Where a consensus is reached on controversial articles in advance, the primary assembly may do little more than ratify the voters' pre-meeting consensus on warrant articles. Similarly, the absence of controversial warrant articles reduces the magnetic attraction of the town meeting. In either situation, voters lacking a strong commitment to the community may conclude that their interests will be protected by the finance committee, planning board, and other town officers.

Case studies in a few towns reveal psychological barriers that work against town meeting attendance. Jane J. Mansbridge studied a Vermont town (fictional name Selby) with a population of about 350 in the 1970s and reported that approximately one-quarter of her interviewees "spontaneously gave some indication that the personal, face-to-face character of the town meeting disturbed them."[9] Many persons are reluctant to speak in public and fear that their comments might be ridiculed. They also may dislike the confrontational nature of the debate on controversial warrant articles and/or fear retaliation for their views by employers and others.

Similarly, retail merchants often are reluctant to participate in a town meeting if divisive issues are listed in the warrant for fear that opponents of the merchants' views may not visit their stores to make purchases.

Also promoting the decline in meeting attendance are federal and state mandates and restraints.[10] A mandate directs a town to initiate a particular course of action that typically costs money, and a restraint forbids a town to take a specified action. In certain instances, a restraint may prove to be costly for a town if a problem has to be solved by a more expensive method. Town meetings can debate the desirability of mandates and restraints but must observe them or face financial penalties. Mandates and restraints reduce the competence of the town meeting to act on specified matters and divert town funds, thereby discouraging voter participation. Furthermore, Massachusetts statutory initiative proposition 2 1/2, which limits the real property tax rate, may discourage meeting attendance by voters interested in initiating a new program or expanding an existing one if the town is at or near its property tax limit.

In the larger towns, only the absence of a significant number of voters makes it possible for the meeting to function with reasonable efficiency and effectiveness. If all voters decided to attend, no auditorium would accommodate them, and the meeting would function with great difficulty in two or three large auditoriums connected by an intercommunications system, which is the practice in a small number of open meeting towns with very large populations. A successful campaign to increase voter participation in the larger towns would necessitate adoption of an RTM or another form of government.

A Representative Assembly?

Who attends town meetings? Do the participants mirror the socio-economic characteristics of the non-attendees? Does a group of voters exercise monopoly control of town meetings? The bulk of the participants at the typical town meeting can be termed "regulars" and are committed deeply to their respective community. With rare exceptions, "regulars" attend every annual town meeting and most special town meetings other than ones called to handle routine matters such as the transfer of funds from one account to another account. Interviews with "regulars" reveal the belief that it is their civic duty to be informed on town issues and problems and to attend town meetings. They recognize that they are performing a representational function by acting on behalf of the large number of non-participating voters. Granted the motivation of "regulars" to attend meeting may not always be altruistic or public-regarding, it is apparent that they take the civic responsibilities seriously.

Whether participants mirror the population depends, in part, upon the degree of socio-economic homogeneity in the town. Surveys reveal that attendees significantly overrepresent the middle-age and older voters and that young voters have an exceptionally low attendance rate. This finding comports with survey findings with respect to those who cast ballots for candidates in national, state, and local elections. Young voters tend to shun the polls, and it is unrealistic to anticipate that these persons will have a high participation rate at town meetings.

Mansbridge found that blue-collar workers constituted approximately one-third of the population of Selby and had a low town meeting attendance rate compared to wealthier citizens.[11] She specifically noted "that the old-timers, the villagers, the elderly, the middle class, and the self-confident are somewhat more likely to attend than are their neighbors."[12] It is important to recognize that her study involved a very small Vermont town with a significant low-income population.

Milton Kotler reported that "the native-born, Protestant, self-employed and professional, educated and middle-aged and older citizens" were the "regulars" who dominated town meetings in the 1970s in Springfield, Vermont, which had a large industrial worker population.[13] Nevertheless, he concluded that the town meeting "is still a freer, more egalitarian, and politically-educative way to govern" than any alternative form of local government.[14]

Professor Frank Bryan of the University of Vermont and his students observed 1,215 town meetings in 210 Vermont towns under 4,500 population between 1970 and 1994. He concluded that there is no "systematic class bias in town meeting attendance" and commented that "[t]he very well off are as apt to be absent from town meeting as the very poor."[15]

Professor Bruce C. Evans of Susquehanna University studied the representativeness of town meeting attendees in rural Chesterfield (1,000) and suburban Wilbraham (12,000), Massachusetts, and found that there were no statistically significant differences between participants and non-participants.[16] Specifically, he reported that participants "were significantly different from those who did not [attend] on the basis of their interest in public affairs."[17] Attendees followed and discussed national and local affairs more often than non-attendees. Evans is convinced that decisions on town policies would not have been different if the non-attendees had participated in the town meetings.[18]

In Wilbraham, the socio-economic characteristics of the "regulars" and the non-attendees were very similar, with the latter more apt to be slightly older, retired, and recipients of a slightly higher income. In Chesterfield, participants and non-participants were nearly mirror images of each other. Both towns are relatively homogeneous in population composition, which is typical of suburban bedroom towns and rural agricultural towns. Industrial towns such as Springfield, Vermont, have a relatively large blue-collar population, which generally is lacking in the suburban and rural towns.

Special Interest Groups

In common with group pressure brought to bear on a city council, supporters also are mobilized by a special interest group to attend the town meeting whenever articles of interest are included in the warrant. For certain groups, such articles appear in every annual meeting warrant and occasionally in special meeting warrants. For other groups, articles of interest appear on the warrant occasionally. No special interest group is concerned with all warrant articles, although a taxpayers' association, if there is one, will be concerned with any article that directly or indirectly increases town spending.

The annual primary assembly of voters should be the epicenter of the town's universe. If a perception exists that the meeting is controlled by a small clique or dominated by powerful interest groups, a portion of the electorate will be discouraged from attending because of their belief that the meeting would be a waste of time and that their presence would not change decisions that will be made on warrant articles.

A Concord, Massachusetts, town meeting study committee reported in 1996 that a number of citizens were convinced that town boards and committees and the town meeting, to a lesser extent, were controlled by a small group of citizens and that the meeting, to a large extent, was simply a confirmation assembly for decisions made in advance.[19] Our survey of New England towns with open meetings produced results that appear to support the latter perception as to previous decisions since the overwhelming number of respondents indicated that their respective town meetings always or most of the time followed the recommendations of the finance committee and the planning board. Furthermore, numerous town officers reported that there is a commonly held citizen belief that the town meeting is dominated by special interest groups. These officers, however, are convinced that this perception is not reality.

A Massachusetts superintendent of town schools described in a 1996 letter how he would employ telephone banks of a local business firm, staffed by volunteers, to urge school supporters to attend the primary assembly whenever an education article of major importance appeared on the warrant. He was convinced that approval of such an article was in the best interest of the town and that extra efforts had to be made by those who believed in the importance of education to ensure that the article was approved. Granted that his organized effort can be described as pressure group action, there is no evidence that such action did not benefit the town.

Sociologists long have had an interest in community power studies. Robert and Helen Lynd, for example, conducted studies in Muncie, Indiana, in the 1920s and 1930s that led to the development of a stratification theory that holds that a community is stratified into groups with distinct socio-economic characteristics and that an economic elite controls decision-making.[20] The findings of an elite power group in cities by sociologists did not attract the attention of most political scientists until sociologist Floyd Hunter published in 1953 a study of Atlanta, Georgia, and identified bankers, manufacturers, and other businessmen as the elite power influentials who controlled the city.[21]

Political scientist Robert Dahl of Yale University was critical of the reputational methodology of the sociologists who asked interviewees to identify individuals who wielded influence in the city and decided to undertake a study of decision-making in New Haven, Connecticut. His book, *Who Governs?*, served as the basis for the theory of pluralism, which posits that there is no power elite in a city and that the decision-making process is open to all groups.[22] Dahl found that the influential groups varied over time according to the issue.

No empirical evidence has been uncovered in New England towns to support the elite theory, but ample evidence supports the theory of pluralism. The finding of factions at town meetings is not a revelation even in relatively homogeneous towns in terms of the socio-economic composition of the population. Factionalism may be geographically based, as in Swanzey, New Hampshire, which contains population clusters in East Swanzey, Swanzey Center, and West Swanzey, and voters tend to look out for the interests of their respective part of the town. More commonly, factionalism develops relative to proposed spending and its impact on the property tax rate. Our surveys reveal that the views of longtime residents often tend to differ on certain subjects from the views of the newer residents. If the latter have young children, interest in improving schools will be high in contrast to older residents who have no school-age children.

The open town meeting allows any resident to organize a group of voters to attend the town meeting and offset ''special interests,'' who tend to be identified as town employees, the school lobby, firemen, policemen, and taxpayers' association. Such a newly organized group, of course, is a special interest group.

The critical challenge to town meeting democracy is to minimize the ability of a special interest group to control a meeting or major warrant articles, thereby negating the preferred policies of the majority of the townspeople. In practice, there has been an effective antidote to pressure groups, and that antidote is the committee system. The expertise brought to the town meeting by the finance and planning committees in particular is an effective offset to special interest groups.

If the low participation rate is responsible for allowing special interest groups to make major decisions that are not in the best interests of the town, we should expect to see *pari passu* special town meetings called by voter petitions to reexamine the decisions and possibly modify or repeal them. In fact, special town meetings seldom are called by voters, according to our surveys. An example of such a rare meeting is one called by 262 Hillsborough, New Hamp-

Table 10.2
Quality of Debate (New England Annual Town Meetings, 1996)

	Excellent		Good		Fair		Poor	
State	#	%	#	%	#	%	#	%
Connecticut	8	14	34	58	12	20	5	8
Maine	19	13	91	64	23	16	10	7
Massachusetts	29	25	89	57	25	16	3	2
New Hampshire	13	18	39	55	16	23	3	4
Rhode Island	2	17	5	41	3	25	2	2
Vermont	18	18	60	60	20	20	2	2

shire, voters in 1997 for the purpose of reconsidering a decision of a recently held special town meeting siting a new town community center.[23] Residents of the area where the center would be constructed argued that it would lower real property values, endanger children who play in the road, and generate noise in a quiet residential neighborhood. Petitioners suggested three alternative sites.

Critics assume that special interest groups control town meetings without examining the quality of town meeting debate and decisions. Table 10.2 contains town officers' judgment of the quality of 1996 town meeting debate in terms of explanations of budget items, exploring pros and cons of proposals, and "neighbors influencing neighbors' opinions on town issues."

It is apparent that the majority of responding town officers believe that 1996 town meeting debate was of excellent or good quality. The unweighted average excellent rating was 17.5 percent, and the weighted average excellent rating was 18.3 percent. The unweighted average good rating was 56.0 percent, and the weighted average good rating was 59.1 percent.

Table 10.3 lists the ratings by town officers of the quality of 1996 town meeting decisions. The evaluations of decision quality were higher than the evaluation of debate quality. The unweighted average excellent rating for decision quality was 20.6 percent, and the weighted average excellent rating was 21.3 percent. The unweighted average good rating for decision quality was 64.6 percent, and the weighted average good rating was 67.7 percent.

PARTICIPANT-FRIENDLY TOWN MEETINGS

Town meetings are not always propitious, in the view of many eligible participants, and this fact accounts, in part, for the typical low attendance. Voters new to a town and newly registered voters often may find the primary assembly unfriendly if they lack experience in an open town meeting and no efforts are made by the town to inform voters of town meeting procedures. Hartland, Vermont, town clerk Clyde A. Jenne commented in 1996 that he "noticed that people do not know how to act in a town meeting. They no longer rise to speak or wait to be recognized by the moderator."

Table 10.3
Quality of Decisions (New England Annual Town Meetings, 1996)

	Excellent		Good		Fair		Poor	
State	#	%	#	%	#	%	#	%
Connecticut	12	19	42	67	9	24	0	0.0
Maine	36	26	92	65	10	7	3	2.0
Massachusetts	28	18	109	68	22	14	1	0.6
New Hampshire	16	24	47	69	4	27	1	7.0
Rhode Island	3	20	7	47	4	27	1	6.0
Vermont	18	17	75	72	11	11	0	0.0

Prolonged debates, extraneous questions, and a long meeting warrant tend to discourage townspeople from participating in future primary assemblies. Adjourned meetings in large towns over the course of two or three weeks to complete action on the warrant depress voter participation to a great extent.

A relatively brief debate-less "pre–town meeting meeting," held on a Saturday or a Sunday afternoon, would be of particular value to new voters, who would be provided the opportunity to question town officers, boards, and committees and gain a better understanding of warrant articles. In addition, town meeting procedures could be explained, and a copy of the moderator's rules of procedure made available. Such a meeting should be publicized widely in advance and broadcast by a local radio station and the community access television channel, if there is one.

The tone of town meeting government is set, in part, by individual town officers, boards, and committees. The Concord study committee reported that a number of citizens complained they "were not well received at committee and board meetings."[24] Recognizing decision-making at town meeting is the product of extensive research by town officers, boards, and committees, and the committee concluded that all public hearings should be conducted in a manner that welcomes all citizens and that the schedule should allow sufficient time for all meetings and public hearings to permit residents to offer comments and raise questions.[25]

Actions can be taken by a town and volunteer citizen groups, such as the League of Women Voters, to facilitate voter participation in town meetings. Assistance should be made available in advance of a meeting to voters desiring to have an article placed in the warrant. In Massachusetts, the Bedford moderator appointed a three-member citizen advisory committee to help citizens draft warrant articles in proper form. A similar action has been taken by the Lexington moderator, who holds a conference in advance of the town meeting to which all article submitters, including town officers and citizens, are invited to attend. In Belmont, the town administrator and the town counsel review all petitions and motions and, with the permission of petitioners, may revise a petition without requiring the submittal of a new petition.

The town moderator has broad discretion relative to the length of debate on an article and the ruling out-of-order of extraneous statements and questions. The moderator should channel the discussion to facilitate decision-making by participants in the shortest amount of time. A very experienced former New Hampshire moderator explained in a 1996 interview that his town meeting typically was concluded within ninety minutes in contrast to a similar neighboring town, which held three to four recessed meetings due to the inexperience of the moderator. This view was reinforced by a newspaper report of the 1997 Rutland, Massachusetts, annual town meeting, where Leonard Gengel of the Economic and Industrial Development Committee asked school superintendent Tutela why a new high school was needed. The critical reporter wrote:

Never mind that there was no article on the warrant that had anything to do with a new high school. Never mind that residents may attend any school committee or school building study committee meeting and ask that same question. Never mind that there will be public hearings . . . to discuss that very subject before anyone is asked to vote on it.

And, most importantly, never mind that Gengel acknowledged, that even as he asked the question, that he already knew the answer and was asking just to give Tutela the opportunity to provide information to others in the hall. . . .

This was not democracy in action. It was democracy inaction.[26]

Voter participation can be increased by the provision of child and elder care and free transportation to and from the meeting hall. In Uxbridge, Massachusetts, members of the high school National Honor Society baby-sit under parental supervision during the town meeting to allow parents of young children to participate. Similarly, elder care makes it possible for a voter to participate in the meeting if he or she has been providing care for an elderly relative who needs continuous supervision or care. Shirley, Massachusetts, offers free transportation to and from the town meeting for senior citizens, and all citizens are informed in advance that the meeting will terminate by approximately 10:00 P.M. The Concord, Massachusetts, Council on Aging arranges free transportation for senior citizens to and from town meetings. This committee in 1996 commended the Girl Scouts for providing in-home child care and recommended that the administration of the Concord-Carlisle High School should be requested to consider granting community service credits to high school students who organize and provide child care services under adult supervision.[27]

State law requires the posting of the town meeting warrant or warning in several public places. The majority of voters, however, do not visit these places as they travel to and from work and shopping. To increase voters' knowledge of the warrant and the importance of attending the town meeting, the Monterey, Massachusetts, town clerk in 1991 persuaded the town meeting to mail a copy of the warrant to every registered voter. Subsequently, attendance at special town meetings has been larger.

No day of the week or hour of the day will be convenient for all town voters. Weekday town meetings exclude many voters who work outside the town as well as in-town workers unable to take the full day or half day off from work or to afford to take the time off with a loss in pay. Weekday evening meetings present similar problems in view of the many activities townspeople engage in during this time period, discourage attendance by elderly citizens, and also involve conflicts with favorite television programs. An alternative is the scheduling of the annual town meeting for a Sunday afternoon in the spring when there are no major athletic games, such as professional football, on television. If the warrant cannot be acted upon totally in one afternoon, a recessed or adjourned meeting could be held the following Sunday afternoon.

A consent calendar can speed up markedly the town meeting and allow more time for discussion and debate on controversial articles. This calendar commonly is used in representative legislative assemblies and, at a town meeting, could include only non-controversial articles with the exceptions of petitioned articles and, in certain cases, zoning by-law amendments. The 1996 Concord, Massachusetts, town meeting had a twelve-article consent calendar, but one article was removed from the calendar at the request of five participants. The remaining articles were acted upon in approximately one-quarter of an hour, thereby reducing the number of articles for individual action from fifty-five to forty-four.

Also in Massachusetts, the Brewster town meeting uses a consent calendar as the first order of business, and the rules stipulate: "If any voter has doubt about passing any motion, SAY IN A LOUD, CLEAR, VOICE WHEN THE NUMBER IS CALLED."[28] The moderator will inquire whether the request is for a question or for debate. If the latter is the case, the article is removed from the calendar and restored to its original warrant position to be acted upon in the customary manner.

The Princeton, Massachusetts, moderator placed an article in the 1997 warrant requesting voters to authorize him at future town meetings to declare a two-thirds majority vote, when such a vote is required, without taking a count to speed up completion of action on warrant articles. His article was amended to allow for a counted vote whenever any participant requested it and was approved by the meeting.

Individual voters may have a special interest in certain articles and do not wish to attend the entire meeting. Many citizens in Burlington, Massachusetts, watch live television coverage of the town meeting and come to the meeting when articles of interest are about to be considered. If all eligible townspersons were present at one time, the auditorium would not be able to accommodate them.

An alternative method to facilitate voter attendance when articles of interest are under consideration is to announce and publicize well in advance the approximate times at which specified high-interest articles will be taken up by the meeting. Should the meeting progress more quickly than anticipated with respect to the early articles, other low-interest articles could be considered to fill the time until the next high-interest article is scheduled to be acted upon.

The 1996 Concord study committee recommended that "a town meeting procedure resource" person should be appointed to answer the procedural questions of participants during a meeting.[29] Lack of knowledge of procedures deters many attendees, particularly new ones, who wish to offer a motion but are reluctant to interrupt the moderator to ask a procedural question that would disrupt the meeting's flow. There is, of course, the rare possibility that the advice of the resource person may not be identical to the moderator's advice, and a motion would be ruled out of order by the moderator.

This study committee also recommended a town meeting held on a weeknight should commence at 7:00 P.M. and that no new article should be considered after 10:00 P.M.[30] The committee's report noted that late-night sessions exact a physical toll on participants and also make it difficult to schedule other commitments to allow attendance at the meeting.

As noted, critics allege that a significant number of voters boycott town meetings because they do not wish to have to declare in public their views on controversial warrant articles or that attendees may not wish to have their votes known on such articles at the meeting. In many towns they may be unaware that a secret ballot vote can be taken on any warrant article. The Concord study committee acknowledged that secret ballot procedures are not known widely and that "[m]any voters, looking at the length of time a standing 'head-count' requires, are extremely reluctant to request a secret ballot, particularly when to do so would require a majority vote of the meeting."[31] In consequence, the committee suggested that a secret ballot should be taken on an article if a petition is signed by twenty-five voters at the meeting or if a request is made immediately prior to the vote on the article in question, and a minimum of twenty-four additional voters stand in support of the request.

The invention of the microphone and loudspeaker led to their rapid adoption in the larger towns to ensure that attendees could hear all announcements and debates and be heard when they spoke. A participant wishing to ask a question or offer comments typically walks to the microphone on the meeting floor and waits to be recognized by the moderator. The result is a mixture of pro and con statements on issues waiting to be made, which makes it difficult for the moderator to guarantee that speakers on each side of an issue have an equal amount of time. A preferable approach is the use of pro and con microphones, which allows the moderator to allocate equal time to the two sides.

The annual town meeting could be shortened considerably in the larger towns if biannual meetings were held, with one meeting held at the traditional time in the spring and the other meeting in the autumn. The first meeting might be a financial meeting only with the possibility of adding emergency articles to the warrant. All other actions could be taken at the autumn meeting or a special town meeting(s). Voters, however, should retain the right to add articles to the spring meeting warrant by petition but could be encouraged by town officers to reserve such articles for the autumn meeting or possibly a special town meeting.

The Concord study committee stressed the importance of the appointment of a communications committee that would be responsible for devising and implementing a communications master plan designed to facilitate the transmission of information on all facets of town government to the citizenry as quickly and fully as possible.[32] The committee's report advocated (1) appointment of a media specialist with specific responsibility for facilitating implementation of the plan, which would include radio and television broadcasts of meetings of the Board of Selectmen, (2) publication of a weekly calendar of events to be posted in various public places, broadcast by radio and channel 8 and included in the Concord World-Wide Web home page, (3) production of a town meeting procedures videotape and a warrant article preview videotape to be available on a loan basis from the town and school libraries, and (4) making important public town documents accessible by the Internet.

Moreover, the committee highlighted the importance of the periodic review of all procedures surrounding town meetings, including placement of articles in the warrant, town elections, and activities of boards and committees.[33] Such a review would be responsive to the complaints and suggestions of citizens, lead to the adoption of changes to make the meeting more informative and shorter, and encourage voter attendance.

Voters dissatisfied with a major annual town meeting decision may petition for the holding of a special town meeting to reconsider most actions taken at the earlier meeting, yet few such special meetings have been held. Their relative lack can be interpreted as evidence that the overwhelming majority of townspeople are satisfied with town meeting decisions, but it is possible that dissatisfied voters may perceive that the meeting is controlled by an elite group and that a special town meeting called to reconsider an earlier decision would be no more than a ratification assembly.

An alternative is the adoption of the protest referendum delaying the implementation of a town by-law, except emergency ones, for a period of time during which voters may petition for the holding of a referendum on the question of repealing the by-law.[34] This participatory device does not involve the convening of a special town meeting, which typically has a small attendance, as the voters go to the polls to vote on the question of repealing the previous decision. The protest or citizen referendum first was authorized by South Dakota in 1898, along with the initiative, to ensure that the state legislature would be responsive to the will of the voters. Where employed, signatures of 2 percent to 15 percent of the registered are required for its use.

The Massachusetts General Court enacted special acts authorizing Hopkinton and Millbury voters to employ the protest referendum to reconsider town meeting decisions. In Millbury, the protest referendum is invoked if 3 percent of the registered voters in each precinct sign petitions.[35] The protest referendum is invoked in Hopkinton by petitions signed by 10 percent of the town's registered voters but may not be used to reconsider a vote to adjourn or to borrow funds in anticipation of tax revenues.[36]

Currently, voters in Connecticut towns with town meetings by petitions—200 voters or 10 percent of the registered voters, whichever is less—may force a referendum on any warrant article.[37] The New Hampshire statutes authorize a limited form of a protest referendum; that is, twenty owners of 20 percent of either the land area or lots may call for a referendum on a change in land use regulations adopted by a town.[38]

According recognition to the fact that unusual circumstances might prevent a faithful participant from attending a town meeting, the Concord study committee suggested that the town meeting should consider the possibility of limited proxy voting, which is employed by a number of representative legislative bodies.[39] Under this proposal, a voter would be authorized to designate another registered voter to act as a proxy at a specified town meeting, but no voter would be authorized to exercise more than one proxy. A proxy authorization form would have to be signed by a voter contemplating absence from town on the meeting day and filed in advance with the town clerk.

THE OFFICIAL BALLOT REFERENDUM SYSTEM

The neoteric trend toward the use of the Australian (official) ballot referendum to decide all warning articles in Bennington, Poultney, Pownal, Rutland, Shelburne, Shrewsbury, West Rutland, and Winooski, Vermont, and certain warning articles in sixty-six other Vermont towns and to decide all warrant articles in thirty-five New Hampshire towns is a significant one that fundamentally changes traditional open town meeting government from participatory democracy to plebiscitary democracy and suggests that a majority of voters prefer the privacy of the polling booth to the public declaration of their votes in the open town meeting.[40] Although Londonderry and Newmarket, New Hampshire, did not adopt the official ballot (OB) referendum statute, each town adopted a state statute providing for the amendment of their charters to authorize voting by official ballot referendum at the election polls on all or certain matters required by general law to be addressed by the annual or a special town meeting.[41] These matters include the annual town budget and transfer of funds among accounts.

As explained in Chapter 4, enactment of the OB referendum statute by the New Hampshire General Court (state legislature) is attributable to the pressure applied by the Granite State Taxpayers Association, which was convinced that major financial decisions should not be made by school district or town meetings attended by a small fraction of the registered voters. In the association's view, the official ballot referendum would increase sharply the rate of voter participation in town meeting decision-making.

Representative Betsey L. Patten, vice chair of the House Municipal and County Government Committee, chaired a subcommittee that surveyed in 1997 voter reactions to the OB referendum system in fifteen OB towns. Admitting that the survey was not scientific, the representative reported that nearly 80 percent of interviewed OB voters believed that they were informed sufficiently to make discriminating decisions on warrant articles and that more than 90 percent indicated they had sufficient time to read the ballot articles prior to voting.[42] Only 16 percent of the interviewed OB voters stated they disliked the system.[43] Limited experience with the OB referendum system suggests it probably will be repealed by few towns because of the difficulty of obtaining the required 60 percent majority vote but will be adopted in the future by other towns where the Granite State Taxpayers Association is strong.

The effect of the OB referendum system in New Hampshire is to destroy the traditional open town meeting and replace it with a referendum voting system that had a 1997 weighted average participation rate of only 27.7 percent of the registered voters, which increased slightly to 31.1 percent in 1998 because of a relatively higher average participation of voters in towns utilizing the SB2 system for the first time in 1998. In general, voter participation declined between 1997 and 1998 in the original OB towns with the sharpest decline, approximately 7 percent, in Charlestown and Sandown. It is too soon to draw definitive conclusions, but it appears that voter interest in the system will decline as its novelty wears off.

Voters participating in an SB2 town meeting on average are not as well informed on complex issues as voters who attend traditional open town meetings. Furthermore, the OB ballot referendum also facilitates private-regarding voting by townspeople so predisposed who at open meeting would be reluctant to display their private interests or would not attend the primary assembly. In addition, this town meeting variant allows the very small minority of voters who attend the deliberative session to amend individual budget articles by reducing amounts sharply or to zero. Of great concern is the potential for use of the OB referendum by special interest groups with ample funds to exert an undue influence on the minority of voters who go to the polls to make decisions on warrant articles that may result in policies not in the best interests of the town.

THE REPRESENTATIVE TOWN MEETING

As explained in Chapter 9, forty-two Massachusetts towns, seven Connecticut towns, one Maine town, and one Vermont town have replaced the open town meeting with a representative town meeting (RTM), which also is known as a limited town meeting since voting is limited to elected town meeting members. Interestingly, 121 Massachusetts towns with an open meeting have a population exceeding the population of Lee (5,798), which is the smallest RTM town.

The theory of the representative town meeting for large towns is supported by logic, yet it is ironic that the system has been beset by major and minor problems in most towns and generally has not been a panacea for the problems of the open town meeting that had been anticipated when the first RTM was adopted by Brookline, Massachusetts, voters in 1915.

The lack of candidates for town meeting members in certain voting precincts in most RTM towns, quorum problems at special town meetings, and the modicum of debate have disturbed students of town government.

Lack of Candidates

The number of candidates for the office of town meeting member is small and frequently is only equal to, or less than, the number of town meeting members to be elected. Only on rare occasions are there two candidates for each position. The number of candidates would be even less except for the active recruitment of candidates by the town clerk and/or other town officers. Experience indicates that the number of candidates for town meeting members in most RTM towns declines with the passage of time.

The most commonly advanced proposal to solve the problem of the relative lack of candidates is a reduction of the size of the RTM so as to increase the number of electoral contests for membership. Currently, the number of town meeting members varies from 50 in Saugus to 429 in Fairhaven, Massachusetts. The voters in the latter town defeated a 1994 referendum proposal to reduce the size of the RTM, as did Framingham voters in 1997.

A second approach to increasing the number of candidates is to reduce the number of town meeting members elected in each precinct and provide for the election of additional town meeting members at large equal in number to the total number of precinct members eliminated. A third possibility is to elect all members at large, which would take advantage of the surplus of candidates in certain precincts. A fourth alternative is a charter provision establishing an earlier date for the filing of petitions for election of precinct town meeting members and authorizing the election of one at large member for each precinct where no candidate has filed a petition for election. Admittedly, this alternative establishes a cumbersome procedure that might be subject to misunderstanding.

Attendance Problems

Town meeting members, in theory, should be more conscientious than other townspeople in attending town meetings, as the former have accepted a civic responsibility by seeking public office. Nevertheless, the representative town meeting has experienced attendance problems at adjourned sessions of the annual meeting and special meetings. Attendance at the annual meeting usually is good if action on the warrant is completed in one evening.

The RTM appears to have operated most satisfactorily in terms of attendance during its early years in a town when interest was high. The reluctance of voters to seek election as town meeting members undoubtedly contributes to the attendance problem, as certain town meeting members apparently lack strong interest in their offices or are very busily engaged in their professions and business firms and were persuaded to seek election by one or more town officers.

A number of towns print the attendance record of town meeting members in the town's annual report in the hope that members will be shamed into attending RTM meetings. Winthrop, Massachusetts, followed this practice and believed that the system was working well until it was discovered that certain members were attending only long enough to have their presence recorded.

In Connecticut, the town clerk calls a special meeting of the town meeting members in a precinct to vote on the question of declaring a seat vacant if the incumbent failed to attend three consecutive meetings. This practice merits serious consideration by Massachusetts RTM towns experiencing attendance problems but desiring to retain a relatively larger RTM.

Quality and Quantity of Debate

The quality of debate at representative town meetings generally is superior to that which takes place at an open town meeting. Extraneous materials and personalities seldom are interjected into the debates. As one would anticipate, the average representative town meeting member is better informed than the average participant in an open town meeting, thereby raising the level of debate. Our survey of officers in RTM towns revealed that debate quality was rated as excellent or good.

One complaint directed against the RTM is the relative absence of debate and the number of town meeting members who attend but never or seldom participate in the debates. There are three major explanations for the modicum of debate.

Debates tend to be limited if many issues have been settled prior to the town meeting as the result of informal meetings and study and consideration of the finance committee's report and recommendations.

Certain town meeting members, especially newly elected ones, may have concluded they are not acquainted sufficiently with major issues to participate in genuine debate. Others may believe their forensic ability is limited.

A town meeting member may be overwhelmed when presented with a town budget of several million dollars. He or she possesses the authority to approve, increase, or reduce the items in the budget but in practice may lack independent and reliable information other than what is provided by the finance committee, which has been scrutinizing town finances over the past year or longer. Consequently, a member may decide that he or she is not in a position to question seriously the committee's recommendations.

RTM Tenacity

Professor William B. Munro prophesied in 1937 that the representative town meeting was a step toward the ultimate, namely, a city government.[44] Technically, his forecast has proven to be inaccurate, as no town has abandoned the RTM by adopting a city charter. *De facto*, however, the prophecy is accurate since nine Massachusetts towns replaced the RTM with a town council. Five of these towns have an elected mayor who is the chief executive, and four towns have an appointed town manager as the chief executive. These towns, in effect, have a form of city government but retain the name "town" because, according to the chair of the Amesbury Charter Commission, the term "describes the community. . . . The name city gives you a picture of a large community that is overcrowded with big high rise buildings and a lot of crime."[45]

Abandonment of the RTM is attributable principally to factors other than disappointment with it as the legislative body. The mayor of Easthampton, a former selectman, explained that the adoption of a "mayor/town council form of government was not necessarily driven by an aversion to town meeting. The principal reason was to provide a single person (mayor), elected by the voters, who could be held accountable for the direction and success of the community."[46]

Amesbury's abandonment of the RTM is ascribed by observers to friction between nine town managers and the Board of Selectmen over the previous fifteen years, which involved, among other things, "an ugly firing of the police chief in 1991 which led to a long-running legal battle (and the reinstatement of the chief)."[47]

The number of Massachusetts RTM towns has remained constant at forty-two since 1966 in spite of its abandonment by eight towns, since an equal number of open meeting towns adopted the RTM. Seekonk, Massachusetts, abandoned the RTM and reverted to an open town meeting because a majority of town voters had become convinced that any citizen sufficiently interested in attending a town meeting should be able to vote on the warrant articles.[48] Webster, Massachusetts, also decided to change from the RTM to an open town meeting.

Framingham, Massachusetts, has a current population of approximately 63,000 and has been subject to growing pressure to adopt a city charter in place of the representative town meeting. Voters in 1996, by an overwhelming margin, approved the election of a commission to draft a new charter, and pro-city advocates secured a majority of the commission seats.[49] The electorate, however, on April 8, 1997, rejected a proposed city charter by a 68 percent to 32 percent margin. The RTM on May 8, 1997, defeated a proposal to reduce its size from 204 to 136 in an effort to increase the percentage of members who attend each RTM. During the debate on this proposal, Philip Frank stated: "If you want to increase the attendance you should raise the size to 300, and then you might have 204."[50]

Voters apparently are satisfied with the decisions made by their respective RTMs, since they have reserved to themselves the right to exercise the protest referendum but seldom do. Furthermore, abandonment of the RTM has involved only a small number of towns.

The RTM is not a perfect instrument of representation, but neither is its alternative: a city or town council. Although beset with certain problems, the RTM is a mechanism that has adapted town meeting government successfully to the larger towns by facilitating the conduct of business by a relatively large number of citizens and reducing the influence of cliques and interest groups.

CONCLUSIONS

Philosophers have been critical of ordinary citizens serving as a legislative assembly and have feared that deliberative democracy would develop into an ocholocracy. Plato, for example, favored a small group of philosophers as the rulers. Pericles, on the other hand, had "a vision that exalted the individual within the political community; it limited the scope and power of the state, leaving enough space for individual freedom, privacy, and the human dignity of which they are a crucial part."[51]

Classical representative government confines the voters to an exceptionally limited, irregular, and principally passive role in the governance process. Political theorist Benjamin R. Barber in 1984 criticized representative government in the following terms:

A well-known adage has it that under a representative government the voter is free only on the day he casts his ballot. Yet even this may be of dubious consequence in a system where citizens use the franchise only to select an executive or judicial or legislative elite that in turn exercises every other duty of civic importance. To exercise the franchise is unhappily also to renounce it. The representative principle steals from individuals the ultimate responsibility for theory values, beliefs, and actions.[52]

Critics assume, without evidence, that the relatively small percentage of the registered voters attending town meetings skews decisions in favor of their private or personal interests and that an elected council would protect the public interest. However, law-making by elected town councillors may foster the illusion that all proposals receive careful scrutiny prior to their approval, amendment, or rejection. While giving the appearance of relative simplicity as a political institution, representative government permits the manipulation of voters. Furthermore, voters who neglected their town meeting responsibilities probably will be no more conscientious in studying the records and views of candidates for election to a town council.

The open town meeting is predicated on the theory that ordinary voters possess the native intelligence to weigh the pros and cons of an issue and the political acumen to make wise decisions and attend meetings out of self-interest to ensure decisions benefit the polity. In other words, the theory is based on an implicit belief in the collective wisdom of assembled voters. We agree with Lowell's 1909 conclusion that debates help the participants in a town meeting to make better decisions, as discussion is an essential preliminary to decision-making on complex issues.[53]

Our evidence supports this theory and highlights the fact the open town meeting is a *de facto* representative legislative body. The meeting increasingly serves as a representative assembly as the population of a town grows, since the relationship between the population size of a town and the percentage of voters participating in a town meeting is isomorphic, with the percentage generally declining as the population size increases.

The leitmotifs of the primary assembly are openness and equality. Majoritarian government is possible at any time. Even the most apathetic voter is invited to participate, as there are no legal barriers to participation, and his or her vote is weighted equally with the vote of a regular attendee. Our study reconfirms the 1835 conclusion of Emerson that town meeting government permits all voters, rich or poor, to counsel the assembly.[54]

We should discard the delusion that special interest groups control town meetings and note that the conclusions of Bryan, Mansbridge, and others that town meeting attendees are not representative of the citizenry at large apply equally to elected town councils.

Is the theoretical equality of each voter at a town meeting a fiction? The answer in part is yes, since a number of participants will not have as much information as others and/or may be hesitant to speak in public. Nevertheless, each participant has an equal influence when a vote is taken.

Evidence is lacking that the "regular" participants, who tend to constitute the majority of attendees, are a threat to town meeting democracy. These individuals have the strongest sense of community, study the warrant carefully prior to a meeting, and listen to, and/or participate in, debates on controversial articles. Their decisions, with few exceptions, are sound ones in the best interest of the town, as confirmed by our surveys of, and interviews with, officers and citizens in New England towns.

We specifically reject Madison's view relative to "the infirmities incident to collective meetings of citizens. Ignorance will be the dupe of cunning and passion the slave of sophistry and declamation."[55] Madison, of course, did not foresee the development of town meeting citizen advisory committees—the finance committee and planning board—which assist voters in making intelligent decisions, acting as a counterpoise to special interest groups. Critics notwithstanding, town voters have been discriminating in examining the pros and cons of warrant articles prior to deciding how to vote. It would be a mistake, however, to conclude that the town meeting is a rubber stamp of the committee's and the board's recommendations, as the unpredictability of the town meeting is proverbial. No warrant article, no matter how insignificant, is immune to comment, amendment, and/or rejection by the town meeting.

Our survey evidence suggests that active devotion to the open town meeting, as reflected by participation, will involve only a small minority of the eligible voters in other than small towns. Special efforts need to be made by town officers and civic leaders to foster participation by inactive townspeople by making the meeting more participant-friendly and thereby increasing attendance, which will enhance the legitimacy of the primary assembly.

Three alternatives exist to the traditional open town meeting—the official ballot referendum meeting, the representative town meeting, and the town or city council. As explained, the first alternative changes dramatically the nature of the primary assembly into a vestigial body whose only important powers are to deliberate on warrant articles and, in New Hampshire, to amend them. The decision-making open town meeting is replaced by a referendum system of law-making with town policies still determined by a minority of the registered voters, who include a significant number of persons not well informed on the pros and cons of complex warrant articles. Results to date indicate that official ballot referendum voters are fiscally conservative and may not appreciate the need for town spending on major projects. Furthermore, the OB referendum system presents opportunities for phraseology of articles by petition or the selectpersons that will confuse a number of voters.

The representative town meeting retains many of the advantages of the open town meeting, including the opportunity for a relatively large number of towns-people to serve as legislators and/or on town committees, but deprives all other voters of the right to vote on warrant articles. Efforts, no doubt, will continue to be made in certain Massachusetts RTM towns to adopt a charter establishing a council and a mayor or a town manager.

The town council system can displace completely town meeting government, as in twenty-seven towns in Massachusetts, Maine, New Hampshire, and Rhode Island. Alternatively, the council can share power with the open town meeting, with the former responsible for all decisions except appropriations or for many, but not all, decisions.

Transfer of all powers to a town council deprives townspeople of the ability to participate directly in the law-making process unless the town charter authorizes the employment of the initiative and the protest referendum, as it does in each of the five New Hampshire towns that adopted charters creating councils. Voters in these towns also may employ the recall to remove elected town officers from office prior to the expiration of their respective term of office.

Proponents of a town or city council maintain that the open town meeting is a maladroit institution that cannot react quickly to problems that arise suddenly and that participants lack the expertise to make decisions on baffling issues. Proponents also advance citizen apathy as a major argument for abandoning the system. However, apathy does not disappear when a representative body is the replacement, since voter turnout in most local elections, requiring little effort on the part of the citizenry, is typically low. For example, only 15 percent of the voters in Keene, New Hampshire, a city of 22,733 residents, participated in the November 4, 1997, city council general election.[56] Furthermore, members of a town council often are elected by the plurality rule, and hence the individual elected member may not necessarily have received a majority of the votes cast if a relatively large number of candidates split the votes.

Representative government as a substitute for the open town meeting inserts intermediaries between the electorate and the decisions who may misinterpret the views of the former. Many citizens and civic reformers distrust representative law-making because of abuses associated with it. Jacksonian democracy's emphasis upon the need to elect all state and local government officers for short terms was a response to the scandals involving state legislatures in the financing of canals and railroads. Constitutional conventions were convened in many states in the nineteenth century to place restrictions upon the powers of the state legislatures to prevent abuses of power. These actions proved to be insufficient, and several reform movements were generated by the unrepresentative nature of many state and local governments. The Populist movement developed the protest referendum and the initiative as *in extremis* tools of popular control that, respectively, allow voters to veto unpopular statutes and initiate adoption of proposals that the legislatures failed to act upon or rejected.

Richard S. Childs, the cofounder with Woodrow Wilson of the National Short Ballot Organization in 1916, wrote:

Although the people may be ready to vote overwhelmingly for a measure, their nominal agents and servants in the representative system will frequently maintain a successful indifference or resistance election after election. Our governments are less anxious to please the people than they are to please the politicians who thus become an irresponsible ruling class with a vast and marketable influence. Our representative system is misrepresentative.[57]

Child's 1916 views remain relevant. The distrust of elected legislative bodies flows, in large measure, from legislative action and inaction on important issues, as witnessed by the continuing efforts to reform the election campaign finance system. Representative government can be a shadow institution if dominated by special interest groups.

Elected legislative assemblies do not mirror the population of their constituents. Men are overrepresented vastly, and many groups are unable to elect one of their members as a representative. Boston had an all-green (Irish Roman Catholic) council for years in a city with many other ethnic religious groups. In addition, the voter occupies an inferior status at a council meeting since he or she may not speak without being recognized by the chair and lacks a vote on motions. A town meeting, in contrast, can mirror the population if non-attendees gain the motivation to participate and does with respect to women, who typically compose one-half or more of the participants.

Although critics allege that town meetings are dominated by special interest groups, the evidence is stronger that such groups exercise considerably more influence in legislative halls of representative bodies where *in camera* decisions occasionally are made and that their influence has tended to undermine citizen confidence in traditional representative governance institutions. Any town citizen can organize a special interest group, and its views will be heard by the town meeting, which may or may not endorse a group's proposal(s). Town meetings successfully have counteracted special interest groups.

Town meeting government has a number of auxiliary benefits that enhance its comparative advantage over its alternatives. Our evidence affirms Bryce's 1888 observation that participants are educated by the town meeting.[58] The primary assembly involves political interactions among equals that educate and socialize the participants. Voting is restricted to registered voters, but other town residents may attend and speak when recognized by the moderator. Citizens also educate elected officers by providing a different perspective on certain public problems. Furthermore, residents who participate in policy decision-making are more apt to support fully implementation of the policies, and town meeting experience serves as a training ground for future state and national elected officers.

Democratic scrutiny of town administrators is another benefit of the primary assembly, as ordinary citizens can question and hold town officers responsible for their actions and inactions, which Lawrence highlighted in 1909.[59] If townspeople are satisfied with the performance of officers, there may be few questions other than ones designed to elicit supplemental information. On the other hand, officers can be grilled if they have exercised power in an arrogant manner and their performance in office has disturbed greatly a number of participants, and the officers' responsiveness to citizens' concerns will improve if they desire to be reelected.

Town meeting government has psychological benefits for participants. Some may discover that their frustration relative to a matter of concern is the result of misinformation, which is corrected at town meeting. Their mental health also may benefit from the fact that a small number of voters can employ a petition to place any matter on the agenda for a town meeting, a fact that contrasts with a town or city council, where the voters typically have no control over the agenda. Professor Lincoln Smith in 1955 commented on the psychological benefits for attendees:

> Town meeting offers not only an emotive outlet but also has certain positive therapeutic values for the taxpayers which cannot be ignored. New Englanders . . . derive much incommunicable satisfaction in their asservations and decisions which they have made in their own sovereign capacities, after an opportunity for full and free discussion.[60]

The primary assembly serves the additional function of helping to preserve local customs and traditions, including the expectation that each citizen may play an active role in the governance of his or her town to the extent desired.

The internal problems faced by New England towns are not attributable to the town meeting. The typical town suffers from the lack of professional management. The town meeting as the legislative body functions adequately, and there is no division between the rulers and the ruled.

The management problem is most acute in large and growing towns lacking a professional town manager. The part-time plural executive, the Board of Selectmen, is ill equipped to deal with town problems in the most economical and efficient manner. A number of Connecticut towns have sought to remedy this problem by providing for a full-time first selectperson, yet this approach is not always satisfactory because power still is confined to a board, and the first selectperson may not be a good administrator.

The solution is adoption of a town manager charter and the employment of a professionally trained individual as town manager. There has been strong resistance in many towns to a manager because of the historical reliance on a decentralized system of part-time administrators and distrust of a strong executive. Ironically, a manager can strengthen the town meeting by providing information that committees and boards may not be able to obtain since they function on a voluntary, part-time basis. In addition, the manager can ensure that town meeting decisions are implemented as quickly and as fully as possible in the most effective and efficient manner.

A small town lacks the resources to employ a full-time professional manager. Two options are available to a Lilliputian town. It may pair with one or more neighboring towns to employ jointly a town manager, which results in an organizational arrangement similar to a school superintendency union where several school districts employ the same individual as superintendent of schools. The other alternative is the adoption of the county manager system in rural Ireland, where the county manager *ex officio* is the manager of all other local governments in the county.[61] This option of a county manager's serving as manager of other local governments is unavailable in Rhode Island and Connecticut, in which organized county government was abolished in 1842 and 1996, respectively. Nevertheless, towns in these two states could jointly employ a manager.

CONCLUDING COMMENTS

The stereotypes of the New England open town meeting advanced by its captious critics are a serious distortion of reality. That the primary assembly has its shortcomings must be admitted, yet one would be premature in sounding its death knell. Critics generally evaluate the meeting either against an idealized version of decision-making by assembled voters conjured up in their minds that never existed or in terms of their subjective and unrealistic standards. Their preoccupation with the supposed evil of low voter participation results in the failure to explore the quality of town meeting decisions and determine whether they are *pro bono publico* ones.

There is no evidence supporting the fears of certain Greek philosophers that an ocholocracy would be the product of law-making by assembled voters. Our conclusion is similar to the one drawn by Munro in 1912:

The basis . . . of the New England town system of government is the principle that even matters of very minor importance shall be decided by referenda of the citizens, and . . . taking the history of New England towns as a whole, it does not appear that voters have shown themselves less capable in determining these things than a body of representatives would have been. Most of those towns are small, it is true, but others, like, Brookline, Mass., are, in point of population, larger than half the so-termed "cities" of the United States, and it does not appear that town government in any way loses its satisfactoriness as the towns grow in population.[62]

Our study of open town meetings reveals that voter superintendence of town affairs has proven to be effective, and there is no empirical evidence that the thousands of small towns and cities with elected councils in the United States in the population range of New England towns are governed better. In fact, an officer of a New Hampshire town that adopted a charter providing for a town council with full legislative authority wrote to the author in 1996 that "[t]he council has made no changes in policies as a result of the change in style of government." Furthermore, Hudson, New Hampshire, abandoned a town council and reverted to the open town meeting as the legislative body.

While lamentable, voter non-participation may be interpreted as a vote of confidence in the "regular" town meeting attendees to represent in a responsible manner the best interests of absent voters. Similarly, the lack of a quorum requirement in most towns and exceedingly low quorum requirements in a few additional towns indicate that townspeople have confidence that even a meeting with a very small attendance will make sound decisions. In fact, the town meeting is synergetic as participants debate the pros and cons of controversial warrant articles and may adopt amendments that will result in an improved policy decision.

In common with elections, the town meeting offers voters the choice whether to participate in electing town officers and deciding all legislative questions. In contrast to a *de jure* representative body, all voters in an open meeting town are free to attend future town meetings and become lawmakers. The latent power of the primary assembly as a self-correcting body should not be underestimated. Whenever the *de facto* representative town meeting makes an unpopular decision, voters by petition can compel the Board of Selectmen to call a special town meeting to reconsider all or most decisions.

The low and generally declining attendance has not invidiously weakened support for deliberative decision-making democracy. The remarkable tenacity of the town meeting is not enigmatic and can be accounted for in terms of the tinkering with the traditional *modus operandi*. Today, the linchpin of town meeting government is the committee system, which performs the research and reference functions typically performed by committees of a representative legislative body. Committee members become subject matter experts and provide advice to the town meeting that is followed most of the time.

We agree with Barber that "democracy is neither government by the majority nor representative rule: it is citizens self-government" and with Jefferson that the town meeting acts as a cement binding the participants together as a community.[63] What is needed is a new conception of town meeting democracy positing that the assembly of voters is a *de facto* representative legislative body with two safety valves—open access to all voters and availability of the initiative to add articles to the warrant and to call special meetings. A third safety valve—the protest referendum—can be adopted by a town meeting.

In retrospect, the open town meeting is not an endangered species and has proved to be a lithe and tenacious institution that has contributed to the art of governance by demonstrating that decision-making by assembled voters functions adequately. The meeting, which is the leading national symbol of grass-roots democracy, has coped successfully with serious problems in the past and should continue to do so in the future until a town's population growth necessitates adoption of a *de jure* representative town meeting or town council.

NOTES

1. M.I. Finley, *Democracy: Ancient and Modern* (London: Hogarth Press, 1985), p. 24.

2. James Bryce, *The American Commonwealth*, 2nd ed. rev. (London: Macmillan and Company, 1891), p. 566.

3. *National Voter Registration Act of 1993*, 107 Stat. 84, 42 U.S.C. § 1973gg-6(d).

4. John Dewey, *The Public and Its Problems* (Denver: Alan Swallow, 1927), pp. 138–39.

5. Lester W. Milbrath, *Political Participation* (Chicago: Rand McNally & Company, 1965), p. 21.

6. Ibid.

7. Charles Johnson, *Nonvoting Americans* (Washington, D.C.: U.S. Bureau of the Census, 1980), p. 8.

8. "Why Citizens Shun the Polling Booth: An Interview with Curtis B. Gans," *The Public Perspective*, February/March 1997, p. 42.

9. Jane J. Mansbridge, "Town Meeting Democracy," in Peter Collier, ed., *Dilemmas of Democracy* (New York: Harcourt Brace Jovanovich, 1976), p. 155.

10. Consult Joseph F. Zimmerman, *Federal Preemption: The Silent Revolution* (Ames: Iowa State University Press, 1991); Joseph F. Zimmerman, *State-Local Relations: A Partnership Approach*, 2nd ed. (Westport, Conn.: Praeger Publishers, 1995), pp. 85–115.

11. Mansbridge, "Town Meeting Democracy," p. 156; Jane J. Mansbridge, *Beyond Adversary Democracy* (New York: Basic Books, 1980), p. 109.

12. Mansbridge, *Beyond Adversary Democracy*, p. 111.

13. Milton G. Kotler, "Politics and Citizenship in New England Towns: A Study of Participation and Political Education" (Unpublished Ph.D. dissertation, University of Chicago, 1974), p. 181.

14. Ibid., p. 213.

15. Frank M. Bryan, "Direct Democracy and Civic Competence," *The Good Society*, Fall 1995, pp. 39, 41.

16. Bruce C. Evans, "Representativeness in Massachusetts Town Meetings," paper presented at the annual meeting of the Northeastern Political Science Association, Boston, November 15, 1996, p. 12.

17. Ibid., p. 28.

18. Ibid., p. 30.

19. *Final Report of the Town Meeting Study Committee* (Concord, Mass.: Town of Concord, 1996), p. 6.

20. Robert S. Lynd and Helen M. Lynd, *Middletown* (New York: Harcourt, Brace, and World, 1929); Robert S. Lynd and Helen M. Lynd, *Middletown in Transition* (New York: Harcourt Brace Jovanovich, 1937).

21. Floyd Hunter, *Community Power Structure* (Chapel Hill: University of North Carolina Press, 1953).

22. Robert Dahl, *Who Governs?* (New Haven, Conn.: Yale University Press, 1961).

23. Jonathan McNeilly, "Town Meeting Called on Community Center," *The Union Leader* (Manchester, N.H.), July 24, 1997, p. A13.

24. *Final Report of the Town Meeting Study Committee*, p. 10.

25. Ibid.

26. Mark E. Ellis, "Democracy Lumbers on as Off-the-Point Meetings Discourage Participation," *Telegram & Gazette* (Worcester, Mass.), June 6, 1997, p. B4.

27. *Final Report of the Town Meeting Study Committee*, p. 9.

28. *Fall Yearly Town Meeting Warrant for Use at Fall Yearly Town Meeting* (Brewster, Mass.: Town of Brewster, November 18, 1996), p. 2.

29. *Final Report of the Town Study Committee*, p. 6.

30. Ibid., pp. 6–7.

31. Ibid., p. 7.

32. Ibid., p. 12.

33. Ibid., p. 13.

34. For details, consult Joseph F. Zimmerman, *Participatory Democracy: Populism Revived* (New York: Praeger Publishers, 1986), pp. 45–67.

35. *Massachusetts Acts of 1954*, chap. 660.

36. *Massachusetts Acts of 1992*, chap. 337.

37. *Connecticut General Statutes*, chap. 90, § 7–7.

38. *New Hampshire Revised Statutes Annotated*, § 675:5(a–b). See also *Disco v. Board of Selectmen*, 115 N.H. 609 (1975).

39. *Final Report of the Town Meeting Study Group*, p. 14.

40. *New Hampshire Laws of 1995*, chap. 164; *New Hampshire Revised Statutes Annotated*, § 40:13.

41. *New Hampshire Laws of 1995*, chap. 53; *New Hampshire Revised Statutes Annotated*, § 49–D3(a).

42. Robert Rand, "Voters Like New Setup," *The Keene (N.H.) Sentinel*, July 17, 1997, p. 1.

43. Ibid., p. 5.

44. William B. Munro, *The Government of the United States*, 4th ed. (New York: Macmillan Company, 1937), pp. 743–44.

45. Letter to author from chair Rosemary Leary of the Amesbury, Mass., Charter Commission, dated October 29, 1996.

46. Letter to author from Mayor Michael A. Tautznik of Easthampton, Mass., dated April 10, 1997.

47. Dave Denison, "Two More Towns Scuttle Town Meeting," *Commonwealth* 1, Summer 1996, p. 10.

48. Letter to author from Seekonk, Mass., town clerk Janet Parker, dated October 9, 1996.

49. Beth Carney, "Framingham Rejects Plan to Become a City," *Boston Globe*, April 9, 1997, p. B4.

50. Dave Denison, "Framingham: Back to the Future," *Commonwealth* 2, Spring/Summer 1997, p. 20.

51. Donald Kagan, *Pericles of Athens and the Birth of Democracy* (New York: Free Press, 1991), p. 273.

52. Benjamin R. Barber, *Strong Democracy: Participatory Politics for a New Age* (Berkeley: University of California Press, 1984), p. 145.

53. A. Lawrence Lowell, *Public Opinion and Popular Government* (New York: Longmans, Green, and Company, 1926), p. 153.

54. Ralph Waldo Emerson, *Miscellanies* (Boston: Houghton, Mifflin, and Company, 1904), vol. 11, pp. 46–47.

55. James Madison, *The Federalist Papers* (New York: New American Library, 1961), p. 360.

56. Deirdre M. Shaw, "Council Turns to Right," *Keene (N.H.) Sentinel*, November 5, 1997, p. 1.

57. Richard S. Childs, *The Short Ballot: A Movement to Simplify Politics* (New York: National Short Ballot Organization, 1916), p. 4.

58. Bryce, *The American Commonwealth*, p. 391.

59. Lawrence, *Public Opinion and Popular Government*, p. 153.

60. Lincoln Smith, "Town Meeting Government," *Social Science*, June 1955, p. 183.

61. For details, consult Joseph F. Zimmerman, "Council-Manager Government in Ireland," *Studies in Comparative Local Government*, Summer 1972, pp. 61–69.

62. William B. Munro, *The Initiative, Referendum, and Recall* (New York: D. Appleton and Company, 1912), p. 24.

63. Barber, *Strong Democracy*; p. 211; *The Writings of Thomas Jefferson* (Washington, D.C.: Thomas Jefferson Memorial Association of the United States, 1904), vol. 15, p. 38.

Appendix I

Marshfield, Massachusetts, Town Meeting Rules and Definitions

1. The conduct of Marshfield's Town Meeting is dictated by Federal and State law, the Town's Charter and By-Laws, local tradition, and the publication entitled, "Town Meeting Time."

2. The Moderator shall preside over the Town Meeting, decide all questions of order and procedure, and announce the results of all votes. The results of all votes as announced by the Moderator shall be final except on a voice vote which may be questioned by seven (7) voters standing immediately after the announced results of a vote. In such a case, a standing vote shall be taken without debate.

3. Non-voters will be seated in a special section unless permission is granted by the Town Meeting to be seated elsewhere. Non-voters may be allowed to address the Town Meeting with permission of the Moderator unless a majority of voters choose to deny such a privilege.

4. Articles in the Warrant give notice of the issues subject to discussion at a Town Meeting and establish the parameters of matters that can be debated and acted on. Amendments, motions and/or debate determined by the Moderator, with the advice of Town Counsel, to be "beyond the scope" of the Articles may not be permitted.

5. In order for the Town Meeting to act on or discuss an Article, a motion must be made. The Moderator will call for a motion on each Article and, if no motion is made after the second call, the Moderator will "pass over" the Article and move on to the next Article. In order to bring back a "pass over" Article for a motion and discussion, there must be an approved "motion for reconsideration."

6. Articles may be postponed by a majority vote or advanced by approval of the Moderator and a 2/3 vote.

7. To address the Town Meeting, a speaker must be recognized by the Moderator and, once recognized, a speaker should first give [his] or her name and address for the record.

No speaker will be recognized while another person is speaking except to raise "a point of order" which is used to question a ruling of the Moderator or the conduct of the Town Meeting. "Points of Order" are not to address the subject matter being discussed.

8. All matters shall be decided by a majority vote unless a 2/3 or greater vote is required. If more than a majority vote is required, the Moderator shall announce the required percentage for passage before calling for the vote.

9. The Moderator may set time limits on all presentations and may terminate debate on a motion when he deems it appropriate. Debate on a motion may also be terminated by a voter "moving the question" which, if accepted by the Moderator as not being premature, shall be voted on without discussion or debate. A motion to "move the question" requires a 2/3 vote for passage.

10. Only two (2) amendments to a motion may be on the floor at any particular time. Amendments over ten (10) words must be submitted to the Moderator in writing and, if over fifty (50) words, sufficient copies must be available to those attending at the entrance of the hall before the start of that particular session.

11. Generally, amendments shall be voted on in the order made and prior to the vote on the motion to be amended. However, amendments relating to amounts to be appropriated shall be voted on in a descending order until an amount gains approval.

12. A motion may be reconsidered once for any reason by a majority vote. No further reconsideration will be permitted unless the Moderator determines that there has been a significant procedural error or that there is new information likely to affect the vote. There will be no reconsideration of a vote either on a subsequent evening or after 10:30 P.M. on the evening of the vote in question.

13. A resolution is a non-debatable, non-binding motion on any matter calling for a consensus of the Town Meeting. If a resolution is over ten (10) words, it must be submitted to the Moderator in writing and, if over fifty (50) words, sufficient copies must be available at the entrance of the hall to those attending.

14. No new business will be taken up after 10:45 P.M. on any evening.

15. When justice or order requires, the Moderator may make exceptions to these rules as he, in his discretion, deems it appropriate under the circumstances.

Respectfully submitted,

Richard E. Levin, Moderator

Reminder – State Law prohibits SMOKING on school property.

Source: Town of Marshfield Special & Annual Town Meeting, April 22, 1996 (Marshfield, Mass., 1996), pp. 1–2.

Appendix II

Stoneham, Massachusetts, Town Government Organization

Citizens Elected:
Board of Selectmen
School Committee
Town Clerk
Board of Assessors
Planning Board
Constables
Library Trustees
Board of Health
* Housing Authority
Moderator
Northeast Metropolitan Regional
Vocational School Representative

Selectmen Appoint:
Town Administrator
Town Counsel
Town Accountant
Selectmen's Office Staff
Council on Aging
Board of Appeals
Conservation Commission
Commission for the Handicapped
Historical Commission
Registrars of Voters
Unicorn Recreational Area Committee
Youth Commission
All multi-member Boards/Committees

* Four Elected, One Appointed by State EOCD

School Committee Appoints:
Superintendent of Schools

Superintendent of Schools Appoints:
School Staff

Library Trustees Appoint:
Library Director

Moderator Appoints:
Finance & Advisor Board
Ad Hoc Committees

Town Administrator Appoints:
Building and Wire Inspectors
Dog Officer
Fire Chief
Police Chief
Town Engineer
Treasurer/Tax Collector
Director of Veterans' Services
All Other Officers and Employees

Source: Town of Stoneham, Massachusetts, 1995 Annual Report (Stoneham, Mass., 1996), p. 17.

Appendix III

Fitzwilliam, New Hampshire, Town Warrant, 1997

To the inhabitants of the Town of Fitzwilliam, in the
County of Cheshire, in said State, qualified to vote in
town affairs, you are hereby notified to meet at the Town
Hall in said Fitzwilliam on Tuesday, the eleventh day of
March next at seven (7:00) o'clock in the afternoon to act
on the following subjects:

ARTICLE 1. To bring in your votes for the election of
one Selectman for three years; one Fireward for three
years; two Planning Board Members for three years, one
Cemetery Commissioner for three years; one Trustee of
the Library for three years; one Trustee of the Trust
Funds for three years; two Budget Committee Members
for three years and three Commissioners of Plante
Memorial Park for one year.

ARTICLE 2. To see if the town will vote to raise and
appropriate the sum of $250,000 for the purchase of land
and buildings owned by Treat and Legg as shown on Tax
Map 20, Lot 16 and Tax Map 20, Lot 16-01 of the Tax
Maps of the Town of Fitzwilliam, said appropriation to
be paid for by authorizing the selectmen to issue bonds or
notes in the amount of $150,000 for three year(s)
requiring $50,000 of the principal to be paid each year
commencing one year from date of issue with terms and
conditions they deem to be in the best interest of the town
and the remaining $100,000 to come from current tax
revenues, further provided that in the event all said real
estate is not necessary for the operation of the town
beach/recreation area, to authorize the Board of
Selectmen to adjust lot lines of said lots and to sell
whatever portion of the land and buildings as are not
necessary for town purposes and to apply the net
proceeds from any such sale to the reduction of the
town's indebtedness on the bonds or notes executed in
connection with the original purchase of this property, or
take any action thereon
(Ballot vote required; two-thirds majority needed for
passage) (Board of Selectmen recommend a price to be
negotiated)

ARTICLE 3. (BY BALLOT). "Shall we modify the elderly exemptions from property tax in the Town of Fitzwilliam, based on assessed value, for qualified taxpayers, to be as follows: for a person 65 years of age up to 75 years, $12,500; for a person 75 years of age up to 80 years, $25,000; for a person 80 years of age or older. $50,000. To qualify, the person must have been a New Hampshire resident for at least 5 years, own the real estate individually or jointly, or if the real estate is owned by such person's spouse, they must have been married for at least 5 years. In addition, the taxpayer must have a net income of not more than $20,000 or, if married, a combined net income of less than $25,000; and own net assets not in excess of $50,000 excluding the value of the person's residence."

Polls will open not later than 2:00 p.m. and close not earlier than 7:00 p.m. or such later time as shall be authorized by vote of the town.

ARTICLE 4 . To hear and act upon the reports of Agents, Committees and Officers, heretofore chosen.

ARTICLE 5. To see if the town will vote to appoint a committee to have charge of the Memorial Day exercises, or take any action thereon.

ARTICLE 6. To see if the town will vote to raise and appropriate the sum of $17,000 to paint the Town Hall and finance said appropriation by withdrawing $7,000 from the Capital Reserve Fund created by ARTICLE #18 at the 1996 Annual Meeting and $10,000 to come from current tax revenues, or take any action thereon. (Recommended by Budget Committee; Recommended by Board of Selectmen)

ARTICLE 7. To see if the town will vote to raise and appropriate the sum of $ 5,900 to install an addition to the exhaust extraction system in the Public Safety Building (for the purpose of removing diesel exhaust fumes), or take any action thereon. (Recommended by Budget Committee; Recommended by Board of Selectmen)

ARTICLE 8. To see if the Town will vote to raise and appropriate the sum of $21,722 to purchase and equip a vehicle for the Police Department, said appropriation to be funded by withdrawing $10,000 from the Capital Reserve Fund created by ARTICLE #15 of the 1995 Annual Meeting and added to with ARTICLE #20 of the 1996 Annual Meeting and $11,722 to come out of current tax revenues, or take any action thereon. (Recommended by Budget Committee; Recommended by Board of Selectmen)

ARTICLE 9. To see if the town will vote to raise and appropriate the sum of $101,493 to repair and maintain (including but not limited to paving and ditching) roads, or take any action thereon. (Recommended by Budget Committee; Recommended by Board of Selectmen)

ARTICLE 10. To see if the town will vote to raise and appropriate the sum of $26,000 for repairs and maintenance to the Rhododendron Road. (This will be paid over to the State of New Hampshire who will add $50,200 and do this repair and maintenance), or take any action thereon. (Recommended by Budget Committee; Recommended by Board of Selectmen)

ARTICLE 11. To see if the town will vote to raise and appropriate the sum of $18,000 to be used for the site plan and development, with minor construction and personnel costs of Map 20, Lot 16, and Map 20 Lot 16-01 for use as a Town Beach and to authorize the Selectmen to appoint a committee including one member of each the Planning Board, Conservation Commission, Recreation Committee, Board of Selectmen and one member at large from the public to oversee this project. This appropriation shall be non-lapsing for up to three years and may be encumbered by the Board of Selectmen. (Recommended by Budget Committee; Recommended by Board of Selectmen).

ARTICLE 12. To see if the town will vote to raise and appropriate the sum of $25,000 for a new platform lift for the physically challenged, at the Town Hall, and to authorize the Board of Selectmen to apply for

Community Development Block Grant Funds through the Cheshire County ADA Project and the New Hampshire Office of State Planning, and if said grant is approved, to authorize the Board of Selectmen to use any funds received from the grant as an offset against this appropriation. (Recommended by Budget Committee; Recommended by Board of Selectmen)

ARTICLE 13. To see if the town will vote to raise and appropriate the sum of $2,000 to support the operation of Meadowood County Area Fire Department, or take any action thereon. (Recommended by Budget Committee; Recommended by Board of Selectmen)

ARTICLE 14. To see if the town will vote to raise and appropriate the sum of $10,000 to be added to the Capital Reserve Fund created by ARTICLE #17 at the Annual Meeting of 1995 for the reassessment of the town, or take any action thereon. (Recommended by Budget Committee, Recommended by Board of Selectmen)

ARTICLE 15. To see if the town will vote to raise and appropriate the sum of $5,000 to add to the Capital Reserve Fund created by ARTICLE #11 of the Annual Meeting of 1969 for the purchase of a fire department vehicle, or take any action thereon. (Recommended by Budget Committee; $10,000 recommended by Board of Selectmen)

ARTICLE 16. To see if the town will vote to raise and appropriate the sum of $2,500 to create a Capital Reserve Fund for the acquisition of a fork lift for use at the Transfer Station, or take any action thereon. (Recommended by Budget Committee; Recommended by Board of Selectmen)

ARTICLE 17. To hear the report of the Budget Committee, and pass any vote in relation thereto.

ARTICLE 18. To see if the Town will vote to authorize the Board of Selectmen to convey an easement to Richard and Beverly Bagster and C. Gonyou over a portion of land owned by the Town situated at the Depot Common

for the purposes of installing, maintaining, repairing and
replacing a septic system leach field, in accordance with
a plan prepared by Carl Hagstrom, provided said system
is fully approved by the Water Supply and Pollution
Control Division of the New Hampshire Department of
Environmental Services, and to further authorize the
Board of Selectmen to provide for such terms and
conditions in the granting of said easement as will
preserve and protect the Depot Common property in the
best interest of the Town.

ARTICLE 19. To see if the town will vote to authorize
the Board of Selectmen to deed to the State of New
Hampshire the boat landing as shown on Tax Map 21,
Lot 05 of the tax maps of the Town of Fitzwilliam, if it is
deemed in the best interests of the Town of Fitzwilliam to
do so, or take any action thereon.

ARTICLE 20. (By Petition) To see if the town will
vote to designate that portion of Rockwood Pond Road
which begins at the Rhododendron Road and ends at the
crossing of the former railroad right of way at the
Rockwood Pond Dam, as a scenic road under the
authorization and provisions of RSA 231:157 and RSA
231:158.

ARTICLE 21. To see if the town wishes to amend the
existing agreement with the Internal Revenue Service
under Section 218 of the Social Security Act, by
excluding the services performed by election workers for
a calendar year in which the remuneration paid for such
service is less that $1,000 until the amended agreement is
modified or rescinded, or take any action thereon.

ARTICLE 22. To see if the town will vote to adopt the
provisions of RSA 202-A:4-d authorizing the library
trustees to accept gifts of personal property, other than
money, which may be offered to the library for any public
purpose, provided, however, that no acceptance of
personal property by the library trustees shall be deemed
to bind the town or the library trustees to raise,
appropriate or expend any public funds for the operation,

maintenance, repair or replacement of such personal property.

ARTICLE 23. To see if the town will vote to rescind the vote on Article #14 of the 1903 Annual Meeting of the Town of Fitzwilliam requiring the Tax Collector "to furnish the Selectmen at the close of each fiscal year the names and amounts of all unpaid taxes and that the Selectmen cause the same to be printed in the annual report", or take any action thereon.

ARTICLE 24. To see if the town will vote to authorize the Board of Selectmen to trade, sell or otherwise dispose of any unusable vehicles or equipment of any of the departments of the town, or take any action thereon.

ARTICLE 25. To see if the town will vote to authorize the Board of Selectmen to accept, on behalf of the town, gifts, legacies, and devices made to the town in trust for any public purpose, as permitted by RSA 31:19, or take any action thereon.

ARTICLE 26. To see if the town will vote to authorize the Board of Selectmen to accept the dedication of any street shown on a subdivision plat by the Planning Board, provided that such street has been constructed in accordance with the approval of the subdivision plat by the Planning Board and has been constructed in accordance with applicable town specifications as determined by the Board of Selectmen or their agent, or take any action thereon.

GIVEN UNDER our hands this 4th day of February in the year of our Lord, nineteen hundred and ninety-seven.

Joan Knight, Chairman

Susan S. Silverman

Jean G. Auperin
BOARD OF SELECTMEN

Appendix IV

Milford, New Hampshire, Absentee Ballot, 1997

ABSENTEE
OFFICIAL BALLOT
ANNUAL ELECTION
MILFORD, NEW HAMPSHIRE
APRIL 8, 1997

Town Clerk

INSTRUCTIONS TO VOTER

A. TO VOTE, completely fill in the OVAL to the RIGHT of your choice(s) like this: ●

B. Follow directions as to the number of candidates to be marked for each office.

C. To vote for a person whose name is not printed on the ballot, write the candidate's name on the line provided and completely fill in the OVAL.

TOWN OFFICES	FOR LIBRARY TRUSTEE	FOR FIRE WARDEN
FOR SELECTMAN	For THREE Years Vote for THREE	For THREE Years Vote for ONE
For THREE Years Vote for TWO	CARA BARLOW ○	ROLAND J. FAUVEL ○
RICHARD D. D'AMATO ○	TIMOTHY BARR ○	JOHN W. RAYMOND ○
ROSARIO "SAROOCH" RICCIARDI ○	SANDRA N. HARDY ○	_____ (Write-in) ○
_____ (Write-in) ○	JOHN "JACK" MATTKE ○	
_____ (Write-in) ○	MARK A. TUNIEWICZ ○	**FOR CEMETERY TRUSTEE**
	_____ (Write-in) ○	For THREE Years Vote for ONE
FOR TRUSTEE OF TRUST FUNDS	_____ (Write-in) ○	ROSARIO "SAROOCH" RICCIARDI ○
For THREE Years Vote for ONE	_____ (Write-in) ○	_____ (Write-in) ○
MARTY WILDE ○		
_____ (Write-in) ○		

ZONING QUESTIONS

1. ARE YOU IN FAVOR OF THE ADOPTION OF AMENDMENT NO. 1 AS PROPOSED BY THE PLANNING BOARD, FOR THE TOWN OF MILFORD ZONING ORDINANCE AS FOLLOWS:

Amend ARTICLE II: GENERAL PROVISIONS by adding the following: 2.050 Any uses of land and/or structures not specifically included in each zoning district as either Acceptable or Acceptable by Special Exception shall be considered as not permitted within that zoning district.

YES ○
NO ○

2. ARE YOU IN FAVOR OF THE ADOPTION OF AMENDMENT NO. 2 AS PROPOSED BY THE PLANNING BOARD, FOR THE TOWN OF MILFORD ZONING ORDINANCE AS FOLLOWS:

Amend ARTICLE III: ZONING MAP - ZONING DISTRICT CHANGES/REZONING OF THE FOLLOWING LOTS by adding #4: 4. Rezone the following parcels on Emerson Road from Residence "R" to Integrated Commercial-Industrial: Map 48, Lots 35, 35-1, 35-2, 37, 38 and 39.

YES ○
NO ○

3. ARE YOU IN FAVOR OF THE ADOPTION OF AMENDMENT NO. 3 AS PROPOSED BY THE PLANNING BOARD, FOR THE TOWN OF MILFORD ZONING ORDINANCE AS FOLLOWS:

Amend/add to ARTICLE IV: SECTION 4.010 Definitions as follows:
Agriculture; Commercial Recreation; Density; Processing and Warehousing; Processing of Natural Resources; Recreational Facility, Commercial; Self-Service Storage Facilities; Warehouse; Light Manufacturing and Bed and Breakfast.

YES ○
NO ○

4. ARE YOU IN FAVOR OF THE ADOPTION OF AMENDMENT NO. 4 AS PROPOSED BY THE PLANNING BOARD, FOR THE TOWN OF MILFORD ZONING ORDINANCE AS FOLLOWS:

ARTICLE V, RESIDENCE "A", SECTION 5.022 - Acceptable Uses and Yard Requirements by Special Exception (add the following)
B. Recreational Facility, Not for Profit; I. Bed and Breakfast, J. Recreational Facility, Commercial. Replace 5.023 - Uses Specifically Excluded with: 5.023 - Uses Not Specified: Any uses of land and/or structures not specifically included in the "A" district as either Acceptable or Acceptable by Special Exception shall be considered as not permitted.

YES ○
NO ○

GO TO TOWN BALLOT TWO TO CONTINUE VOTING

5. ARE YOU IN FAVOR OF THE ADOPTION OF AMENDMENT NO. 5 AS PROPOSED BY THE PLANNING BOARD, FOR THE TOWN OF MILFORD ZONING ORDINANCE AS FOLLOWS:

ARTICLE V, RESIDENCE "B", SECTION 5.032 - Acceptable Uses and Yard Requirements by Special Exception (add the following)
G. Recreational Facility, Not-for-profit; J. Recreational Facility, Commercial and I. Bed and Breakfast. Replace **YES** ◯
5.033 - Uses Specifically Excluded with the following: 5.033 - Uses Not Specified: Any uses of land and/or **NO** ◯
structures not specifically included in the "B" district as either Acceptable or Acceptable by Special Exception shall be considered as not permitted.

6. ARE YOU IN FAVOR OF THE ADOPTION OF AMENDMENT NO. 6 AS PROPOSED BY THE PLANNING BOARD, FOR THE TOWN OF MILFORD ZONING ORDINANCE AS FOLLOWS:

ARTICLE V, RESIDENCE "R" DISTRICT, SECTION 5.041 - Acceptable Uses - Replace: B. Farm, agricultural or nursery uses with "Agriculture"; Delete - E. Recreation and community center buildings; 5.042 - Acceptable uses by Special Exception (add) - K. Bed & Breakfast, L. Processing of Natural Resources on **YES** ◯ parcels of a minimum 10 acres in size, M. Recreational Facility, Not-for-profit, N. Recreational Facility, **NO** ◯ Commercial, O. Self-service storage facilities in accordance with Section 10.024. Replace 5.043 - Uses Specifically Excluded with the following: 5:043-Uses Not Specified: Any uses of land and/or structures not specifically included in the "R" district as either Acceptable or Acceptable by Special Exception shall be considered as not permitted.

7. ARE YOU IN FAVOR OF THE ADOPTION OF AMENDMENT NO. 7 AS PROPOSED BY THE PLANNING BOARD, FOR THE TOWN OF MILFORD ZONING ORDINANCE AS FOLLOWS:

ARTICLE V, COMMERCIAL DISTRICT, SECTION 5.051 - Acceptable Uses (amend as follows): Replace K: Commercial Recreation with Bed & Breakfast; Add: R. Recreational Facility, Not-for-Profit: S. Recreational **YES** ◯ Facility, Commercial: 5.052 - Acceptable Uses by Special Exception (delete the following) - C. Recreation **NO** ◯ and community center buildings........ Replace 5.053 - Uses Specifically Excluded with: 5.053 - Uses Not Specified: Any uses of land and/or structures not specifically included in the "Commercial" district as either Acceptable or Acceptable by Special Exception shall be considered as not permitted.

8. ARE YOU IN FAVOR OF THE ADOPTION OF AMENDMENT NO. 8 AS PROPOSED BY THE PLANNING BOARD, FOR THE TOWN OF MILFORD ZONING ORDINANCE AS FOLLOWS: **YES** ◯

ARTICLE V, INDUSTRIAL DISTRICT, SECTION 5.061 - Acceptable Uses - add the following: F. Processing **NO** ◯ and Warehousing. Replace 5.062 - Uses Specifically Excluded with 5.062 - Uses Not Specified: Any uses of land and/or structures not specifically included in the "Industrial" district as either Acceptable or Acceptable by Special Exception shall be considered as not permitted.

9. ARE YOU IN FAVOR OF THE ADOPTION OF AMENDMENT NO. 9 AS PROPOSED BY THE PLANNING BOARD, FOR THE TOWN OF MILFORD ZONING ORDINANCE AS FOLLOWS: **YES** ◯

NO ◯

ARTICLE V, LIMITED COMMERCIAL-BUSINESS DISTRICT, SECTION 5.072 - Acceptable Uses and Yard Requirements by Special Exception - Replace 5.072.C Recreation and community center buildings.........with 5.072.C - Recreational Facility, Not-for-Profit. Replace 5.073 - Uses Specifically Excluded with: 5.073 - Uses Not Specified: Any uses of land and/or structures not specifically included in the "Limited Commercial-Business District as either Acceptable or Acceptable by Special Exception shall be considered as not permitted.

10. ARE YOU IN FAVOR OF THE ADOPTION OF AMENDMENT NO. 10 AS PROPOSED BY THE **YES** ◯ PLANNING BOARD, FOR THE TOWN OF MILFORD ZONING ORDINANCE AS FOLLOWS:

NO ◯

ARTICLE V. INTEGRATED COMMERCIAL-INDUSTRIAL DISTRICT, SECTION 5.081 - Acceptable Uses - Add - N. Processing and Warehousing; 5.082 Acceptable Uses by Special Exception - Add: B. Recreational Facility, Not-for-Profit; C. Recreational Facility, Commercial; and D. Processing of natural resources. Replace; 5.083 - Uses Specifically Excluded with: 5.083 - Uses Not Specified: Any uses of land and/or structures not specifically included in the "Integrated Commercial-Industrial District." as either Acceptable or Acceptable by Special Exception shall be considered as not permitted.

11. ARE YOU IN FAVOR OF THE ADOPTION OF AMENDMENT NO. 11 AS PROPOSED BY THE **YES** ◯ PLANNING BOARD, FOR THE TOWN OF MILFORD ZONING ORDINANCE AS FOLLOWS: **NO** ◯

ARTICLE IX - BOARD OF ADJUSTMENT - SECTION 9.020 - Delete the following from the first sentence: "and no member shall hold any elective or appointive position in the Town of Milford".

GO TO TOWN BALLOT THREE TO CONTINUE VOTING

12. ARE YOU IN FAVOR OF THE ADOPTION OF AMENDMENT NO. 12 AS PROPOSED BY THE PLANNING BOARD, FOR THE TOWN OF MILFORD ZONING ORDINANCE AS FOLLOWS:

ARTICLE X - ADMINISTRATIVE RELIEF: Add
10.024 Self-Service Storage Facilities
A. In all cases involving self-service storage facilities in the Residence "R" district, the following shall be minimum performance conditions of approval, in addition to any other conditions the Board of Adjustment may require:
(1) The self-service storage facility shall be located specifically on, and have frontage on, Route 13 North, Route 13, South and/or the following parcels of land on North River Road; Map 8, Lots 11,11-1, 19, 48, 49, 50, 51, 53, and 53-5.
(2) In order to screen facilities and insure their compatibility with surrounding land uses, there shall be a minimum fifteen (15') feet perimeter landscaped buffer along all sides of the parcel. This buffer shall be planted and maintained with evergreen trees, minimum 6' in height, at intervals 15' on-center, alternately staggered along the length of the buffers. This type of evergreen tree shall be subject to the approval of the Planning Board.
(3) If the Board of Adjustment determines that existing landscaping and/or topographic conditions already create an effective perimeter screen, the Board of Adjustment may waive all or a part of the evergreen tree screening requirement.   YES ◯
(4) There shall be no outside storage.   NO ◯
(5) Each structure shall be set back at least 50' from the front lot line.

TOWN WARRANT ARTICLES

QUESTION 3 - MILFORD DISTRICT COURT FACILITY
Shall the Town vote to raise and appropriate the sum of $1,920,000, and authorize the Selectmen to borrow and issue bonds or serial notes, under the Municipal Finance Act (RSA Chapter 33), for the construction and equipping in cooperation with the State of New Hampshire, a Milford District Court Facility said costs to be offset by a twenty year, lease purchase payment agreement with the State and as more particularly set forth in   YES ◯
Warrant Article 3?   NO ◯

QUESTION 4 - WATER MAIN IMPROVEMENTS
Shall the Town vote to raise and appropriate the sum of $764,000, and authorize the Selectmen to borrow and issue bonds, bond anticipation notes or serial notes, under the provisions of the Municipal Finance Act (RSA Chapter 33), for the installation of approximately 8100 linear feet (LF) of water main and appurtenances;   YES ◯
consisting of the following: West St. from Crosby St. to Osgood Rd.; Spaulding St. from West St. westerly; and   NO ◯
Osgood Rd. to its intersection with Mason Rd., as more particularly set forth in Warrant Article 4?

QUESTION 5 - MILFORD DISTRICT COURT BOND COSTS
In the event that Question 3, the Milford District Court Bond, passes, shall the Town vote to raise and   YES ◯
appropriate the sum of $26,000 for the bond issuance fees and bond anticipation note costs associated with   NO ◯
Article 3 as described in Article 5?

QUESTION 6 - WATER MAIN IMPROVEMENT BOND COSTS
In the event that Question 4, the Water Main Improvement Article passes, shall the Town vote to raise and   YES ◯
appropriate the sum of $10,104 for bond fees and bond anticipation note costs associated with Article 4 as   NO ◯
described in Article 6?

QUESTION 7 - OSGOOD POND
Shall the Town vote to establish a Capital Reserve Fund under RSA 35:1 for the purpose of cleaning, dredging   YES ◯
and restoring Osgood Pond and to raise and appropriate the sum of $25,000 as described in Article 7?   NO ◯

QUESTION 8 - MILFORD MILLENIUM
Shall the Town vote to establish a Capital Reserve Fund under the provisions RSA 35:1 for the purpose of   YES ◯
planning and presenting a Milford Millennium Celebration in the year 2000 and to raise and appropriate the   NO ◯
sum of $0 as described in Article 8?

QUESTION 9 - BROX PROPERTY
Shall the Town vote to raise and appropriate the sum of $0 for an appraisal of the Brox property by a certified   YES ◯
appraiser as described in Article 9?   NO ◯

QUESTION 10 - SAVAGE ROAD IMPROVEMENTS
Shall the Town vote to raise and appropriate the sum of $97,500 to improve a 4,000 LF. section of Savage   YES ◯
Road as described in Article 10?   NO ◯

QUESTION 11 - WRESTLING
Shall the Town vote to authorize, in accordance with NH RSA 285:20, the conducting of a wrestling   YES ◯
competition(s) as described in Article 11 and as requested by the Milford Lion's Club?   NO ◯

GO TO TOWN BALLOT FOUR TO CONTINUE VOTING

QUESTION 12 - NEW MILFORD SCHOOL LAND AGREEMENT (QUEENS QUARRY)
Shall the Town, at the request of the Milford School Board, vote to authorize the Board of Selectmen to enter into a purchase and sale agreement to convey the premises owned by the Town known as Map 47, Lot 28, located on Old Brookline Road and consisting of approximately twelve (12) acres, said agreement to be on such terms and conditions as the Selectmen deem expedient as described in Article 12?

YES ○
NO ○

QUESTION 13 - FIREWORKS
Shall the Town vote to raise and appropriate the sum of $0 for the purpose of providing a Fourth of July type of fireworks display as described in Article 13?

YES ○
NO ○

QUESTION 14 - HIGHWAY CAPITAL RESERVE
Shall the Town vote to raise and appropriate the sum of $25,000 to add to the established Highway Capital Reserve Fund as described in Article 14?

YES ○
NO ○

QUESTION 15 - MIDDLE STREET SIDEWALK
Shall the Town vote to raise and appropriate the sum of $0 for the construction of two hundred feet of brick banded concrete sidewalk on the north side of Middle Street as described in Article 15?

YES ○
NO ○

QUESTION 16 - WASTEWATER FACILITY
Shall the Town vote to raise and appropriate the sum of $1,320,692 to operate and maintain the Wastewater Treatment Facility, and the Sanitary Sewer Collection System as described in Article 16?

YES ○
NO ○

QUESTION 17 - WATER DEPARTMENT
Shall the Town vote to raise and appropriate the sum of $754,942 to operate and maintain the Water Department as described in Article 17?

YES ○
NO ○

QUESTION 18 - FIRE DEPARTMENT CAPITAL RESERVE
Shall the Town vote to raise and appropriate the sum of $25,000 to be paid into the established Capital Reserve Fund to finance the acquisition of fire apparatus and equipping thereof, as described in Article 18?

YES ○
NO ○

QUESTION 19 - FIRE STATION CLEANING/PAINTING
Shall the Town vote to raise and appropriate the sum of $19,936 to clean and repaint the interior bays of the Milford Fire Station as described in Article 19?

YES ○
NO ○

QUESTION 20 - TOWN'S OPERATING BUDGET
Shall the Town of Milford raise and appropriate as an operating budget, not including appropriations by Special Warrant Articles, the amounts set forth on the budget posted with the Warrant, for the purposes set forth therein, totaling $6,774,995. Should this Article be defeated, the operating budget shall be $6,457,698, which is the same as last year, with certain adjustments required by previous actions of the Town, or by law, or the governing body may hold one special meeting, in accordance with RSA 40:13, X and XVI, to take up the issue of a revised operating budget only?

YES ○
NO ○

QUESTION 21 - ROUTE 13 TRAFFIC SAFETY
Shall the Town vote to raise and appropriate the sum of $20,000 as the Town's share of traffic safety improvements at the Rte. 13 and Emerson Road intersection and other conditions as described in Article 21?

YES ○
NO ○

QUESTION 22 - AMBULANCE DIRECTOR VEHICLE
Shall the Town vote to raise and appropriate the sum of $10,000 to purchase or lease a new or used replacement vehicle for the Ambulance Director as described in Article 22?

YES ○
NO ○

QUESTION 23 - AMUBULANCE CAPITAL RESERVE
Shall the Town vote to raise and appropriate the sum of $12,000 to be paid into the established Ambulance Capital Reserve Fund to finance the acquisition and equipping thereof as described in Article 23?

YES ○
NO ○

QUESTION 24 - LIBRARY CONSULTING
Shall the Town vote to raise and appropriate the sum of $7,500 towards the cost of hiring a consulting firm to perform a professional library needs analysis as described in Article 24?

YES ○
NO ○

QUESTION 25 - LIBRARY GIFTS
Shall the Town vote to authorize the Library Trustees, in accordance with RSA 202-A:4-d, to accept gifts of personal property, other than money, and not be required to hold a public hearing unless the gift is valued at over $5,000, said authorization to continue until recinded by Town Meeting vote, as described in Article 25?

YES ○
NO ○

QUESTION 26 - TOWN REVALUATION
Shall the voters of the Town instruct the Board of Selectmen to plan for a town-wide revaluation and to seek funds for the same at the 1998 Annual Town Meeting as more particularly described in Article 26?

YES ○
NO ○

QUESTION 27 - CONSERVATION COMMISSION LAND FUND
Shall the Town vote to raise and appropriate the sum of $30,000 to be added to the fund created in accordance with NH RSA 36-A, for the acquisition of property and other RSA 36-A conservation purposes as the Town may direct in accordance with the provisions of NH RSA 36-A as described in Article 27?

YES ○
NO ○

GO TO TOWN BALLOT FIVE TO CONTINUE VOTING

211

QUESTION 28 - NEW ELDERLY EXEMPTION

Shall we modify the elderly exemption from property tax in the Town of Milford, based on assessed value, for qualified taxpayers to be as follows: for a person 65 years of age up to 75 years of age $20,000; for a person 75 years of age and up to 80 years $30,000; for a person 80 years of age or older $40,000. To qualify the person must have been a New Hampshire resident for at least 5 years, own real estate individually or jointly, or if the real estate is owned by such person's spouse, they must have been married for at least five years. In **YES** ○
addition, the taxpayer must have a net income of not more than $18,400 or, if married, a combined net income of less than $26,400; and own net assets not in excess of $35,000 excluding the value of the person's **NO** ○
residence.

QUESTION 29 - RIVERSIDE CEMETERY   **YES** ○

Shall the Town vote to raise and appropriate the sum of $12,800 to construct a 24 by 20 foot addition onto the **NO** ○ existing storage building at Riverside Cemetery as described in Article 29.

QUESTION 30 - TOWN HALL ROOF REPAIR   **YES** ○

Shall the Town vote to raise and appropriate the sum of $80,000 to shingle the Town Hall roof and install **NO** ○ and/or repair the gutters as described in Article 30?

QUESTION 31 - TAX EXEMPT CHARITABLE PROPERTIES   **YES** ○

Shall we adopt the provision of RSA 72:23-n, allowing for otherwise tax-exempt charitable properties to enter **NO** ○ into an agreement with the Town to make payment in lieu of taxes as described in Article 31?

QUESTION 32 - "SENATE BILL 2"   **YES** ○

Shall the provisions for voting by official ballot on all issues before the Town of Milford under New Hampshire **NO** ○ Revised Statutes Annotated 40:13 be limited to the election of officers and certain other questions?

END OF TOWN BALLOT VOTING

Bibliography

BOOKS AND MONOGRAPHS

Adams, Charles Francis et al. *The Genesis of the Massachusetts Town, and the Development of Town Meeting Government*. Cambridge: John Wilson and Son, 1892.

————. *Three Episodes of Massachusetts History*. Boston: Houghton, Mifflin and Company, 1892. 2 vols.

Adams, Herbert B. *The Germanic Origin of New England Towns*. Baltimore: Johns Hopkins University Studies in Historical and Political Science, 1892.

————. *Norman Constables in America*. Baltimore: Johns Hopkins University Studies in Historical and Political Science, 1883.

Arendt, Hannah. *On Revolution*. New York: Viking Press, 1963.

Aronson, Stephen. *The Legal Powers of Town Councils in Rhode Island*. Kingston: Bureau of Government Research, University of Rhode Island, n.d.

Bachrach, Peter, and Baratz, Morton S. *Power and Poverty*. New York: Oxford University Press, 1967.

Banfield, Edward C., and Wilson, James Q. *City Politics*. Cambridge: Harvard University Press and MIT Press, 1963.

Barber, Benjamin R. *Strong Democracy: Participatory Politics for a New Age*. Berkeley: University of California Press, 1984.

Baylies, Francis. *Historical Memoir of the Colony of New Plymouth*. Boston: Wiggin & Lunt, 1866.

Belknap, Jeremy. *The History of New Hampshire*. Boston: Isaiah Thomas and Ebenezer T. Andrews, 1791. 3 vols.

Bolan, Robert P. *Handbook for Massachusetts Selectmen*. Amherst: Bureau of Government Research, University of Massachusetts, 1956.

Bolton, Geoffrey. *A Handbook for Town Moderators*. 2nd ed. Boston: Massachusetts Federation of Taxpayers Associations, 1954.

Bridenbaugh, Carl. *Cities in the Wilderness*. New York: Ronald Press Company, 1938.

Bryan, Frank M. *Politics in the Rural States: People, Parties, and Processes*. Boulder, Colo.: Westview Press, 1981.

———. *Yankee Politics in Rural Vermont*. Hanover, N.H.: University Press of New England, 1974.

———, and McClaughry, John. *The Vermont Papers: Recreating Democracy on a Human Scale*. Chelsea, Vt.: Chelsea Green Publishing Company, 1989.

Bryce, James. *The American Commonwealth*. 2nd ed., rev. London: Macmillan and Company, 1891.

Callahan, Ellen E. *Hadley: A Study of the Political Development of a Typical New England Town from the Official Records (1659–1930)*. Northampton, Mass.: Smith College Studies in History, 1930.

Canfield, Cass. *Samuel Adams's Revolution: 1765–1776*. New York: Harper & Row Publishers, 1976.

Caruso, John C., and Coduri, Joseph E. *Home Rule Charters in Rhode Island*. Providence: Rhode Island Office of Municipal Affairs, 1995.

Chamberlain, Mellen. *A Documentary History of Chelsea: 1624–1824*. Boston: Massachusetts Historical Society, 1908.

Chandler, Alfred D. *Local Self-Government*. Brookline, Mass.: Riverdale Press, 1908.

Channing, Edward. *The Narragansett Planters*. Baltimore: Johns Hopkins University Studies in Historical and Political Science, 1886.

———. *Town and County Government in the English Colonies of North America*. Baltimore: Johns Hopkins University Studies in Historical and Political Science, 1884.

Conley, Patrick T. *Democracy in Decline: Rhode Island's Constitutional Development 1776–1841*. Providence: Rhode Island Historical Society, 1977.

Dahl, Robert. *Who Governs?* New Haven, Conn.: Yale University Press, 1961.

Daniels, Bruce C. *The Connecticut Town: Growth and Development, 1635–1790*. Middletown, Conn.: Wesleyan University Press, 1979.

DeBard, Stuart. *Massachusetts Finance Committee Handbook*. Boston: Association of Town Finance Committees, 1992.

DeSantis, Victor W. *Open Town Meetings in Massachusetts: Issues and Evaluation*. Bridgewater, Mass.: Institute for Regional Development, Bridgewater State College, 1997.

de Tocqueville, Alexis. *Democracy in America*. New York: Harper Perennial, 1988.

Dewey, John. *The Public and Its Problems*. Denver: Alan Swallow, 1927.

De Wold, Austin. *The Town Meeting: A Manual of Massachusetts Law*. Boston: George B. Reed, 1890.

Dowling, Edward T. *The Office of First Selectman in Connecticut Local Government*. Storrs: Institute of Public Service, University of Connecticut, 1976.

Drake, Francis A. *The Town of Roxbury*. Boston: Municipal Printing Office, 1905.

Drake, Samuel G. *The History and Antiquities of Boston, from Its Settlement in 1630 to the Year 1770*. Boston: Luther Stevens, 1856.

Dwight, Timothy. *Travels in New England and New York*. Cambridge: Belknap Press of Harvard University Press, 1969.

Emerson, Ralph W. *Miscellanies*. Boston: Houghton, Mifflin and Company, 1904.

Fairlie, John A. *Local Government in Counties, Towns, and Villages*. New York: Century Company, 1906.

Farrar, Cynthia. *The Origins of Democratic Thinking*. Cambridge: Cambridge University Press, 1988.

The Federalist Papers. New York: New American Library, 1961.

Finley, M. I. *Democracy: Ancient and Modern*. 2nd ed. London: Hogarth Press, 1985.

Ford, Paul L., ed. *The Writings of Thomas Jefferson*. New York: G. P. Putnam's Sons, 1894.

Foster, William E. *Town Government in Rhode Island*. Baltimore: Johns Hopkins University Studies in Historical and Political Science, 1886.

Gould, John. *New England Town Meeting: Safeguard of Democracy*. Brattleboro, Vt.: Stephen Daye Press, 1940.

Guide for Establishing a Representative Town Meeting. Amherst: Bureau of Government Research, University of Massachusetts, 1957.

Haller, William, Jr. *The Puritan Town-Planting in New England Colonial Development 1630–1660*. New York: Columbia University Press, 1951.

Hansen, Mogens H. *The Athenian Democracy in the Age of Demosthenes*. Oxford: Basil Blackwell, 1991.

Hardy, Henry W. *The Role of the Town Counsel*. Amherst: Bureau of Government Research, University of Massachusetts, 1960.

Harlow, Ralph V. *Samuel Adams: Promoter of the American Revolution*. New York: Henry Holt and Company, 1923.

Harvey, Lashley G. *The Walled Towns of New England*. Boston: Boston University, 1964.

Haskins, George L. *Law and Authority in Early Massachusetts*. New York: Macmillan Company, 1960.

Haynes, George H. *Representation and Suffrage in Massachusetts, 1620–1691*. Baltimore: Johns Hopkins University Studies in Historical and Political Science, 1884.

Hicks, Granville. *Small Town*. New York: Macmillan Company, 1947.

Home Rule Charters in Rhode Island. Providence: Rhode Island Office of Municipal Affairs, 1995.

Hormell, Orren C. *Maine Towns*. Brunswick, Maine: Bowdoin College Bulletin, 1932.

Hosmer, James K. *Samuel Adams, the Man of the Town Meeting*, vol. 2, no. 4. Baltimore: Johns Hopkins University Studies in Historical and Political Science, 1884.

Howard, George E. *Local Constitutional History of the United States*. Baltimore: Publication Agency of Johns Hopkins University, 1889.

Hunter, Floyd. *Community Power Structure*. Chapel Hill: University of North Carolina Press, 1953.

Jackson, W. Eric. *Local Government in England and Wales*. Hardmonsworth, Middlesex: Penguin Books, 1959.

Jager, Ronald. *Last House on the Road: Excursions into a Rural Past*. Boston: Beacon Press, 1994.

Jameson, J. Franklin, ed. *Johnson's Wonder-Working Providence: 1628–1651*. New York: Barnes & Noble, 1952.

Johnson, Richard B., Trustman, Benjamin A., and Wadsworth, Charles Y. *Town Meeting Time*. Boston: Little, Brown, and Company, 1962.

Jowett, Benjamin, trans. *Aristotle's Politics*. New York: Carlton House, n.d.

Kagan, Donald. *Pericles of Athens and the Birth of Democracy*. New York: Free Press, 1991.

Kittredge, Henry C. *Barnstable 1639–1939*. Barnstable, Mass.: Tercentenary Committee, 1939.

Levermore, Charles H. *The Town and City Government of New Haven*. Baltimore: Johns Hopkins University Studies in Historical and Political Science, 1886.

Levin, Murray B. *The Alienated Voter*. New York: Holt, Rinehart & Winston, 1960.

Levitan, Donald, and Mariner, Elwyn E. *Your Massachusetts Government*. 8th ed. Newtown Centre, Mass.: Governmental Research Publications, 1978.

Lippincott, Bertram. *Indians, Privateers, and High Society*. Philadelphia: J. B. Lippincott Company, 1961.

Locke, John. *The Second Treatise of Government*. Indianapolis: Bobbs-Merrill Company, 1952.

Lockridge, Kenneth A. *A New England Town: The First Hundred Years*. New York: W. W. Norton & Company, 1970.

Lopach, James J., and McKinsey, Lauren S. *Handbook of Montana Forms of Local Government*. Missoula: Bureau of Government Research, University of Montana, 1975.

Lowell, A. Lawrence. *Public Opinion and Popular Government*. New York: Longmans, Green and Company, 1926.

Lynd, Robert S., and Lynd, Helen M. *Middletown*. New York: Harcourt, Brace, and World, 1929.

———. *Middletown in Transition*. New York: Harcourt Brace Jovanovich, 1937.

MacLear, Anne B. *Early New England Towns: A Comparative Study of Their Development*. New York: Columbia University Press, 1908.

Maine Moderators Manual. 5th ed. Augusta: Maine Municipal Association, 1989.

Mann, David L. *Handbook for New Hampshire Selectmen and Local Officers*. Concord: New Hampshire Municipal Association, 1965.

Mansbridge, Jane J. *Beyond Adversary Democracy*. New York: Basic Books, Publishers, 1980.

Martin, Roscoe C. *Grass Roots: Rural Democracy in America*. New York: Harper & Row Publishers, 1964.

Milbrath, Lester W. *Political Participation: How and Why Do People Get Involved in Politics?* Chicago: Rand McNally & Company, 1965.

Modernizing Local Government. New York: Committee for Economic Development, 1966.

Mumford, Lewis. *The City in History*. New York: Harcourt, Brace, & World, 1961.

Munro, William B. *The Government of the United States*. 4th ed. New York: Macmillan Company, 1937.

———. *The Initiative, Referendum, and Recall*. New York: D. Appleton and Company, 1912.

Notestein, Wallace. *The English People on the Eve of Colonization*. New York: Harper & Row, Publishers, 1954.

Nuquist, Andrew E. *Town Government in Vermont*. Burlington: Government Research Center, University of Vermont, 1964.

———, and Nuquist, Edith W. *Vermont State Government and Administration*. Burlington: Government Research Center, University of Vermont, 1996.

Ober, Josiah. *Mass and Elite in Democratic Athens*. Princeton: Princeton University Press, 1989.

Padover, Saul. *The Complete Jefferson*. New York: Sloan and Pearce, 1943.

Paige, Lucius R. *History of Cambridge, Massachusetts: 1630–1877*. Boston: H. O. Houghton and Company, 1877.

Parker, Joel. *Origin, Organization, and Influence of the Towns of New England*. Cambridge: Press of John Wilson and Son, 1867.

Pateman, Carole. *Participation and Democratic Theory*. New York: Cambridge University Press, 1970.

Pitkin, Hanna F. *Representation*. New York: Atherton Press, 1969.

Powell, Lyman P., ed. *Historic Towns of New England*. New York: G. P. Putnam's Sons, 1899.

Powell, Sumner C. *Puritan Village: The Formation of a New England Town*. Middletown, Conn.: Wesleyan University Press, 1963.

Reid, John P. *The Concept of Representation in the Age of the American Revolution*. Chicago: University of Chicago Press, 1989.

Riker, William H. *Liberalism against Populism: A Confrontation between the Theory of Democracy and the Theory of Social Choice*. San Francisco: W. H. Freeman Company, 1982.

Roberts, Kenneth L. *Local Government in Maine*. Augusta: Maine Municipal Association, 1979.

Rousseau, Jean-Jacques. *The Social Contract*. Chicago: Henry Regnery Company, 1954.

Schattschneider, E. E. *The Semisovereign People: A Realist's View of Democracy in America*. New York: Holt, Rinehart, and Winston, 1960.

Shipton, Clifford K. *Roger Conant*. Cambridge: Harvard University Press, 1944.

Shurtleff, Nathaniel B., ed. *Records of the Governor and Company of the Massachusetts Bay in New England*. Boston: From the Press of William White, 1853. 2 vols.

————. *Records of the Colony of New Plymouth in New England*. Boston: From the Press of William White, 1855.

Sinclair, R. K. *Democracy and Participation in Athens*. Cambridge: Cambridge University Press, 1988.

Sly, John F. *Town Government in Massachusetts (1620–1930)*. Cambridge: Harvard University Press, 1930.

Snider, Clyde F. *Local Government in Rural America*. New York: Appleton-Century-Crofts, 1957.

Starr, Chester G. *The Birth of Athenian Democracy*. Oxford: Oxford University Press, 1990.

Stockton, David. *The Classical Athenian Democracy*. Oxford: Oxford University Press, 1990.

Stuart, Patricia. *The Connecticut Town Meeting*. Storrs: Institute of Public Service, University of Connecticut, 1984.

————. *Handbook for Connecticut Selectmen*. Storrs: Institute of Public Service, University of Connecticut, 1984.

Susemihl, Franz, and Hicks, Robert D. *The Politics of Aristotle*. London: Macmillan and Company, 1894. Books I–V.

Switzerland. Berne: Kümmerly & Frey, 1994.

Syed, Anwar. *The Political Theory of American Local Government*. New York: Random House, 1966.

Tercentenary of the Landing of the Popham Colony at the Mouth of the Kennebec River, August 19, 1607. Portland: Maine Historical Society, 1907.

Tilden, Robert J. *How Town Meeting Functions*. Falmouth, Mass.: Falmouth Enterprise, 1957.

Tinder, Glenn. *Community: Reflection on a Tragic Ideal*. Baton Rouge: Louisiana State University Press, 1980.

Town Meeting and Elections Manual. Augusta: Maine Municipal Association, 1994.

Trumbull, Benjamin. *A Complete History of Connecticut: Civil and Ecclesiastical*. New London, Conn.: H. D. Utley, 1898. 2 vols.

Usher, Roland G. *The Pilgrims and Their History*. New York: Macmillan Company, 1918.

Vidich, Arthur J., and Bensman, Joseph. *Small Town in Mass Society: Class, Power, and Religion in a Rural Community*. Princeton: Princeton University Press, 1968.

Waugh, H. Bernard, Jr. *Town Meeting & School Meeting Handbook*. Concord: New Hampshire Municipal Association, 1995.

Webber, Edwin W. *Rhode Island Local Government and Administration*. Kingston: Bureau of Government Research, University of Rhode Island, 1963.

Webster, Clarence M. *Town Meeting Country*. New York: Duell, Sloan & Pearce, 1945.

Wertenbaker, Thomas J. *The Puritan Oligarchy: The Founding of American Civilization*. New York: Charles Scribner's Sons, 1947.

Whitmore, William H. *The Massachusetts Civil List for the Colonial and Provincial Periods, 1630–1774*. Albany, N.Y.: J. Munsell, 1870.

Wickwar, W. Hardy. *The Political Theory of Local Government*. Columbia: University of South Carolina Press, 1970.

Wilcox, Delos F. *Government by All the People or the Initiative, the Referendum, and the Recall as Instruments of Democracy*. New York: Macmillan Company, 1912.

Winthrop, John. *The History of New England from 1630 to 1649*. Boston: Little, Brown, and Company, 1853.

Woliver, Laura R. *From Outrage to Action: The Politics of Grass-Roots Dissent*. Urbana: University of Illinois Press, 1993.

Wood, Robert C. *Suburbia: Its People and Their Politics*. Boston: Houghton Mifflin Company, 1958.

Worcester, Alfred. *The Origin of the New England Town Meeting*. Waltham, Mass.: Waltham Historical Society, 1925.

The Writings of Thomas Jefferson. Washington, D.C.: Thomas Jefferson Memorial Association of the United States, 1904. Vol. 15.

Zimmerman, Joseph F. *Federal Preemption; The Silent Revolution*. Ames: Iowa State University Press, 1991.

———. *The Federated City: Community Control in Large Cities*. New York: St. Martin's Press, 1972.

———. *The Massachusetts Town Meeting: A Tenacious Institution*. Albany: Graduate School of Public Affairs, State University of New York at Albany, 1967.

———. *Participatory Democracy: Populism Revived*. New York: Praeger Publishers, 1986.

———. *The Recall: Tribunal of the People*. Westport, Conn.: Praeger Publishers, 1997.

———. *State-Local Relations: A Partnership Approach*. 2nd ed. Westport, Conn.: Praeger Publishers, 1995.

Zuckerman, Michael. *Peaceable Kingdoms: New England Towns in the Eighteenth Century*. New York: Alfred A. Knopf, 1970.

GOVERNMENT DOCUMENTS AND REPORTS

Athol, Mass. *Report of the Committee "To Consider the Subject of a Representative Form of Town Government."* (May 15, 1963).

Auburn, Mass. *Report of the Representative Town Meeting Committee.* (January 14, 1963).

Boston. *Dorchester Town Records. Fourth Report of the Record Commissions of the City of Boston,* 2nd ed. Boston: Rockwell and Churchill, 1883.

————. *A Report of the Record Commissioners of the City of Boston, Containing the Boston Records from 1700 to 1728.* Boston: Rockwell and Churchill, 1883.

————. *Report of the Town Convention.* 1804.

————. *Second Report of the Record Commissioners of the City of Boston.* Boston: Rockwell and Churchill, 1877.

————. *Several Rules, Orders, and By-Laws Made and Agreed Upon by the Freeholders and Inhabitants of Boston of the Massachusetts, at Their Meeting, May 12, and September 22, 1701.* Boston: Bartholomew Green, 1702.

————. *A Volume of Records Relating to the Early History of Boston Containing Boston Town Records, 1784 to 1796.* Boston: Municipal Printing Office, 1903.

————. *A Volume of Records Relating to the Early History of Boston Containing Boston Town Records, 1796 to 1813.* Boston: Municipal Printing Office, 1905.

————. *A Volume of Records Relating to the Early History of Boston Containing Boston Town Records, 1814 to 1822.* Boston: Municipal Printing Office, 1906.

Cambridge, Mass. *The Records of the Town of Cambridge (Formerly Newtowne) Massachusetts 1630–1703.* Cambridge: Printed by order of the City Council under direction of the City Clerk, 1901.

Commonwealth of Massachusetts. *The Acts and Resolve of the Province of the Massachusetts Bay.* Vol. 1. Boston: Wright and Potter, 1869.

————. *The Acts and Resolves of the Province of Massachusetts Bay.* Vol. 2. Boston: Wright and Potter, 1879.

————. *The Acts and Resolves of the Province of the Massachusetts Bay.* Vol. 3. Boston: Wright and Potter, 1878.

————. *The Constitution of the Commonwealth of Massachusetts.* Boston: Secretary of the Commonwealth, 1984.

————. *Opinion of the Justices to the House of Representatives.* 347 Mass. 792 (1964).

————. *Report of the Commission to Complete the Work of Revising and Codifying the Laws Relating to Towns.* Boston: Senate No. 2 (1920).

————. *Report Submitted by the Legislative Research Council Relative to Town Meetings in Regional Schools.* Boston: House of Representatives No. 3687. (December 27, 1961).

Fall Yearly Town Meeting Warrant for Use at Fall Yearly Town Meeting, November, 1996. Brewster, Mass.: Town of Brewster, 1996.

The Federal and State Constitutions, Colonial Charters, and Other Organic Laws. Washington, D.C.: Government Printing Office, 1909.

Final Report of the Charter Commission of Southbridge, Massachusetts. (January 1, 1970).

Final Report of the Official Ballot Referenda Study Committee. Concord, N.H.: Senate, 1997.

Final Report of the Town Meeting Study Committee. Concord, Mass.: Town of Concord, 1996.

The Form of Government in Large Towns. Boston: Legislative Research Bureau, 1971.

Framingham, Mass. *Report of the Committee Studying Changes in the Town Government*. (March 1965).

General By-Laws of the Town of Shrewsbury. Shrewsbury, Mass.: n.d.

Holden, Mass. *Report of the Committee to Study the Representative Form of Town Meeting for Holden* (n.d.).

A Model Charter for Towns in Massachusetts. Boston: Massachusetts Department of Community Affairs: n.d..

1995 School District Annual Report. Bedford, N.H.

1997 Municipal Census Report. Montpelier: Vermont League of Cities and Towns, 1997.

Preliminary Findings from the Concord Town Meeting Survey: Report of the Work Group. Concord, Mass.: Town of Concord, 1995.

Population and Local Government. Montpelier: Vermont Secretary of State, 1990.

Report and Recommendations of the Advisory Committee for the Year 1970. Winthrop, Mass.: Town of Winthrop, 1970.

Report of the Committee to Consider the Use of the Australian Ballot to Vote on Issues Presented and Debated at Town Meeting. Westboro: Massachusetts Moderators Association, 1997.

Study Report on the Constitution of Finance Committees in Representative Town Meeting Systems. Boston: Massachusetts Department of Community Affairs, 1973.

Thorpe, Francis, N., ed. *The Federal and State Constitutions, Colonial Charters, and Other Organic Laws*, vol. 4. Washington, D.C.: Government Printing Office, 1909.

A Town Meeting Committee Guide. Stoughton, Mass.: Town of Stoughton, 1992.

Town of Marshfield Special & Annual Town Meeting. Marshfield, Mass.: 1996.

Town of Stoneham, Massachusetts, 1995 Annual Report. 1996.

Town Report. Brookline, Mass.: 1915.

Articles

"Acid Rain Resolution Passed at 197 N.H. Town Meetings." *Keene (N.H.) Shopper News* (May 25, 1983): 5.

Adams, Charles F. "The Genesis of the Massachusetts Town and the Development of Town Meeting Government." *Proceedings of the Massachusetts Historical Society* 7 (January 1892): 172–211.

Adams, Patricia. "Ballot Law Is a Boon to N.H. Democracy." *Keene (N.H.) Sentinel* (September 1, 1995): 8.

Adlow, Elijah. "Lemuel Shaw and Municipal Corporations." *Massachusetts Law Quarterly* 44 (July 1959): 53–98.

Aldrich, Eric. "Peterborough Buys Police Station, Trims Spending." *Keene (N.H.) Sentinel* (March 14, 1994): 3.

———. "Tempers Soar at Ski Meeting." *Keene (N.H.) Sentinel* (December 1, 1995): 1.

Alexander, John W. and Berger, Morroe. "Is the Town Meeting Finished?" *The American Mercury* (August 1949): 144–51.

Amsden, Roger. "High Court OK's Special Belmont Meeting on Town Beach Purchase." *Union Leader* (Manchester, N.H.) (July 25, 1997): A5.

Atkins, Richard A. "The Old and the New in Massachusetts Towns." *National Municipal Review* 29 (June 1940): 361–66.

———— and Ziegler, Lyman H. "Citizen Budgeting in Massachusetts." *National Municipal Review* 30 (October 1941): 568–73.

Baker, Gordon E. "The Impulse for Direct Democracy." *National Civic Review* 66 (January 1977): 19–23, 35.

Banning, Kendall. "Is the Town Meeting Democratic?" *National Municipal Review* 24 (March 1935): 152–55.

Bates, Frank G. "Village Government in New England." *The American Political Science Review* 3 (August 1912): 367–85.

Bogart, Walter T. "State-Local Relations in Vermont." In Rolf N. B. Haugen and E. William Steele, eds., *Vermont—The 14th Original State*. Burlington: Government Clearing House, University of Vermont, 1959.

Bryan, Frank M. "Direct Democracy and Civic Competence." *The Good Society* 5 (Fall 1995): 36–44.

————. "Does the Town Meeting Offer an Option for Urban America?" *National Civic Review* 67 (December 1978): 523–27.

————. "Town Meeting Debate." *Vermont Life* (Spring 1986): 36–39.

————. "Town Meeting Government Still Supported in Vermont." *National Civic Review* 61 (July 1972): 348–51.

————. "Trouble in the Vermont Hills." *Newsweek* (March 5, 1984): 15.

Carney, Beth. "Framingham Rejects Plan to Become a City." *Boston Globe* (April 9, 1997): B4.

Chandler, Alfred D. "Remarks of Alfred D. Chandler." *Massachusetts Law Quarterly* 4 (February 1919): 71–91.

Clark, Raymond P. "Maybe It's Sloppy, but It's Good Government." *Boston Globe* (February 22, 1985): 14.

Cunningham, Richard H. "Every Citizen a Legislator: But It Takes Good Citizens." *Worcester (Mass.) Telegram* (March 5, 1964): 6.

————. "Forty Massachusetts Communities Now Use the Representative Town Meeting Idea." *Worcester (Mass.) Telegram* (March 4, 1964): 6.

————. "Representative Town Meetings: The Shrewsbury Experience." *Worcester (Mass.) Telegram* (March 6, 1959): 6.

————. "What's Gone Wrong with the Old Town Meeting?" *Worcester (Mass.) Telegram* (March 3, 1959): 6.

Daley, Yvonne. "Town Meeting Day Voters Undercut Act 200." *Boston Globe* (March 8, 1990): 26.

Daniels, Bruce C. "Contrasting Colony–Town Relations in the Founding of Connecticut and Rhode Island." *The Connecticut Historical Society* 3 (April 1973): 60–64.

"The Decay of Town Government." *The Nation* 65 (September 2, 1897): 180–81.

Denison, Dave. "Developments in Plymouth." *Commonwealth* 1 (Spring 1996): 5–6.

————. "Discord in Concord." *Commonwealth* 1 (Summer 1996): 8– 9.

————. "Framingham: Back to the Future." *Commonwealth* 2 (Spring/Summer 1997): 12–13, 20.

————. "Has History Caught Up to the Town Meeting?" *Boston Sunday Globe* (April 7, 1996): 64.

————. "A Professor's Survey." *Commonwealth* 2 (Winter 1997): 13.

————. "Two More Towns Scuttle Town Meeting." *Commonwealth* 1 (Summer 1996): 10–11.

"Do Budgetary Meetings Work: The Reaction in Yarmouth, Maine Is Mixed." *(White River Junction, Vt.) Valley News* (March 31, 1981): 10-S.

Doyle, William, and Milburn, Josephine F. "Citizen Participation in New England Politics: Town Meetings, Political Parties, and Interest Groups." In Josephine F. Milburn and Victoria Schuck, eds., *New England Politics*. Cambridge: Schenkman Publishing Company, 1981.

"11 of 13 Vermont Towns Refuse to Join Hydropower Project." *Keene (N.H.) Sentinel* (March 8, 1983): 9.

Ellis, Mark E. "Democracy Lumbers on as Off-the Point Meetings Discourage Participation." *(Worcester, Mass.) Telegram & Gazette* (June 6, 1997): B4.

————. "Plan to Speed Things Takes Its Time." *(Worcester, Mass.) Telegram & Gazette* (May 21, 1997): B3.

"The Fading Town Meeting." *National Civic Review* 54 (October 1965): 464–65, 522.

"54 Towns Support Death Penalty: Westminster, Rockingham Say No." *Keene (N.H.) Sentinel* (March 8, 1989): 8.

Flint, Anthony. "Petersham Lost." *Boston Globe* (September 17, 1996): B1, B3.

Ford, Royal. "Town Meetings: Relic of the Past?" *Boston Globe* (March 3, 1991): 49–50.

Forry, Kathryn. "Too Many Demands, Too Few Thanks Make the Selectman's Job Tough." *Keene (N.H.) Sentinel* (January 21, 1983): 1, 3.

Fossel, Peter V. "How Best to Run a Small Town." *Yankee* 41 (December 1977): 108–11, 114–18.

Gere, Edwin A., Jr. "Open Town Meeting: Vital Institution or Inefficient Anachronism?" *The Municipal Forum* (Winter 1981): 11–18.

Good, Jeffrey. "Vermont Spoilers." *New York Times* (March 16, 1983): 23.

"Greenfield, Mass., Council Opposes City Government Led by a Mayor." *Keene (N.H.) Sentinel* (June 6, 1997): 3.

Gross, Melanie B. "Political Poison at the Grass Roots." *New York Times* (May 4, 1996): 19.

Hart, John. "Rye Residents OK Mandated Sewer." *(Manchester, N.H.) Union Leader* (November 18, 1989): 6.

Harvey, Lashly G. "First Break in New Hampshire." *National Municipal Review* 35 (November 1946): 521–24.

Hayward, Mark. "Times Change, Towns Change." *Keene (N.H.) Sentinel* (March 12, 1991): 1, 10.

Herman, Geoffrey. "Municipal Charters: A Comparative Analysis of 75 Maine Charters." *Maine Townsman* (August 1992): 5–15.

Hollister, Timothy S. "The Myth and Reality of Home Rule Powers in Connecticut." *Connecticut Bar Journal* 59 (1985): 389–403.

"How Voters Get Muscle: Maine Citizens Arm Themselves with Petitions." *(White River Junction, Vt.) Valley News* (March 31, 1981): 11–S.

Howes, Robert G. "Letter to the Editor." *The Massachusetts Selectman* 19 (October 1960): 34–35.

Kalijarvi, Thorsten V. "Town Meeting vs. Town Management." *National Municipal Review* 29 (August 1940): 540–44.

Knowles, Howard S. "How Massachusetts Towns Choose Their Officers." *(Worcester, Mass.) Sunday Telegram* (February 12, 1961): B-1.

LaPlante, John G. "What Killed the Town Meeting?" *The Nation* 123 (February 1, 1958): 96–98.

Leahy, Patrick J. "America's Thinking Is a Citizens' Job." *New York Times* (April 10, 1982): 22.

Long, John A. "N.E. Town Fights for Landscape." *Christian Science Monitor* (February 13, 1965): 2.

Lord, Arthur. "The Representative Town Meeting in Massachusetts." *Massachusetts Law Quarterly* 4 (February 1919): 49–74.

Lukas, J. Anthony. "Urban Problems Beset Old Yankee Community." *New York Times* (March 27, 1970): 1.

MacNeil, Allen et al. "Official Ballot Bill Tears Away at the Wrong Thing." *(Laconia, N.H.) Citizen* (March 2, 1996): 2.

Mansbridge, Jane J. "Town Meeting Democracy." In Peter Collier, ed., *Dilemmas of Democracy: Readings in American Government*. New York: Harcourt Brace Jovanovich, 1976, 148–67.

Marks, Paul. "The Town Meeting: Alive, but Ailing." *Hartford Courant* (July 14, 1996): 1, A5.

McGrory, Mary. "Weston and Foreign Policy." *(Worcester, Mass.) Evening Gazette* (March 23, 1983): 16.

McGuire, Mark. "12% on State's Voter Rolls Are Dead or Have Moved." *(Albany, N.Y.) Times Union* (October 30, 1996): B2.

McNeilly, Jonathan. "Town Meeting Called on Community Center." *(Manchester, N.H.) Union Leader* (July 24, 1997): A13.

Miller, Amy. "Moderators Walk Fine Line of Order as They Lead Town Business." *Keene (N.H.) Sentinel* (March 12, 1984): 8.

Moroney, Tom. "Modern Life Challenges Town Meeting Tradition." *Boston Sunday Globe* (April 21, 1996): 1, 9.

Morris, Jeanne. "New Meeting Style: 'Slightly Baffling.' " *(Manchester, N.H.) New Hampshire Sunday News* (March 23, 1997): 1, 19A.

Nuquist, Andrew E. "March Meeting." *Vermont Life* (Spring 1947): 9–11, 39.

Parker, Joel. "The Origin, Organization, and Influence of the Towns of New England." *Proceedings of the Massachusetts Historical Society* 9 (1866–1867): 14–65.

Peairs, C. A. "Introduction." *Boston University Law Review* 38 (Summer 1958): 339–46.

Preer, Robert. "Meeting Needs of a Democracy?" *Boston Globe* (May 13, 1995): 13, 20.

Rimer, Sara. "In Region of Its Birth, Town Meeting Cedes Tradition to the Television Age." *New York Times* (March 8, 1993): A12.

Robbins, L. H. "Democracy, Town Meeting Style." *New York Times Magazine* (March 23, 1947): 24, 35, 38.

Rousmaniere, James A., Jr. "Fitzwilliam Road Agent Target at Town Meeting." *Keene (N.H.) Sentinel* (December 1, 1995): 5.

Sale, Kirkpatrick. "The Importance of Size for Democracy." *The Good Society* 6 (Fall 1996): 6–10.

"Saugus Selectmen Recalled." *Worcester (Mass.) Telegram* (August 24, 1961): 6.

Shaw, Deirdre M. "Council Turns to Right." *Keene (N.H.) Sentinel* (November 5, 1997): 1.

Shribman, David. "The Town Meeting, New England Staple, Faces Tide of Change." *Wall Street Journal* (March 7, 1986): 1, 24.

Smith, Lincoln. "Leadership in Local Government—the New England Town." *Social Science* 29 (June 1954): 147–57.

———. "Town Meeting Government." *Social Science* 30 (June 1955): 174–85.

Specter, Michael. "In New England, Outgrowing the Quaint and Historical Town Meeting." *Washington Post* (May 12, 1991): A3.

Stetson, Fred. "The Brattleboro Way." *Vermont Life* (Spring 1989): 17–19.

Thompson, Carl D. "The Vital Points in Charter Making from a Socialist Point of View." *National Municipal Review* 2 (July 1913): 416–26.

Tilden, Robert J. "Separation of Powers and the Representative Town Meeting." *Massachusetts Law Quarterly* 42 (March 1957): 24–28.

———. "Some Fundamentals of Town Meetings." *Massachusetts Law Quarterly* 47 (June 1962): 165–74.

———. "Town Government." *Boston University Law Review* 38 (Summer 1958): 347–89.

Thürer, Georg. "The 'Landsgemeinde' of Switzerland." *Pro Helvetia* (July 1972): 1–7.

"Vermonters Come Out against Revising State Election Laws." *Keene (N.H.) Sentinel* (March 31, 1983): 15.

"The Warning for Town Meeting." *VLCT News* (December 1996): 1, 12.

Waugh, H. Bernard, Jr. "How to Make SB 2 Work." *New Hampshire Town & City Counsel* (May 1996): 1–8.

"Why Citizens Shun the Polling Booth: An Interview with Curtis B. Gans." *The Public Perspective* 8 (February/March 1997): 42–44.

Zimmerman, Joseph F. "Can Cities and Towns Meet the Challenges of the Space Age?" *New Hampshire Town and City* 15 (June 1972): 4/104–4/110.

———. "Chaos or Correction?" *National Civic Review* 54 (July 1965): 348–49, 396.

———. "Citizen Budgeting in Massachusetts Towns." *The Massachusetts Selectman* 27 (January 1968): 7–10.

———. "Commonwealth-Town Relations." *The Massachusetts Selectman* 24 (April 1965): 7–9.

———. "Council-Manager Government in Ireland." *Studies in Comparative Local Government* 6 (Summer 1972): 61–69.

———. "Electoral Systems and Direct Citizen Law-Making." *Diskussionsbeitrage (Forschungs-Schwerpunkt Historische Mobilität und Normenwandel, Universität Gesamthochscule, Siegen, Deutschland)* (April 1988): entire issue.

———. "Enhancing Representational Equity in Cities." In Wilma Rule and Joseph F. Zimmerman, *United States Electoral Systems.* Westport, Conn.: Greenwood Press, 1992): 209–20.

———. "Evolving State-Local Relations in New England." In Stephanie Cole, ed., *Partnership within the States: Local Self Government in the Federal System.* Urbana and Philadelphia: Institute of Government and Public Affairs of the University of Illinois and Center for the Study of Federalism of Temple University, 1976: 213–47.

———. "Executive Secretary Plan in Massachusetts." *The Massachusetts Selectman* 26 (October 1967): 17–18, 20–21, 28.

————. "Genesis of the Massachusetts Town." *Social Science* 41 (April 1966): 76–83.

————. "The Heart of Grass Roots Democracy." *Worcester (Mass.) Sunday Telegram Feature Parade* (March 28, 1965): 30–32.

————. "Home Rule in Massachusetts: Some Historical Perspectives." *Home Rule in Action.* Chestnut Hill: Bureau of Public Affairs, Boston College, 1970: 1–20.

————. "Initiative, Referendum, and Recall: Government by Plebiscite?" *Intergovernmental Perspective* 13 (Winter 1987): 32–35.

————. "Law Making by Citizens in the United States." *Diskussionsbeitrage (Forschungs-Schwerpunkt Historische Mobilität und Normenwandel, Universität Siegen, Deutschland)* (Winter 1985): entire issue.

————. "Limitations on Cities and Towns under Home Rule." In Robert J. M. O'Hare, ed., *Municipal Home Rule.* Chestnut Hill: Bureau of Public Affairs, Boston College, 1965: 22–26.

————. "Local Discretionary Authority in New England." *Suffolk University Law Review* 15 (December 1981): 1125–56.

————. "Maximization of Local Autonomy and Citizen Control: A Model." *Home Rule & Civil Society.* Abiko, Japan: Local Public Entity Study Organization, 1989: 175–89.

————. "The New England Town Meeting: Pure Democracy in Action?" *The Municipal Year Book 1984.* Washington, D.C.: International City Management Association, 1984: 102–6.

————. "New Hampshire Mandates." *Comparative State Politics* 11 (October 1990): 38.

————. "On the Other Hand." *National Civic Review* 55 (January 1966): 14–20.

————. "The Open Town Meeting: A Tenacious Institution." *Civic Affairs* 13 (October 1965): 16–19.

————. "Regionalism." *The Massachusetts Selectman* 31 (April 1972): 7–8, 10, 15–16.

————. "Relieving the Fiscal Burdens of State and Federal Mandates and Restraints." *Current Municipal Problems* 19, no. 2 (1992): 216–24.

————. "Representative Town Meeting." *The Massachusetts Selectman* 25 (April 1966): 7–8, 10, 30.

————. "Representative Town Meeting: An Evaluation." *The Massachusetts Selectman* 25 (July 1966): 17–18.

————. "The Role of Local Government in Massachusetts." *The Municipal Voice* 2 (November 1964): 4–8.

————. "Selectmen—Origins." *The Massachusetts Selectman* 25 (January 1966): 17.

————. "Solving Areawide Problems in Rhode Island." In Robert W. Sutton Jr., ed., *Rhode Island Local Government: Past, Present, Future.* Kingston: Bureau of Government Research, University of Rhode Island, 1974: 121–28.

————. "State Mandate Relief: A Quick Look." *Intergovernmental Perspective* 20 (Spring 1994): 28–30.

————. "Town Manager Plan in Massachusetts." *The Massachusetts Selectman* 25 (October 1986): 17–18, 20, 22.

————. "Town Manager Plan in Massachusetts, Part II." *The Massachusetts Selectman* 26 (January 1967): 11–14, 28–30.

————. "Twentieth Century Selectmen." *The Massachusetts Selectman* 25 (January 1966): 23–24.

————. "Whither Town Government." *The Massachusetts Selectman* 29 (October 1970): 11–16, 18–20, 28–31.

Unpublished Materials

Alger, John. "Survey of Rumney Voters concerning Annual Meeting." Available from author, R.R. #1, Box 133, Rumney, N.H. 03266.

Bracco, Donato, and Frasier, Cline. "Voting in Concord in 1997." Available from Donato Bracco, 348 Hayward Mill Road, Concord, Mass. 01742.

Bryan, Frank M. "Comparative Town Meetings: A Search for Causative Models of Feminine Involvement in Politics with New Operational Definitions of a Well Calloused Dependent Variable." Paper presented at the annual meeting of the Rural Sociological Society, San Francisco, August 1975.

————. "Direct Democracy in the New England Town Meeting: Establishing Empirical Parameters." Paper presented at the annual meeting of the American Political Science Association, Washington, D.C., August 30, 1986.

————. "Open Democracy: Correlates of Participation in the New England Town Meetings." Paper presented at the annual meeting of the Southern Political Science Association, Atlanta, November 1976.

————. "Real Democracy: What It Looks Like: How It Works" (work in progress).

————. "Town Meeting in Mass Society—What Role Remains?" Paper presented at the annual meeting of the New England Political Science Association, Durham, N.H., April 1979.

————. "What If We Held a Democracy: Would Anyone Come?" (work in progress).

DeSantis, Victor S. "Patterns of Citizen Participation in Local Politics: Evidence from New England Town Meetings." Paper presented at the 1998 annual meeting of the American Political Science Association, Washington, D.C.

———— and Renner, Tari. "Democratic Traditions in New England Town Meetings: Myths and Realities." Paper presented at the 1997 annual meeting of the Midwest Political Science Association, Chicago.

Evans, Bruce C. "Representativeness in Massachusetts Town Meetings." Paper presented at the annual meeting of the Northeastern Political Science Association, Boston, November 15, 1997.

Hagerman, Robert L. "Roster of Certain Vermont Municipalities with Special Charters or Charter Amendments," 1981. Available from the Vermont Secretary of State, 109 State Street, Montpelier, Vt. 05602.

Hixon, Vivian S. "The New Town Meeting Democracy: A Study of Matched Towns." Unpublished Ph.D. thesis, Michigan State University, 1974.

Kotler, Neil G. "Politics and Citizenship in New England Towns: A Study of Participation and Political Education." Unpublished Ph.D. dissertation, University of Chicago, 1974.

Leiffler, Donald B. "Town Manager Government in Massachusetts." Unpublished Ph.D. dissertation, Harvard University, 1939.

Melick, Richard P. "Memo to Town Meeting Members." Natick, Mass., March 8, 1953 (mimeographed).

"Model By-Laws for Massachusetts Towns." Boston: Massachusetts Federation of Taxpayers Associations, 1940 (mimeographed).

"NH City & Town Clerks' Position on SB2 Official Balloting." Available from Town Clerk Gwendolyn M. Jones, P.O. Box 637, Alton, N.H. 03809.

"Representative Town Meetings in Massachusetts." Boston: Massachusetts Federation of Taxpayers Associations, June 1945 (mimeographed).

Soule, Lewis. "The New Hampshire Town Meeting." Copy provided by Deputy New Hampshire Secretary of State Robert Ambrose, n.d.

"Your Opinion Counts! Study of Concord's Town Meeting." Concord, Mass.: Town Meeting Study Committee, 1996.

Zimmerman, Joseph F. "Can Cities and Towns Meet the Challenges of the Space Age?" Paper presented at the annual meeting of the New Hampshire Municipal Association, Manchester, May 11, 1972.

————. "The Evolving New England Town Meeting." Paper presented at the annual meeting of the Massachusetts Moderators Association, Natick, November 8, 1996.

————. "Home Rule in Massachusetts: Some Historical Perspectives." Paper presented at the Massachusetts Municipal Training Institute, Boston College, June 3, 1970.

————. "Law Making by Citizens in the United States." Paper presented at the Forschungs-Schwerpunkt Historische Mobilität und Normenwandel, Universität Gesamthochschule, Siegen, Federal Republic of Germany, November 9, 1984.

————. "The New England Town Meeting and *De Facto* Representation." Paper presented at the annual meeting of the Northeastern Political Science Association, Philadelphia, November 13, 1997.

————. "Town Meeting Government: New Hampshire Style." Paper presented at the annual meeting of the Northeastern Political Science Association, Boston, November 15, 1996.

————. "Whither Town Government?" Paper presented at a Seminar on Strengthening Municipal Government sponsored by the Association of Town Finance Committees, Wrentham, Mass., April 14, 1970.

Index

About the Author

JOSEPH F. ZIMMERMAN is Professor of Political Science at the Graduate School of Public Affairs of the State University of New York. A member of the editorial boards of *Publius*, *National Civic Review*, *Voting and Democracy Review*, and *Representation*, Professor Zimmerman was the first chairman of the section on Representation and Electoral Systems of the American Political Science Association. He is the author of numerous books, including *The Recall: Tribunal of the People* (Praeger, 1997) and *Interstate Relations: The Neglected Dimension of Federalism* (Praeger, 1996).

ISBN 0-275-96523-6

90000>

EAN

9 780275 965235

HARDCOVER BAR CODE